Consider the seed from which you are sprung:
you were not made to live like animals,
but to pursue excellence and knowledge.

(Ulysses exhorting his aged and timid colleagues
through the Gates of Hercules
to the unknown ocean beyond)
DANTE INFERNO 26.118-20

Rethinking Peter Singer

A Christian
Critique

**GORDON
PREECE**
Editor

InterVarsity Press
Downers Grove, Illinois

InterVarsity Press
P.O. Box 1400, Downers Grove, IL 60515-1426
World Wide Web: www.ivpress.com
E-mail: mail@ivpress.com

InterVarsity Press® *is the book-publishing division of InterVarsity Christian Fellowship/USA*®*, a student movement active on campus at hundreds of universities, colleges and schools of nursing in the United States of America, and a member movement of the International Fellowship of Evangelical Students. For information about local and regional activities, write Public Relations Dept., InterVarsity Christian Fellowship/USA, 6400 Schroeder Rd., P.O. Box 7895, Madison, WI 53707-7895, or visit the IVCF website at <www.ivcf.org>.*

Scripture quotations, unless otherwise noted, are from the New Revised Standard Version of the Bible, copyright 1989 by the Division of Christian Education of the National Council of the Churches of Christ in the USA. Used by permission. All rights reserved.

Cover photograph: Princeton University/Ron Carter

ISBN 0-8308-2682-3

Printed in the United States of America ∞

Library of Congress Cataloging-in-Publication Data

Rethinking Peter Singer: a Christian critique/edited by Gordon Preece.
    p. cm.
    Includes bibliographical references.
    Contents: The unthinkable and unlivable Peter Singer/Gordon Preece—Singer, preference utilitarianism, and infanticide/Andrew Sloane—Professor Peter Singer on Christianity: characterized or caricatured?/Graham Cole—Human beings, species or special?: a critique of Peter Singer on animals/Lindsay Wilson—Rethinking Singer on life and death/Gordon Preece.
    ISBN 0-8308-2682-3 (pbk.: alk. paper)
    1. Singer, Peter, 1946- I. Preece, Gordon R., 1954-

B5704.S554 R48 2002
170'.92—dc21

                                               2002023276

P	20	19	18	17	16	15	14	13	12	11	10	9	8	7	6	5	4	3	2	1
Y	18	17	16	15	14	13	12	11	10	09	08	07	06	05	04	03	02			

To Graham Cole
Principal, Mentor, Colleague, Friend

CONTENTS

Acknowledgments

Without turning this into an Academy Awards speech there is a "great cloud of witnesses" and helpers in the production of this book, some of whom should be thanked by name. Professor Hans Reinders of the Free University of Amsterdam generously allowed access to "Debunking the Sanctity of Life," chapter two of his unpublished manuscript *Should We Prevent Handicapped Lives? Reflections on the Future of Disabled People in Liberal Society.*

At IVP my editor, Gary Deddo, having himself heard Peter Singer at Princeton, has been a Barnabas to me and this book. Copyeditor Ruth Goring's exactitude and eagle eye have made the manuscript into a more user-friendly book.

The Ridley College Council generously provided study leave in the second semester of 2000, and colleagues kindly and ably covered for me. My family and I swapped a house, a study and nearly everything else with the Higginson family of our sister college, Ridley Hall, Cambridge. We were received very warmly there, and our time in that magical place was one to remember. Archie and Jenny Ferguson's hospitality knew no bounds, while St. Barnabas's Church provided great spiritual sustenance. My wife Susan's humor and patience gave me a sense of proportion about the project.

Scholars at the Ridley College graduate seminar and the Australian Association for Professional and Applied Ethics helped sharpen the book's content. Colleagues at Ridley College—Jill McCoy, Kathryn Duncan, Peter Angelovski and Ruth Millard—kindly and cheerfully used their detective skills to provide bibliographic assistance.

Finally, a note of explanation for the unusual dedication to Graham Cole, one of the contributors, who was obviously kept unaware. It appropriately marks his transition from principal of Ridley College and founder of its Centre of Applied Christian Ethics to being professor of biblical and systematic theology at Trinity Evangelical Divinity School, Deerfield, Illinois. Graham gave two of us our opportunity in full-time theological education and has been a model to us of that Christian practice and of Christian friendship and leadership.

Gordon Preece

Permissions

Permission is gratefully acknowledged to reproduce the following:

Graham A. Cole, "Professor Peter Singer on Christianity: Characterised or Caricatured?" *Reformed Theological Review* 57, no. 2 (1998): 80-90.

Andrew Sloane, "Singer, Preference Utilitarianism and Infanticide," *Studies in Christian Ethics* 12, no. 2 (1999): 47-73.

Substantial quotes have been drawn from Jenny Teichman, *Social Ethics: A Student's Guide* (Oxford: Blackwell, 1996).

Table 2, "A Case Against Voluntary Euthanasia," is taken from Robert G. Twycross, "Where There Is Hope, There Is Life: A View from the Hospice," in *Euthanasia Examined: Ethical, Clinical and Legal Perspectives*, ed. John Keown (Cambridge: Cambridge University Press, 1995), p. 165.

INTRODUCTION

Peter Singer—Hero or Herod?

GORDON PREECE

Peter Singer is the world's most famous or perhaps infamous contemporary philosopher. His controversial advocacy of infanticide, euthanasia and recently bestiality make headlines. Some even say that Singer is the world's most significant living philosopher. Given the magnitude of the issues he raises and popularizes, this is probably true too, even for those who, like the authors of this book, disagree with him. His significance is shown by his authorship of over twenty books, including the highly influential bestseller *Animal Liberation* (written at the age of only twenty-nine) and *Practical Ethics* (voted one of the hundred most influential philosophy texts of the twentieth century), and his controversial and highly publicized appointment as Ira W. DeCamp Professor of Bioethics in the Princeton University Center for Human Values.

Despite these impressive academic achievements and though personally pleasant and mild-mannered, Singer is a divisive figure. People love or hate him, seeing him either as a hero or a Herod figure.

I was discussing Singer in a café when the eavesdropping waitress, a young college student, told me, "I love the man." His advocacy of animal rights and ecological issues, the last innocents in a world of sullied human heroes, gains him reflected glory.

My college-student daughter, in a bar discussion with a new acquaintance, mentioned that her father taught ethics. She was immediately asked, "What does he think of Peter Singer?" as if ethics and Singer are almost automatically associated.

Another bright young acquaintance, upon hearing that I was an ethics teacher, told me how he had been spaced out on drugs and drink but pulled himself together by determining to lead an ethical life. For him, Peter Singer, the ethicist, animal rights advocate and environmentalist, was the epitome of such a life. I encouraged him in his ethical quest and affirmed Singer's concern for animals and the environment, not wanting to plunge him back into his pre-Singer daze. But when asked my opinion of Singer, I gently mentioned Singer's advocacy of infanticide (of which my young friend, like many, was ignorant) and used it to downgrade Singer's hero status relative to Christ. This book is written for ethical seekers like these, whom we believe are being misled by Singer.

They are not the only ones—some Christians too seem quite unaware of the incompatibility between their faith and Singer's views. I have heard Singer speak to church groups advocating voluntary euthanasia to the agreement of most in the audience. I have seen his books read, seemingly uncritically, in a prominent evangelical church. We hope this book will enable them to read critically and Christianly in the future.

Many Christians and people of conscience find key aspects of Singer's thinking abhorrent, even evil. George Pell, then Roman Catholic bishop of Melbourne, now archbishop of Sydney, describes Singer as "Herod's propaganda chief" and an apologist for the "culture of death."[1] Singer, like Herod, advocates the acceptability of killing the innocent or infanticide (cf. Mt 2:16-19) and seems threatened by the Messiah's claim to kingship and our ethical discipleship.

Singer's advocacy of infanticide for newborns motivated vociferous protests by disabled and prolife groups when he spoke in Germany (where Nazi euthanasia programs are not forgotten) and against his appointment to Princeton University. At Princeton disabled groups with such names as Not Dead Yet chanted, "We love our crippled lives!" and blocked administration building entrances. When an interviewer suggested that Singer would not have advocated infanticide for those disabled activists, Singer protested "No, it is possible." Of course, since as infants they would have been too young to have preferences, Singer thinks it would not have mattered to them.[2] Princeton Students Against Infanticide (PSAI) argued that Singer's appointment both legitimizes infanticide and violates Princeton's own "Commitment to Community" inclusive of all, including the disabled. Yet Singer cleverly played the free speech card and Princeton played the academic freedom card—the right of anyone, especially any academics, to think and say what they want.[3]

[1]Quoted in Richard Egan, "Herod's Propaganda Chief," News Weekly, October 21, 1995, p. 14. Cf. "Saintly or Satanic?" Time (Australia), November 2, 1989.
[2]In Peter Singer, "Playing God," interview by Marianne Macdonald, Herald-Sun (Melbourne), July 29, 2001, Sunday Magazine, p. 15.
[3]See Deidre King Hainsworth, "Mr. Singer Goes to Princeton," Zadok Perspectives 64 (Winter 1999): 11-12.

Unfortunately Singer's resort to rights language in his own case is somewhat disin-genuous, given that he denies the right to life to infants and is "not convinced that the notion of a moral right is a helpful or meaningful one . . . except as a shorthand way of referring to more fundamental moral considerations." For as a consequentialist he can quite easily cancel out rights if the consequences suggest that is preferable.[4]

The Man, the Mind and the Movement

Hastings Center bioethicist Daniel Callahan claims (disapprovingly) that "the first thing" bioethics had to do to establish itself as a profession/specialty was "to push reli-gion aside."[5] Singer has been particularly prominent in this attempt to establish a new secular specialty as the most prominent branch of applied ethics. This book rep-resents a religious determination to stay put and debate with its high priest.

---

[4]Peter Singer, *Practical Ethics*, 2nd ed. (Cambridge: Cambridge University Press, 1993), p. 96. (All subsequent references to *Practical Ethics* are to this second edition unless followed by the date 1979, indicating the first edition.) Contrast p. 359, where Singer applies Voltaire's famous dictum to his own case: "I disapprove of what you say, but I will defend to the death your *right* to say it" (my emphasis). Singer uses rights language as shorthand for utilitarian preferences and interests, but rights need to be helpful and meaningful in themselves if he doesn't want his right to discuss eutha-nasia and infanticide in Germany or the United States to be outweighed in utilitarian terms by pub-lic interest or preference. If there are intrinsic rights of free speech, then public interests cannot outweigh them. See Jacqueline A. Laing, "Innocence and Consequentialism: Inconsistency, Equiv-ocation and Contradiction in the Philosophy of Peter Singer," in *Human Lives: Critical Essays on Consequentialist Bioethics*, ed. David S. Oderberg and Jacqueline A. Laing (London: Macmillan, 1997), pp. 223-24 n. 45. Cf. Jenny Teichman, "Humanism and Personism: The False Philosophy of Peter Singer," *Quadrant*, December 1992, p. 26, who argues that "false philosophy can be danger-ous, and . . . if circumstances prevent its being refuted in print, it is probably all right, in extreme cases, to try to silence it in other ways." The parallel with racial vilification legislation is a pertinent one. In Jenny Teichman, "Freedom of Speech and the Public Platform," *Journal of Applied Philoso-phy* 11, no. 1 (1994): 101, 105, she argues that letters to a newspaper editor have no intrinsic right to be published, especially if deemed offensive to public decency. She considers that Singer's views resemble some Nazi views, and she believes that Germans are best able to judge the potential nega-tive consequences of allowing those views to be disseminated. Further, as a guest in Germany, Singer should not display "gross insensitivity." Dale Jamieson defends Singer's right to speak ("Singer and the Practical Ethics Movement," in *Singer and His Critics*, ed. Dale Jamieson [Oxford: Blackwell, 1999], p. 16 nn. 20-21). However, he misses the fact that Singer's views raise issues of national significance, beyond academic free speech issues, especially in Germany.

　　Catholic philosopher Tony Coady, regarding intellectual work as inherently risky and less influ-ential in practice than often thought, supports Singer's right to speak. He still disagrees profoundly with Singer's views on infanticide and other matters. See his "Morality and Species," *Res Publica* 8, no. 2 (1999): 9. Certainly, while Singer's objectionable views may not be owed hospitality, his per-son should not be treated with hostility or violence.

[5]Quoted by Wesley J. Smith, *The Culture of Death: The Assault on Medical Ethics in America* (n.p.: Encounter, 2001), quoted in a review, Richard M. Doerflinger, "Matters of Life and Death," *First Things*, August/September 2001, p. 68. Callahan makes clear his disapproval of the antireligious trend in bioethics in a letter to *First Things* (December 2001, pp. 8-9, citing an article published in

Singer is high priest, but he is not without acolytes—assistants, followers and col-leagues in what we could call a "Singerian" program in applied ethics. This program would still be advocated, though less publicly and articulately, "even if Peter Singer were himself to give up doing ethics."[6] Singer's rise corresponded with the birth of applied ethics out of the 1970s period of antiwar, feminist and ecological activism, movements in which Singer was personally involved. A rash of new journals appeared: *Philosophy and Public Affairs* (1971), the first volume of which included Singer's significant essay "Famine, Affluence and Morality"; *Journal of Medicine and Philosophy* (1976); *Environmental Ethics* (1979); *Journal of Business Ethics* (1982).[7]

This book will focus on Singer's ideas rather than his person, except where his life illustrates the impracticality of some key ideas. We do not want to demonize Singer but to discern where his ideas are right and where wrong. However, it is worth asking, who is this man who has caused such a fuss? Singer comes from a Jewish background of considerable intellectual pedigree. His maternal grandfather, David Oppenheim, was a collaborator with and member of Sigmund Freud's famous Wednesday Circle. Oppenheim's wife, Amalia, was an outstanding mathematician who once worked with Albert Einstein. Singer's paternal grandmother, Philippine Ernst, was related to the Pulitzers who migrated to the United States and gave their name to the famous Pulitzer Prize. Singer is a long-standing atheist, having refused his bar mitzvah at thir-teen, yet his paternal grandfather's line boasts rabbis going back generations.

Singer's family of origin has suffered considerable tragedy. His father Ernst and mother Cora fled Vienna to avoid persecution at the time of the Nazi *Anschluss* (union) with Austria. Sadly, their parents and extended family (about whom Singer is writing a book) were nearly all killed. There is thus an oft-remarked irony in the

---

Daedalus, Fall 1999): "The decline of religious contributions [to bioethics is] a misfortune, leading to a paucity of concepts, a thin imagination, and the ignorance of traditions, practices, and forms of moral analysis of great value." Cf. his article "Religion and the Secularization of Bioethics," supple-ment to *Hastings Center Report*, July/August 1990.

[6]Bernadette Tobin, review of *Human Lives: Critical Essays on Consequentialist Ethics, Quadrant,* July-August 1997, p. 109. Some of the most prominent Singerians are Michael Tooley, author of *Abortion and Infanticide* (Oxford: Oxford University Press, 1983), whose ideas on infanticide Singer has popularized; Jonathon Glover, author of *Causing Death and Saving Lives* (Harmondsworth, U.K.: Penguin, 1977); Helga Kuhse, author of *The Sanctity of Life Doctrine in Medicine: A Critique* (Oxford: Clarendon, 1987); James Rachels, author of *The End of Life: Euthanasia and Morality* (Oxford: Oxford University Press, 1986); and a number of those writing in *Singer and His Critics,* ed. Dale Jamieson (Oxford: Blackwell, 1999). Smith's *Culture of Death* shows how Singer's basic views on human worth are shared by more bioethicists than we might think. However, Christian bioethi-cist Gilbert Meilaender's review (*Weekly Standard,* February 12, 2001) warns against Smith's ten-dency to anathematize the whole profession of bioethics. Doerflinger's "Matters of Life and Death," pp. 69-70, also notes the way utilitarianism matches the mood of much of Western society.

[7]Jamieson, "Singer and the Practical Ethics Movement," p. 4.

hostile reception Singer received in Germany from disabled and antieuthanasia groups as another Hitler. Singer is no racist. He claims that Nazi extermination on racial grounds of Jews who had a real interest in prolonging their lives is different from his advocacy of infanticide or euthanasia or genetic screening of unborn children or babies, who are not yet thinking persons with an interest in prolonging their lives. Yet his philosophy could lead to the wholesale elimination of many deemed undesirable on genetic or health grounds that the Nazis also used as criteria for euthanasia.

Singer's parents migrated to Australia in 1938. Ernst was a coffee importer/exporter, linguistic pedant and animal lover (abhorring abbatoirs and fishing), while Cora was a doctor.[8] This helps explain their second child (born 1946) Peter's eventual interests in analytical philosophy, animal liberation and bioethics.

After studying at Melbourne University, Singer earned his philosophical stripes at Oxford University, gaining a Ph.D. in the 1970s under R. M. Hare. But Singer has never been a mere academic. His concern for animal welfare was catalyzed by some Canadian vegetarians he met at Oxford in 1970. His name then became widely known for defending the well-being of animals against "speciesism"—prejudice in favor of one's own species, similar to racism or sexism. His *Animal Liberation* soon gave its name to a movement and became its bible.

As professor of philosophy and deputy director of the Centre for Human Bioethics at Melbourne's Monash University for twenty years, Singer has turned his thinking to issues of life, death, artificial conception and genetic engineering. The one hiccup in his success story was when he unsuccessfully attempted to enter the Senate of the Australian Parliament as a Greens candidate in 1996. His political career was short-lived, as he received only a small percentage of the vote. Singer's appointment as professor of philosophy at Princeton University's ironically named Center for Human Values has already brought him even greater prominence and notoriety.

Chapter by Chapter
This book is written by four Australians, from a secular, pluralist society similar to the one that spawned Singer. We believe that we provide a helpful perspective for other societies, like the United States, that may be moving down a similar, dangerous road. The book began life at the inaugural (1996) Ridley College Centre of Applied Christian Ethics (CACE) annual conference but has been updated considerably. It focuses on Singer's unthinkable and thinkable ideas. The only other book-length cri-

---

[8]David Leser, "The Man in the Black Plastic Shoes," *HQ*, Winter 1992, pp. 54-56.

tique, *Singer and His Critics*, edited by Dale Jamieson,[9] is really a tribute. Though philosophically sophisticated, it is relatively soft on Singer and in particular lacks a critique of his more unthinkable ideas in the realm of bioethics.[10] This is a good reason for our relatively strong but not exclusive focus on bioethical issues at the beginning and end of human life. Our book is the first critique of Singer from a specifically Christian perspective, though we argue in ways designed to establish ethical contact points with concerned people of conscience.

Singer's prominence and the magnitude of the issues he addresses make it imperative that there be an appropriate Christian response to some of today's major ethical apologetic issues—a response written as accessibly as much of Singer's work. Believers in the "optimism of grace" (Graham Cole), we pray that Singer and many of his followers on animal rights issues, who often know little of his ideas concerning infanticide, may even rethink his philosophy. The following chapters in this book are offered in this hope.

The first chapter, written by the book's editor, Gordon Preece, attempts a broad, readable introduction to Singer and examines a number of the critiques made of his thought. First it addresses its "unthinkability," Singer's violation of our inbuilt "yuck factor" with his advocacy of infanticide and bestiality. I argue that our perhaps inarticulate reaction of shock and shame, while not infallible, and while needing articulation, should not be lightly set aside unless very good reasons are given. Singer has so far not come up with them. Second, I argue that Singer's ethics fails its crucial self-proclaimed test of practicality. Though Singer is a man of integrity and consistency according to his lights, "walking the talk" of his moral theory, at certain crucial points he is unable to live it out. This was particularly so in relation to his mother's Alzheimer's disease and his unwillingness to euthanize her. Such inconsistencies demonstrate the impossible and inhuman demands his impartiality ethic makes. Third, I argue that Singer's theory is crudely reductionistic. Its rigid rationality fails to do justice to the roles of intuition, social location and power, tradition and revelation in reasoning. Despite Singer's attraction to the concreteness of utilitarianism, at crucial points it abstracts from the basic realties of human relationships from which all ethics emerges.

As Andrew Sloane shows in our key second chapter, Singer's advocacy of infanticide demonstrates in some ways the chilling consistency of his philosophy. Singer's support of infanticide is no isolated idea in his system but is integral to it and a good

---

[9]Oxford: Blackwell, 1999.
[10]Cf. Jenny Teichman, "Peter Singer: Jekyll and Hyde," *News Weekly*, January 27, 2000, pp. 16-18, for a strong critique of Jamieson's lack of criticism.

test case of its validity. Singer rejects the alleged wrongness of killing a newborn human. First, he argues, an infant is not a person (self-aware) and so has no interests or preferences concerning living or dying—in classic postmodern teenage terms, "whatever." Second, her death may benefit her parents and family (if they don't want her), future children and the infant herself.

Singer's allowing of (but not insisting on) infanticide expresses his ethical theory of preference utilitarianism. Utilitarianism was founded by Jeremy Bentham in the late eighteenth century and modified by John Stuart Mill in the early nineteenth century. It focuses on consequences or goals of action, not character (virtue) nor divine commands or any absolute rules, though in some forms like Singer's conventional moral rules are acceptable as regular means to suitable consequences. Actions are not wrong in themselves but only in terms of their results. Results are evaluated in terms of the greatest happiness (or pleasure over pain) of the greatest number concerned. Singer's modification of utilitarianism, known as preference utilitarianism, consists in maximizing the preferences or choices of the greatest number of all rational, choosing persons and minimizing the pain of all sentient (feeling) creatures. Utilitarianism's popularity is due to its objective and scientific appearance; it seems to provide a simple way of measuring social policies and is readily communicated in short sound bites to the media. Sloane questions this alleged objectivity.

Sloane shows that for Singer infanticide is justified when guided by a preference utilitarian criterion: an action (or rule) is right if and only if it maximizes the interests of all those affected by it. Just being born of the human species gives one no automatic interests. Only persons have interests or preferences. So by redefining *persons* as more specific in some ways than *humans* (only including humans with preferences) and yet more general in other ways (allowing some intelligent animals with interests), Singer abolishes any automatic right to life.

Crucially, Sloane demonstrates the clear connections between Singer's particular arguments for infanticide and his general ethical theory. For example: infants are not persons, as they have no "future-oriented" interests; thus their death cannot thwart their interests. The consequences of infanticide, in terms of maximizing interests of persons affected by the decision, on balance, determine its rightness or wrongness.

To be fair, Sloane observes some strengths in preference utilitarianism: it is (relatively) consistent; it shows some of the intellectual and practical problems of overly strict sanctity-of-life ethics; it reminds us to consider the consequences of our actions.

However, it has many flaws:

☐ Singer's reliance on poor and unfair arguments *ad absurdum* (showing the absurdity of Christian and objective moral views) to partly justify his own. They often knock down "straw men" but cannot positively justify his own theory.

☐ The classic clash between justice and utilitarianism. The latter can justify horrendous things, such as torture of alleged terrorists in the name of the social utility of getting information about bombs from them.

☐ Its reductionist nature. Preference utilitarianism ignores many realities of human life, morality and meaning beyond mere happiness or preference.

The horrific and counterintuitive nature of Singer's views on infanticide and their consistency with his overall theory show not that the "traditional ethic" should be abandoned but that his theory should be rejected. Sloane therefore concludes that Singer's theory is unjustifiable, especially for Christians.

Singer, of course, seeks to do away with outmoded relics of the Christian view of life and ethics. He has many criticisms of the Christian Scriptures, history and doctrine, especially surrounding speciesism, reflected in the teaching that human beings are in the image of God, that human life is sacred and potentially immortal, and that humans rule other species. For him, none of these ideas can be justified in a post-Enlightenment, modern world.

This leads Graham Cole to ask in our third chapter, has Singer rightly characterized Christianity or has he caricatured it? Cole argues that Singer produces a cartoon version of Christianity. Singer caricatures by disproportionate emphasis of certain features, by omission and by association with evil. For example, Singer caricatures the biblical story of creation as advocating human domination by omitting the Genesis 2 story of Adam's call to "care for and keep" Eden and of the animals as companions. Likewise, the flood story of God's judgment found in Genesis 9 is mentioned without the balancing picture of God as the preserver of species through the ark in Genesis 6—7. Scripture places high value on humanity, as Singer says. But Singer omits the evidence that Jesus and Christians still valued animals.

Singer considers that Christian ethics are based on a mistaken expectation of Jesus' immediate return and self-interested concern for the rewards and punishments it will bring. But Singer's wooden literalism is mistaken on the former and misses the complex, self-giving motivation of disciples drawn by love of Christ (Jn 14:15). Singer uses texts out of context as a pretext for condemning Christianity. It is not an ethical form of interpretation or argument.

Singer does rightly remind us that the environment and animals matter. But he misses the fact that they matter *to God* and that the many Christian failures in this area stand under God's judgment. The very Bible that he caricatures provides the necessary corrective.

In our fourth chapter, Lindsay Wilson addresses Singer's popularization of the term *speciesism*, on analogy to racism or sexism, to describe unfair discrimination against animals. Singer's innovation in utilitarianism was to expand the range of beings whose pleasure over pain is counted, so that all sentient beings are included and some animals are counted as persons. For him anything short of this constitutes irrational prejudice or preference for our own species, or *speciesism*. According to Singer, all sentient beings, not only human beings, have morally significant interests to be promoted. Further, all self-conscious sentient beings (adult mammals and most humans) are persons with preferences to be maximized. This counts out all cruelty to animals, including some research experiments, and the killing of self-conscious animals. It has inspired the growing trend toward vegetarianism among the young.

A biblical theology of animals describes humans as both like and unlike animals. We are both kin with them and kings and queens over them. We are part of creation but set over it as God's image and its rulers. Animals provide some company but not the fully personal companionship of another human being. The immense diversity of the animal kingdom "according to their kinds" is blessed, and these distinctions are preserved after the flood, when Genesis 9:8-17 speaks of a covenant between God and all creatures. With the flood's judgment on human violence, humans' original vegetarianism is modified, allowing the eating of meat, but within limits. In the Pentateuch animals can be eaten and offered in sacrifice. In New Testament times the Jewish food laws are set aside in Christ, but eating of meat is still permitted. Despite these effects of the Fall, the Bible delights in the animal world and God cares for it. Yet he cares for humans even more.

My (Preece's) concluding essay agrees with Singer that his program, as summarized in *Rethinking Life and Death*, is a wholesale assault on the traditional Western "sanctity of life" ethic. For Singer, just as the first Copernican revolution showed scientifically that the earth and humanity are not the center of the universe, a new Copernican revolution has come with the recognition that humanity is not "the centre of the *ethical* universe, we are just one species among others, and nothing special."[11]

Singer scores some points against the sanctity-of-life ethic, but usually by setting up fundamentalist straw men. He caricatures an absolutist sanctity-of-life position and a Christian ethic based on arbitrary divine commands constraining people's free, rational choices. The extreme cases that Singer cites to justify his revolution do not make good law. In fact Singer reverses the usual, logical and preferred order of argument to argue from liberal and pluralistic polity and legality to morality.

Singer also replaces the sanctity-of-life ethic with a set of modestly entitled "new commandments" of his own devising, based on "quality of life" criteria. But these

---

[11]Peter Singer, *Rethinking Life and Death* (Melbourne: Text, 1994), p. 1.

will ultimately undermine the very liberty of the people he purports to represent, as the Dutch euthanasia experiment shows. Today's *choice* to be euthanized may well, in an increasingly economically rationalist health system, become tomorrow's *obligation* or *commandment*. We are on a very slippery slope indeed.

In the end Singer's song is a sad song, though sincerely sung. For all its liberal and sometimes liberating appearance, his utilitarian philosophy ultimately leads to a state in which people are used as instruments of social utility. Like an inebriated karaoke singer, his philosophy is out of tune with the created ecology and end of God's world and our common humanity. Singer's support of infanticide, euthanasia and bestiality shows the consistency of an anti-Christian, ultimately antihuman philosophy. A true Christian humanism thus shines in stark relief, affirming the correct intuitions of others that all creatures have worth for their own and God's sake, not mere utility.

1

The Unthinkable
& Unlivable Singer

GORDON PREECE

T his chapter aims to show in five sections that despite Peter Singer's commendable concern for the poor and animals, some of his key ideas are (1) unthinkable, (2) "yucky" or morally outrageous, (3) inconsistent, (4) impractical/unlivable and (5) based on a reductionistic model of humanity, ecology, rationality and morality. To unpack this a little, I argue, first, that infanticide and bestiality should not even be thought about or countenanced. Second, our inbuilt "yuck factor," though not infallible, is not irrational either and should be respected. Third, for all his impartiality and consistency of logic and lifestyle, Singer himself could not euthanize his mother, Cora Singer, who was suffering from Alzheimer's. Fourth, Singer's rarefied rationalism of almost total impartiality is thus impossible to live out and fails his basic test of the practicality of ethics. Fifth, Singer's theoretical abstraction is symptomatic of his blindness to the basic relational and ecological nature of human life and morality and to the intuitions that reflect this. It reduces the rich tapestry of relationships to a few threads of an allegedly transcendent reason. He is not without compassion or emotion, just inconsistent in his application of it, more to animals than to human unborns or newborns.

The "Morally Unthinkable"
Philosopher Raimond Gaita finds some of Singer's ideas "morally unthinkable."

> It used to be unthinkable that we should kill children four weeks old or less merely because we didn't want them. You might, for example, have been offered the job you had always desired and your newly born child stands in the way of accepting it. Rather

than pass up the opportunity you could kill it . . . without wronging it. Peter Singer believes that we would not seriously wrong the children if we did it. That belief is undisguised in his book, *Practical Ethics*, and he is right to believe that the extent to which people are now seriously prepared to consider his reasons for it marks a shift in the moral boundaries which partially define our culture. . . . It appears not to have troubled an intelligentsia which generally accords Singer untroubled esteem . . . because what he says are thought to be views that anyone should take morally seriously. Examples such as these show that in the cultural realm, . . . the morally unthinkable . . . is a barrier whose breach is not always dramatic. Singer breached it without much protest.[1]

This should remind us of the well-known parable of the frogs in the kettle of hot water. If they were thrown into boiling water they would immediately jump out. But already immersed in the water while it was gradually heated up, they would slowly die.

Historian Paul Johnson's antiacademic advice applies to Singer's more unthinkable ideas.

One of the principal lessons of our tragic century, which has seen so many millions of innocent lives sacrificed in schemes to improve the lot of humanity, is—beware intellectuals. . . . Above all, we must at all times remember what intellectuals habitually forget: that people matter more than concepts and must come first. The worst of all tyrannies is the heartless tyranny of ideas.[2]

Having challenged society's "unthinking" prescriptions against euthanasia and infanticide, Singer now wants us to think seriously about bestiality. He claims, like someone from *Star Trek*, to think where no one has thought before. Not content to defend one widely discredited Dutch experiment, euthanasia, Singer now defends a double Dutch experiment, Dutch pop naturalist Midas Deckers's apologia for human-animal sex, *Dearest Pet*.[3] It's an ironic Midas touch indeed, turning the gold of human sexuality into the dross of animality. Even the *San Francisco Chronicle* proclaimed: "You could say Singer's take on animal rights is: you can have sex with them, but don't eat them."[4]

Singer foresees the inevitable evolutionary passing of the last sexual taboo of bestiality. He attacks taboos as irrational, prejudiced leftovers of an outmoded Christian ethic. Singer's assumption of a historically inevitable, progressive dismantling of

---

[1]Raimond Gaita, "Forms of the Unthinkable," Part 2, *Ethics Education* 5, no. 4 (October 1999): 6-7. Cf. his *A Common Humanity* (Melbourne: Text, 1999), pp. 157-86, esp. pp. 182-86.

[2]Paul Johnson, *Intellectuals* (New York: Harper & Row, 1989), p. 342. This should not be taken in a totally anti-intellectual way. Johnson himself is, after all, a public intellectual.

[3]Midas Dekkers, *Dearest Pet: On Bestiality*, trans. Paul Vincent (London: Verso, 2000).

[4]Quoted without date in Gay Alcorn, "Singer Stirs up a Hornet's Nest," *The Age*, March 31, 2001, p. 3.

sanctity-of-life and sexual taboos and traditions falsely equates change with progress. It is a modern Western parochialism of the present.

Singer parades as a liberal champion of ethical consumers' and animals' interests in noncruel, cross-species sex. But his utilitarian pleasure maximization principle makes animals and humans mere instruments of instinct. True, positive freedom can be judged only by an entity's nature. Knives are free to cut, humans to love. Bestiality reduces our holistic, relational and sexual humanity to the sexuality of animals in heat. Not only the intrinsic dignity and uniqueness of individual humans but also the lesser but still substantial dignity of animals is undermined by Singer's seeing both as mere units of total utility.

Singer's apology for bestiality appeals to Albert Kinsey's findings that 8 percent of males and 3.5 percent of females have practiced bestiality. But many of Kinsey's conclusions were based on unethically and illegally obtained and massively skewed samples from sexually experimental subjects.[5] Singer even cites Decker's urban myth that 50 percent of rural males have had sex with animals. Even if such figures were true, they represent a sociological form of the naturalistic fallacy. They are merely *descriptive*, not *prescriptive*; they do nothing to justify the logical jump from what *is* to what *ought* to be. If a majority of Germans in Hitler's time were anti-Semitic, does that make it right? This is typical of Singer's political-pollster approach to ethics. He reverses the normal procedure of making politics subject to ethics.

Christian opponents are stereotyped by Singer as absolutely against quality of life or pleasure, in favor of an absolute sanctity of (human) life and procreation ethic based on an unfathomable gulf between humans and animals. Yet most Christians incorporate some quality-of-life considerations into a sanctity-of-life ethic, do not suffer from pleasure phobia, do not reduce sexual satisfaction to procreation (though many do link the two), and oppose cruelty to animals. In fact Singer's demanding universal utilitarianism is much more opposed to individual pleasure and almost infinitely guilt-inducing compared to Christianity, as I shall show in the next section.

The Judeo-Christian creation accounts portray humans and animals as different "kinds" or species. Creation includes built-in boundaries between species. Yet while humans are kings and queens over animals, we are also kin with them. We have a common origin and destiny with the animals. "You are dust, and to dust you shall return," God says to Adam in Genesis 3:19. We are part of creation, but also set apart from the rest of it as God's image-bearers, to rule over it responsibly and carefully (Gen 1:26-28; Gen 2). No animal but only the woman Eve can quench Adam's loneli-

---

[5]See *Kinsey, Sex and Fraud: The Indoctrination of a People,* ed. J. Gordon Muir and John H. Court (Lafayette, La.: Huntington House, 1990), pp. 19, 45-46, 170, 174, 177-78.

ness (Gen 2:18), as together they reflect God's image in their sexual complementarity.

The "Yuck Factor"

Contrary to Singer's attempt to present taboos against infanticide or bestiality as out-moded Christian traditions, these creation accounts reflect something more univer-sal, what philosopher Mary Midgely (among others) calls "the "yuck factor," a prerational but not *ir*rational "sense of disgust and outrage"[6] which ethical theories rationally reflect or reject. A taboo (an intuitive sense of moral boundaries or shame) should not be accepted uncritically, but neither should taboos be rejected out of hand. Christians believe they often (but not always) reflect our very nature as God's creatures. Others see these moral feelings as reflecting our conscience, humanity or sense of the natural.

Midgely affirms the role of the yuck factor by outlining a moral perspective that is more holistic than Singer's rationalism. She argues against emotional and ethical illiteracy:

> Feeling is an essential part of our moral life, though of course not the whole of it. Heart and mind are not enemies or alternative tools. They are complementary aspects of a sin-gle process. Whenever we seriously judge something to be wrong, strong feeling neces-sarily accompanies the judgment. Someone who does not have such feelings—someone who has merely a theoretical interest in morals, who doesn't feel any indigna-tion or disgust and outrage about things like slavery and torture—has missed the point of morals altogether.[7]

Midgely's both-and approach joins intuitive notions of intrinsic wrongness of acts (heart) and allegedly rational calculations of consequences (head). The heart's yuck factor reflects deep, sometimes inarticulate moral intuitions that often take time to rise to the head and be thought and spoken out.

> Feelings always incorporate thoughts—often ones that are not yet fully articulated—and reasons are always found in response to particular sorts of feelings. On both sides, we need to look for the hidden partners. We have to articulate the thoughts that under-lie emotional objections and also note the emotional element in contentions that may claim to be purely rational. The best way to do this is often to start by taking the intrin-sic objections more seriously. If we look below the surface of what seems to be mere feeling we may find thoughts that show how the two aspects are connected.[8]

---

[6]Mary Midgely, "Biotechnology and Monstrosity: Why We Should Pay Attention to the "'Yuck Factor,'" *Hastings Center Report*, September-October 2000, p. 9.
[7]Ibid.
[8]Ibid., p. 8.

Feelings like the yuck factor are not infallible but often are intimate notions about the natural, and what is fitting or grotesquely unfitting, that should not be simply dismissed as irrational reactions to the unfamiliar. Their abuse does not necessarily deny their use.

Our gut reactions against infanticide and bestiality reflect a sense of the specialness of our species and also of the differences between species. Midgely shows how the best of the Enlightenment tradition (in which Singer claims to stand) through people like Montaigne—and I might add the evangelical Clapham sect of William Wilberforce and others, rather than being merely rationalist, developed enlightened feelings against judicial torture, abuse of animals and slavery as *"monstrous, unnatural,* and *inhuman."* She defends these notions, particularly that of "the monstrous," against the transgressing of species boundaries. Mad cow disease illustrates her point, as it arose through the feeding of sheep's brains to cows—a violation of species boundaries with catastrophic consequences.[9] While she doesn't apply her argument to bestiality, it fits perfectly. It shows that bestiality would be speciesist—not in Singer's sense of exalting humans over animals, but in a biblical and biological sense, of violating species' differences and boundaries. In this way bestiality violates our sexual ecology.

Midgely rightly argues against easy dismissal of moral intuitions about the intrinsic wrongness of certain acts as emotional and subjective. Singer's allegedly objective alternative—calculation of future consequences—is often too unclear to enable reasoned decisions. In fact only God can really be a consequentialist or utilitarian, because only God knows the future. Midgely therefore rejects Singer's either-or.

> Consequentialism is not the only alternative to blind taboo, and is certainly not the core that gives life to all our ordinary moral thinking. It cannot simply supersede it, and must therefore show its continuity with it, must show reasons why it should prevail. . . . It is useful as a hammer to break down prejudice, but not as a tool of construction.[10]

I now turn to showing how Singer's hammerlike consequentialism fails to show sufficient continuity with our ordinary moral thinking and feeling and fails its own test of practicality. Then to save its practicality it resorts to inconsistency.

Singer's Consistency and Inconsistency
But we should first recognize Singer's relative consistency and integrity. He practices

---

9Ibid. Cf. Mary Midgely, *Heart and Mind: The Varieties of Moral Experience* (London: Methuen, 1981), and her "Alchemy Revived," *Hastings Center Report,* March-April 2000, pp. 41, 43.
10Mary Midgely, "Consequentialism and Common Sense: A Review of Peter Singer, *Practical Ethics,*" *Hastings Center Report,* October 1980, p. 44.

what he preaches, from head to plastic (i.e., nonanimal product) shoe-covered toe. "Discussion is not enough," he rightly says. "What is the point of relating philosophy to public (and personal) affairs if we do not take our conclusions seriously? In this instance, taking our conclusion seriously means acting upon it."[11] Or to quote Friedrich Nietzsche: "The only critique of a philosophy that . . . proves something, mainly trying to see whether one can live in accordance with it, has never been taught at universities: all that has ever been taught is a critique of words by means of other words."[12]

Singer often lives up to his own test. He gives generously of his time and money—10 to 20 percent of his income to animal, environmental and poverty relief—but still feels that is not enough. He has been arrested and had his glasses smashed at demonstrations—the former against animal mistreatment and the latter against his views of human infanticide and euthanasia.[13] He belies the notion of the ivory-tower intellectual, being perhaps one of the last public intellectual activists. In fact, Singer's *Animal Liberation* was the only philosophy book ever to contain a vegetarian recipe for egg foo yong.[14] Robert C. Solomon claims that "of all the moralists and social reformers I know" Singer is least vulnerable to charges of inconsistency between theory and practice, although he notes humorously that the Singer cat, fed on a vegetarian diet, is a champion mouse hunter. Singer is Solomon's best contemporary exemplar of Nietzsche's "philosopher as example."[15]

While Singer is admirably consistent, in this book we argue that he is consistently wrong on some key philosophical and practical issues. Not only are key ideas intrinsically wrong, they would have catastrophic consequences if put into practice, judged by his own consequentialist standards. Midgely argues that

> some consequences are not just a matter of chance. Acts that are bad in themselves can be expected to have bad effects of a particular kind that is not just accidental. . . . There is a rational, conceptual link between them and their results. These consequences are a sign of what was wrong with the act in the first place. . . . Anyone who acts in this way invites . . . getting what [they] asked for.[16]

[11]Peter Singer, "Famine, Affluence and Morality," *Philosophy and Public Affairs* 1, no. 3 (Spring 1972): 242.
[12]Friedrich Nietzsche, "Schopenhauer as Educator," sec. 8, in *The Complete Works of Friedrich Nietzsche*, vol. 2, trans. Richard T. Gray (Stanford, Calif.: Stanford University Press, 1995), quoted in Robert C. Solomon, "Peter Singer's Expanding Circle: Compassion and the Liberation of Ethics," in *Singer and His Critics*, ed. Dale Jamieson (Oxford: Blackwell, 1999), p. 65.
[13]David Leser, "The Man in the Black Plastic Shoes," *HQ*, Winter 1992, pp. 54-56.
[14]Peter Singer, *Animal Liberation: A New Ethics for our Treatment of Animals* (London: Jonathan Cape, 1976), p. 282 (part of appendix 1, "Cooking for Liberated People").
[15]Solomon, "Peter Singer's Expanding Circle," p. 67.
[16]Midgely, "Biotechnology and Monstrosity," p. 8.

A good example is the way regular lying destroys trust in human relationships.

Singer stands in an intellectual tradition, consequentialism or utilitarianism, that prides itself on the practicality and concreteness of its basic idea of maximizing pleasure over pain. Singer's ideas are the ammunition fired by activists in the animal liberation and voluntary euthanasia movements. The very practicality of his ideas makes them influential, for good and evil. Good consequences have flowed from Singer's advocacy for animals and from his genuine concern to counter selfishness and help the poor, by advocating and practicing tithing (with its Judeo-Christian roots). However, his underlying philosophy is seriously flawed, and its practical implementation in relation to the unborn, newborn, disabled and vulnerable via infanticide and euthanasia would have catastrophic consequences for any society considering itself humane or civilized, not to say Christian. Singer's philosophy, rather than the traditional sanctity-of-life ethic he caricatures in his *Rethinking Life and Death*, thus requires rethinking.

This rethinking could begin with Singer's heavily criticized inconsistency in the case of his own mother. Singer and his sister hired healthcare workers at considerable cost to look after his mother, who was tragically ailing with Alzheimer's disease. Singer said at the time, "I'm pretty clear that my mother would not have wanted to go on living the way she is."[17] After her death in August 2000, Singer said that her situation

> has made me realise how difficult it is, in some cases, to put into effect what you believe are the person's wishes. My mother was a member of the Voluntary Euthanasia Society and, if she'd had cancer, was suffering and was mentally competent, there's no doubt in my mind that there would have come a time when she said, "I've had enough. I want to die . . ." Because she lost her capacity gradually and never seemed fully aware of what was happening, there was no opportunity to ask what she wanted. It was much harder to carry out what I believed her wishes were. She wasn't suffering greatly. I think that influenced my feelings a lot. . . . As for my sister and I, well, we could cope with it. I wasn't prepared—and I don't think my sister would have wanted me to—to risk jail for her.[18]

---

[17]Quoted by Gay Alcorn, "U.S. Hostility Mounts As Professor's University Posting Nears," *The Age*, May 1, 1999. His mother's no longer recognizing him freed Singer to leave for America. Presumably, in terms of units of utility or her current inability to have preferences, care by strangers as opposed to a son would make no difference. Chris Browning ("A Tale of Two Philosophers," *News Weekly*, May 22, 1999, p. 5), contrasts Singer's mother's situation with that of the philosopher Iris Murdoch, also suffering from Alzheimer's. While Murdoch was reduced to the most banal tasks and entertainments, watching *Teletubbies* on TV, her husband John Bayley, a fellow Oxford academic, devoted himself to her care, without considering her life not worth living, to the very end. See John Bayley, *Iris: A Memoir of Iris Murdoch* (London: Abacus, 1999), and the movie *Iris*.

[18]Peter Singer, "Playing God," interview by Marianne Macdonald, *Herald-Sun* (Melbourne), July 29, 2001, *Sunday Magazine*, p. 18.

But as Peter Berkowitz notes, Singer's mother

> has lost her ability to reason, and to remember, and to recognize others. She has
> ceased to be a person in her son's technical sense of the term. In these circum-
> stances, Singer's principles surely require him to give the substantial sums of money
> that he uses to maintain her in comfort and in dignity to feed the poor.[19]

Singer, the usually unsentimental rationalist, admits that from the perspective of
utilitarian theory this is "probably not the best use you could make of my money."
"Despite Singer's view that from the perspective of maximizing human utility universally we should treat friends and family no different to strangers, to his credit, he
now honestly admits in a *New Yorker* interview that 'Perhaps it is more difficult than
I thought before, because it is different when it's your mother.'"[20]

Singer had claimed consistency by arguing, "My mother is not suffering pain
from her condition, because she lacks the self-awareness that would lead her to suffer
from it. So it's not like the cases of euthanasia that I've written about." But it *is* like
those cases: because she was not self-aware, she had no interest or ability to live her
life, as Singer says elsewhere, "from the inside, not just moment by moment but over
a period of time. I see those [capacities] as significant for the wrongness of killing."[21]

Singer's Impractical Impartiality

Further, "from a purely abstract point of view," killing his mother would be consequentially advisable, for the money for her care could have been better used elsewhere. Singer also claims unclarity about his mother's wishes; this seems to show the
impracticality of euthanasia, even for a member of the Voluntary Euthanasia Society.
On his grounds her euthanasia would not be against her interests, as she has none.
He decided it was against his and his sister's interests for him to euthanize his mother
and risk being jailed. Overall, as one interviewer noted, "the nub of the issue [is] that
life can't really be lived in an abstract way." To which Singer replies, "It depends
what you mean by 'can't really.' I . . . think it's clearly possible to do it . . . if I were a
more saintly person."[22] But "saintliness" and humanity seem to part here.

In supporting equality of consideration for the interests of loved ones and strangers,[23] Singer argues, for instance, that if you faced the choice of saving your own three

---

[19]Peter Berkowitz, "Other People's Mothers," *The New Republic*, January 10, 2000, p. 27.
[20]Ibid.
[21]Peter Singer, "Opinion Interview: Only Human," interview by Nell Boyce, *New Scientist* 165, no.
   2220 (2000): 36.
[22]Singer, "Playing God," p. 18.
[23]Peter Singer, *Practical Ethics*, 2nd ed. (Cambridge: Cambridge University Press, 1993), pp. 12-14, chap.
   1. (All subsequent references are to this edition unless followed by 1979, indicating the first edition.)

children or forty strangers from fire, you should save the strangers and let your children die, because the total number of interests served would be greater. He says, "I think it becomes ethically dubious, but humanly understandable [to save your own children]. . . . I guess I would probably save my own children, but I don't know that I would feel that I had done the right thing." [24] Singer's elder sister, Joan Dwyer, agrees: "He would, too [save his own children], because he is real. . . . There's another component that you can't quite reduce to logic. . . . And I suppose that example . . . proves that when it comes to the bottom line, even he agrees." Singer replies that his ethic "is a very demanding one. I think that I go a fair distance towards being that, but I certainly don't go as far as I should. . . . It's really too difficult to do everything that one could do that would have the best consequences in this world." [25] But that honest admission makes the total equality or impartiality of his utilitarianism another form of impractical idealism.

The problem begins with Singer's quest for a rarefied rational ethic of pure objectivity or "REASON." [26] This moves "beyond our own personal point of view to a standpoint like that of the impartial spectator who takes a universal point of view." Singer says we should identify with the "point of view of the universe." [27] But Richard Neuhaus aptly calls this a "view from nowhere," because nobody lives nowhere or everywhere. "We are situated creatures." [28] Bernard Williams somewhere calls this

---

[24] That the ethical and the humanly understandable are opposed for Singer is highlighted by a true example of the kind of society his equality principle seems to support. Some years ago a villager in China, when his village was being flooded, chose to save Comrade X, the local Communist Party chairman, rather than the villager's wife and children. Most people would agree that "any system that would require such conduct as a moral duty is outrageous on the face of it. Similarly, we have our doubts about a system that implies—if it does—that whenever we buy a $100 dollhouse for our children, we do grave moral wrong, since we could, instead, have sent $99 to distant lands, thus saving the lives of several people. . . . Utilitarianism . . . looks on the face of it as though it should and at least could" (Jan Narveson, "Equality vs. Liberty: Advantage, Liberty," 1985, quoted in Russel Blackford, "Singer's Plea for Selflessness," *Quadrant*, October 2001, p. 30). This is not to deny the general obligations of individuals to feed hungry strangers (e.g., through World Vision) but to say that it does not automatically outweigh particular obligations to show special care for family. See Mk 7:9-13; 1 Tim 5:8.

[25] Leser, "Man in the Black Plastic Shoes," p. 61.

[26] Anne Maclean, *The Elimination of Morality: Reflections on Utilitarianism and Bioethics* (London: Routledge, 1993), sees Singer confusing "*human* reason" with an abstract Enlightenment "Equality Principle" which he identifies as the standard of "REASON" or what he calls "the autonomy of reasoning" (p. 63). As in Jonathan Swift's *Gulliver's Travels*, his ideal world is populated by "Houyhnhnms," a race of "walking REASONS" (p. 66).

[27] Quoting the utilitarian Henry Sidgwick's phrase. See Peter Singer, *Practical Ethics* (Cambridge: Cambridge University Press, 1979), pp. 206, 220, cf. 9; *The Expanding Circle* (Oxford: Oxford University Press, 1983), p. 93; *How Are We to Live? Ethics in an Age of Self-Interest* (Melbourne: Text, 1993), 225-33; "About Ethics," in *Writings on an Ethical Life* (London: Fourth Estate, 2001).

[28] Richard John Neuhaus, "A Curious Encounter with a Philosopher from Nowhere," in *First Things*, February 2002, p. 4 <www.firstthings.com>.

exalted Enlightenment claim to a God's-eye view a "mid-air stance." It forgets that we are earthly, finite creatures living in time and space with particular people and commitments, not disembodied rational angels or dualistic Gnostics. As Russel Blackford says, "There is no sense in which acting 'from the point of view of the universe' is more rational than living our own lives with projects and commitments of our own."[29] Singer's principle of universal equality of interests for all sentient beings, if "taken literally, . . . may sink the concept of equality in a sea of universality; if everything equally is our business, nothing is."[30]

Singer's universalism and inhuman demands undermine our ability to invest in our own lives and those of our loved ones, enslaving us to universal utility or infinite interests. His equality principle turns unique individuals, ourselves and others, into replaceable items of total interest or benefit. This is incompatible with loving individuals for themselves. "A utilitarian must suppress the dispositions to show love or loyalty, or friendship or tenderness, if she ever believes they are detracting from the goal of maximizing utility. Yet, it is questionable whether someone who possessed these dispositions conditionally truly possessed them at all."[31]

Singer, however, qualifies his universalism at the abstract, critical level by arguing also for a bottom-level, more conventional, intuitive view. Indirectly, in the long term, it is best for total utility for people to normally take primary responsibility and give some preference to their next of kin over others. Singer believes his theory can be accepted in principle, at the critical level, without our necessarily being motivated by universal utility-maximizing considerations when we make everyday decisions. Singer argues for impartial justification of anyone's having the right or duty to help their mother commit suicide, but for some partiality at the everyday decision-making level.[32] He showed such partiality toward his own mother.

Singer makes similar concessions to personal relations in the second edition of *Practical Ethics* and *How Are We to Live?* But his principle of "equal consideration of equal interests" is not merely *formally* impartial at the higher philosophical, long-term level, but *substantially* impartial at the everyday decision-making level. "It is unclear . . . how the two-level strategy can work for Singer's substantial impartiality requirement." This is because Singer uses impartial and *universal* equivocally or in more than one sense. He misses "an important distinction between the scope of morality, formal impartiality, and substantive impartiality within moral

[29]Blackford, "Singer's Plea," p. 33.
[30]Midgely, "Consequentialism," p. 44.
[31]Blackford, "Singer's Plea," 30.
[32]Peter Singer et al., "What Is the Justice/Care Debate *Really* About?" *Midwest Studies in Philosophy*, 1996.

theories."[33] Samuel Scheffler argues rightly that "impartiality is sometimes represented merely by universalization; that is, the prerogative to act from a personal point of view must be granted to everyone."[34] For example, not only I but all people in general have special obligations to their dying parents. Singer correctly uses the terms in this sense to describe a formally consistent application of such rules or principles. He is right that simple self-interest by itself is not an ethical justification.

But Singer slips in a stronger sense of universal or impartial as selfless, giving our own particular interests and commitments no more weight than those of all strangers. Our interests are only a drop in the ocean of universal interests.[35] If we assumed this stronger sense, utilitarianism might follow. Yet Singer never justifies it, he only assumes it, despite its implausibility.[36] Singer is so focused on justice at a universal level that he can give value to care at a basic, personal level only as a means to the former. Despite his attraction to utilitarianism's concreteness, Singer's consequentialist theory in the end abstracts from the concrete caring relationships that are essential to our ethical development.[37]

Besides this logical inconsistency, there is a personal inconsistency in Singer's two-level view. As Michael Stoker notes, it "creates the 'schizophrenic' situation where our subjective motives are different from our ultimate reasons for our actions, as given by the theory." Singer's two-level view leads either to an ethical schizophrenia between our emotional/relational investments and our ethics or "a life deeply deficient in what is valuable."[38]

Singer's two-level view appears to be humane only by being parasitic on other princi-

---

[33]Lori Gruen, "Must Utilitarians Be Impartial?" in *Singer and His Critics*, ed. Dale Jamieson (Oxford: Blackwell, 1999), pp. 141-42, 147 n. 16. Cf. McLean, *Elimination of Morality*, chap. 4, esp. pp. 56-60 on Singer's confusion about impartiality.

[34]Samuel Scheffler, *The Rejection of Consequentialism* (Oxford: Oxford University Press, 1982), chap. 3.

[35]Statistically, on utilitarianism's mathematical model, the interests of strangers count as much as the interests of our loved ones. As Richard J. Neuhaus writes: "My family, my friends, my country— each must give way to the universal. Each person counts as one and no more than one" ("Curious Encounter," p. 3).

[36]Blackford, "Singer's Plea," p. 32.

[37]See Singer et al., "What Is the Justice/Care Debate Really About?" Colin McGinn ("Our Duties to Animals and the Poor," in *Singer and His Critics*, ed. Dale Jamieson [Oxford: Blackwell, 1999], p. 159) argues that our duties to others are greater the closer they are to us socially. Cf. F. M. Kamm, "Famine in Ethics: The Problem of Distance in Morality and Singer's Ethical Theory," in *Singer and His Critics*, pp. 162-208

[38]Michael Stocker, "The Schizophrenia of Modern Ethical Theories," *Journal of Philosophy* 63 (1976): 453-66, quoted in Blackford, "Singer's Plea," p. 30. Maclean also sees Singer's view as schizophrenic, cutting us off from our human emotions, natures and commitments, even as demonstrated by sociobiology concerning kin preference (*Elimination of Morality*, p. 64).

ples, motivations or intuitions, often Christian ones encoded in our culture. It is a form of "impure utilitarianism" that "admits values or ideals which are independent of utility." Singer's "Equality Principle"—equal consideration for the interests of all persons affected—is one of these. It is separate from and cannot be reduced to utility. Yet it is so secularized and abstracted as to become impossibly demanding and inhuman, even causing inequality based on the extent to which one is a vehicle of utility or interest.[39]

Interests for Singer include our own well-being or "pleasurable states of consciousness" and autonomy or self-determination. These are "the two main values to which human life gives rise."[40] But this is very much a value judgment that needs to be argued for, not assumed. We could argue instead that "*no* amount of pleasure is equal to any amount of virtue, that in fact virtue belongs to a higher order of value," incommensurable with it.[41] As an example, what about sacrificial suffering for loved ones?

Singer makes a little room for loved ones:

> The element of truth in the view that we should first take care of our own, lies in the advantage of a recognized system of responsibilities, with families looking after their own rather than big impersonal bureaucracies. . . . The breakdown of the system of family and community responsibility would be a factor to weigh in the balance of a *small* degree of preference for family and community.[42]

But imagine the scene:

> Professor Singer is proposing to the woman whom he wishes to marry. "Darling," he says, "I have decided that you are the person towards whom I should like it to be morally permissible to show a moderate degree of partiality." What decent, upright woman could resist such an overture? Unfortunately, Singer fails to see that even this allowance completely destroys the basis of his philosophy.[43]

---

[39]Maclean, *Elimination of Morality*, p. 15. She notes, paradoxically, how Singer's equality principle leads to some people's being more equal than others as vehicles of greater value or utility (p. 67). So we should rescue the cancer specialist on the verge of a cure rather than our own mother.

[40]Ibid., p. 13, quoting Peter Singer and Helga Kuhse, "Allocating Health Care Resources and the Value of Life," in *Death and the Value of Life*, ed. David Cockburn, *Trivium* 27 (1992): 9.

[41]W. D. Ross, *The Right and the Good* (Oxford: Clarendon, 1930), p. 150. The same lack of comparison applies to autonomy and certainly to knowledge, on which Singer also puts inordinate value. Ross rightly says that "moral goodness is infinitely better than knowledge" (p. 152).

[42]Singer, *Practical Ethics*, 1979, p. 172, emphasis mine. Cf. "moderate" in Singer, *Rethinking Life and Death*, p. 196. On Singer's use of conventional or commonsense morality see Roger Crisp, "Teachers in an Age of Transition," in *Singer and His Critics*, ed. Dale Jamieson (Oxford: Blackwell, 1999), pp. 98-99. And for a vigorous statement of its inconsistency with his utilitarianism see Jenny Teichman, "Peter Singer: Jekyll and Hyde," *News Weekly*, January 27, 2000, pp. 16-18.

[43]Anthony Daniels, "Utilitarianism Undermines the Hippocratic Oath," *News Weekly*, October 6, 2001, p. 19. Full version at <www.newcriterion.com>.

Utilitarians like Singer, for all their grudging concessions to partiality in personal relationships, still fail to do justice to the "independence of the personal point of view" in marriage, parenthood, friendship, as an end in itself.[44] For Singer, the personal and relational is still instrumental, a means to total, rational interest or utility.

Another aspect of the impracticality or unlivability of Singer's moral theory already touched on is its often well-motivated tendency to produce infinite moral demands and guilt. Singer states that it is the duty of everyone to donate every cent above that needed for personal and family necessities to alleviate world hunger. Thus we would also live at very near the level of a Bengali beggar.[45] Anything less, because acts and omissions are equivalent, would be an act of murder, even mass murder.[46] Though rightly concerned to alleviate hunger and the massive discrepancy between rich and poor, Singer engages in literal overkill by his consequentialist equating of all acts and omissions (see chapter five in this book). Singer's view that the person who helps their own family member rather than a complete stranger is selfish "is plausible only if 'own' is taken in a property sense" rather than in the nonproperty sense of our "own" elected representative or employer or church.[47]

However, Singer again makes a concession to moderation and intuition, settling for relief of *absolute* poverty and the donation of 10 percent of our income.[48] Now the tithe suggestion makes much sense (though he hasn't allowed for taxation). But this is a grudging, guilt-laced concession. One side of Singer feels guilty whenever he goes to a restaurant, or spends anything beyond bare necessities, not just on himself but on loved ones. Philosopher Bernard Williams says, "Some utilitarian writers aim to increase a sense of indeterminate guilt in their readers. Peter Singer is an example, and in his book *Practical Ethics* . . . (1980) he is evidently more interested in producing that effect than he is in the theoretical basis for it, which gets very cursory treatment."[49] As Midgely notes, "Infinite guilt is a most impractical concept,"[50] highlighting what Marilyn Friedman calls "the

[44]Scheffler, *Rejection of Consequentialism*, chap. 3.

[45]Blackford, "Singer's Plea," p. 35. Cf. Berkowitz, "Other People's Mothers," p. 27, on Singer's *New York Times Sunday Magazine* article in early September 1999 pushing the same form of secular monasticism, not for a few who are called but for all.

[46]Singer, *Practical Ethics*, pp. 222-29.

[47]Brenda Almond, *Exploring Ethics: A Traveller's Tale* (Oxford: Blackwell, 1998), p. 216.

[48]Singer, *Practical Ethics*, p. 246.

[49]Bernard Williams, *Ethics and the Limits of Philosophy* (London: Fontana, 1985), p. 212.

[50]Midgely, "Consequentialism and Common Sense," p. 44. Gruen refers to the "demandingess" of utilitarianism generally and asks, "When, if ever, can I as a utilitarian agent relax when there is more good to promote?" ("Must Utilitarians Be Impartial?" p. 148 n. 30). She cites John Cottingham's example of a relaxing holiday weekend spoiled by my interest in maintaining my house by painting it. This is then extended because my interests are no more important than anyone else's,

impracticality of impartiality."[51]

Anthony Daniels pushes Singer's view to its logical extreme:

> No Bach cantatas or Sistine Chapel for Professor Singer; for him it is strictly grub first,
> then culture. To buy a Singer book is to murder a baby in Bolivia who might have been
> saved by the diversion of its cost to medical treatment there. Since Singer's books have
> sold by the hundreds of thousands, he has clearly been responsible for untold numbers
> of deaths. He should withdraw his books from the market at once.[52]

To be fair, however, Singer's common sense again partly balances his consequentialism, while still rightly challenging our consumerism.

> An ethical approach to life does not forbid having fun or enjoying food or wine, but it
> changes our sense of priorities. The effort and expense put into buying fashionable
> clothes, the endless search for more and more refined gastronomic pleasures, the aston-
> ishing additional expense that marks out the prestige car market . . . all these become
> disproportionate to people who can shift perspective long enough to take themselves, at
> least for a time, out of the spotlight.

But this is quite different to lowering our lifestyle to a Bengali refugee's—and this
shows again some real inconsistency between the two levels in Singer's position.[53]

Singer is right that the pursuit of personal happiness is self-defeating and that putting aside some of our interests for others' is a major part of what makes life meaningful. He is also right to highlight hypocritical discrepancies in some of those advocating
strong family values and absolutist sanctity-of-life ethics at the edges of life (abortion
and euthanasia) while displaying indifference to deadly poverty in the midst of life. But
that hypocrisy simply highlights a higher consistency in those advocating and acting
against *all* threats to life, such as Ronald Sider, John Stott, Cardinal Bernadin, J. Ever-
ett Koop, Mother Teresa, and above all Jesus Christ, whom they imitate.

---

and so I should paint my neighbor's house which is in more need ("Ethics and Impartiality," *Philosophical Studies* 43 [1983]: 86). Without being complacent about others' needs, utilitarianism's
strict works righteousness makes me grateful for Christian doctrines of grace, liberty and rest.

[51]Marilyn Friedman, "The Impracticality of Impartiality," *Journal of Philosophy* 86 (November 1989):
645-56. As an alternative she suggests that "our conceptual reference points should be particular
forms of partiality, that is, named biases whose distorted effects on moral thinking we recognize. . . .
The methods for eliminating recognizable biases from critical moral thinking" would stress "interpersonal and public dialogue" (p. 655).

[52]Daniels, "Utilitarianism Undermines," p. 19. Blackford is less colorful but equally dismissive of
Singer's position, which he paraphrases thus: "If we take the point of view of the universe, we can
recognize the urgency of doing something about the pain and suffering of others, before we even
consider promoting (for their own sake rather than as a means to reducing pain and suffering) other
possible values like beauty, knowledge, autonomy, or happiness" ("Singer's Plea," p. 29).

[53]Blackford, "Singer's Plea," p. 35.

Singer also minimizes the fact that charity begins at home. In opposing Singer's overly strict stress on the universal, we do need his reminder that charity does not end at home. But it is charity or love, not abstract interests or utility, that we are talking about.

In effect, Singer secularizes and universalizes the parable of the good Samaritan (Lk 10:25-37). The Samaritan who helps the beaten Jew lying by the side of the road takes seriously the neighborly responsibility that nearness lays upon him. He is moved to compassionate action, unlike the Levite and priest, who walk by on the other side of the road, deliberately distancing themselves. Singer's utilitarian and Promethean pursuit of an infinite, Godlike perspective does not take account of our finitude and creatureliness, and the difference that nearness, though not race or other differences, makes to the requirement of neighborliness.[54]

"The parable of the good Samaritan works by extending the notion of neighborliness in a way already implicit in it—Christ's hearers already know the answer when he asks 'Who was that man's neighbor?' Traditional morality is not bankrupt here. But there really is a change in the world, making our business crop up in areas where it actually did not for our ancestors,"[55] who may not have been aware of what was happening on the other side of the world as we do. This makes the tension between knowing about the neediest and personally knowing our nearest and dearest more difficult but not insurmountable.[56]

The notion of nearer and farther neighbors returns us to Singer's mother's case. The "real" relational dimension of life that Singer's sister and many women recog-

---

[54]Cf. ibid., pp. 33-34, for a demonstration of the inadequacy of Singer's examples of universal obligation. Also note James S. Fishkin, *The Limits of Obligation* (New Haven, Conn.: Yale University Press, 1982), esp. chap. 19, for a helpful philosophical and institutional alternative to individuals' being overwhelmed by obligation in a world of instant and almost infinite information about need. Fishkin quotes Marcus Singer's reference to "moral fanaticism" (*Generalization in Ethics* [London: Eyre, 1963], p. 185) and Anthony Quinton on "moral totalitarianism" in ways that are applicable to Peter Singer. Ethics, despite Singer, is not everything. The good things of God's creation are given to us to enjoy. We can turn our utilitarian moral calculators off every now and then.

[55]Midgely, "Consequentialism and Common Sense," p. 44.

[56]A helpful Christian perspective on the neediest versus nearest dilemma is Garth L. Hallett, *Priorities and Christian Ethics* (Cambridge: Cambridge University Press, 1998). Hallett shares some of Singer's and the New Testament's legitimate concerns for the neediest (such as the starving, p. 112) but honestly notes that the New Testament's "multiple intimations, even when combined, *do not certainly favor the neediest over the nearest*" (p. 54). Nor do they favor an exclusive preference for the nearest. My own suspicion is that the notion of vocation or calling to particular responsibilities provides a way forward here. See Gordon R. Preece, *The Viability of the Vocation Tradition in Trinitarian, Credal and Reformed Perspective* (Lewiston, N.Y.: Edwin Mellen, 1998). The need is not necessarily the call. This is filled out philosophically in Robert Merrihew Adams, "Vocation," *Faith and Philosophy* 4, no. 4 (October 1987): 448-61. He argues for "irreduceably individual ethical facts" that are universalizable for "anyone in a sufficiently similar situation," e.g., a parent.

nize should not be regarded by him as a concession to conventional morality instead
of the very heart of life. In a Judeo-Christian perspective the rational, though important, serves the relational and personal. Fortunately for his mother, Singer is a better
son and person than ethicist. "Does this mean that Singer is a moral fraud who says
one thing and does another? A kinder assessment would simply be that Singer, for all
his tough-mindedness, is a bundle of contradictions—just like the rest of us."[57] Yet as
Berkowitz says, despite Singer's integrity in admitting the difficulty of the difference
it makes when it's your mother,

> the ethicist's innocence, at this late date in his career, of the most elemental features of
> his subject matter boggles the mind. Indeed it is hard to imagine a more stunning
> rebuke to the well-heeled discipline of practical ethics than its most controversial and
> influential star, at the peak of his discipline, after an Oxford education, after 25 years as
> a university professor, and after the publication of thousands of pages laying down clear
> cut rules on life-and-death issues, should reveal, only as a result of a reporter's prodding,
> and only in the battle with his own elderly mother's suffering, that he has just begun to
> appreciate that the moral life is complex.[58]

Singer's rarefied rationalism hit moral *terra firma* in the particular and personal
moral claim of his mother's suffering. She is not merely a universalized unit of utility
or a nonperson.

The Singerian program is practical ethics applied to a range of life and death
issues. Despite some welcome features of the applied ethics movement—for
instance, its concern for objective truth—"the movement has been dominated by
ideas which undermine and devalue the core intuition which is at the heart of any
sound ethics: respect for, and cherishing of, other human beings whatever their age,
their abilities, their health, their rationality."[59] Thankfully, Singer seems to have got-
ten in touch with that intuition just in time for his memoryless mother. But even
though we can commend Singer's practical moral decency to his mother, it is disqualified by his own universal criteria of maximizing the interests of persons and
minimizing the pain of sentients. His concession to conventional morality at the
lower level of his theory leaves us with a schizophrenic motivation, torn between
head and heart. The clash between the infinite universal demands of his consequentialist equation of acts and omissions and the daily demands of particular persons
makes for infinite guilt and a lack of joy in life. This shows that it is impractical and
unlivable. In *Practical Ethics* Singer rightly states that an ethical theory must be able

[57]Hugh Mackay, "So Professor Singer Is Just Like All of Us," *The Age*, October 2, 1999, opinion page.
[58]Berkowitz, "Other People's Mothers," p. 27.
[59]Tobin, review of *Human Lives*, p. 109.

to guide us in practical life decisions, something his theory is unable to do:

> Ethics is not an ideal system that is noble in theory but no good in practice. The reverse
> of this is closer to the truth: an ethical judgement that is no good in practice must suffer
> from a theoretical defect as well, for the whole point of ethical judgment is to guide
> practice.[60]

Reductionistic Ecological Rationalism

Besides the unthinkable nature of some of Singer's key ideas and the impracticality of his philosophy, we can more broadly challenge its reductionistic rationalism. Here I will do so in ten interrelated points demonstrating its lack of ecological wholeness and awareness of creation and humanity as ends in themselves and its inability to overcome utilitarianism's tendency toward counterintuitive and totalitarian conclusions.

1. *Singer's consequentialism rejects the intrinsic value of creatures, whether humans, animals or biosphere.* They are only empty, replaceable vessels for holding the abstract value of interests in pleasure over pain. If other (nonrational, nonpersonal) humans or animals could be reproduced with greater prospects of increasing the total amount, the existing ones are replaceable (if painlessly). Feminist scholar Nel Noddings spots the oddness of this. "We are no longer considering how we shall meet the particular other but how we shall treat a vast group of interchangeable entities."[61] As animal rights advocate Tom Regan also says, "The grounds for finding unjust any practice that treats individuals who have inherent value as renewable resources are distinct from considerations about the consequences of such practices."[62]

Despite Singer's argument that Christianity has devalued animals, the doctrine of creation sees each part of creation as originally and intrinsically good (Gen 1), though it is after the creation of humanity that the whole creation is pronounced "very good" (Gen 1:31). In contrast, the utilitarian asks, "Good for what?" Where Christians have seen creation only in such utilitarian terms, they have failed to live up to the Bible's teaching and been party to ecological destruction.

2. *Singer's program uncritically adopts utilitarianism founder Jeremy Bentham's metaphysical assumption that the key criterion of the moral importance of a creature is "Can it suffer?"* This abstracts one allegedly black or white element from the

---

[60]Singer, *Practical Ethics*, p. 2.

[61]Nel Noddings, *Caring: A Feminine Approach to Ethics and Moral Education* (Berkeley: University of California Press, 1984), p. 154.

[62]Thomas Regan, *The Case for Animal Rights* (Berkeley: University of California Press, 1983), pp. 344-45.

great multicolored rainbow of existence. Even nonsentient (unfeeling) beings are still morally significant if they can flourish or be diminished according to their distinctive created end or purpose. All creatures and their purposes, especially humans, cannot be reduced to mere pleasure-over-pain machines. Bentham and Singer's criterion for moral significance of suffering or pleasure and pain "has an attractive air of moral urgency," but as the only criterion it suffers "ethical tunnel vision."[63]

Singer is like the man in the cartoon who says, "I'm an Idea man." He develops it more subtly than anyone else, but it is still essentially one idea, one that is not good enough to explain everything. It's "one size fits all" for all creatures. Daniels explains:

> Starting from the premise that it was wrong to inflict suffering without good cause, he came too swiftly to the utilitarian conclusion that this was the only possible wrong. If a being were not capable of self-conscious suffering, it could be done no wrong. A newborn baby is not capable of such suffering, and therefore infanticide is possible.[64]

For Singer, like Bentham,

> capacity for suffering—for pleasures and pains—becomes the common measure for both animal and human lives. . . . A further consequence is that human lives, just like animal lives, are of value only according to the satisfactions they deliver. Any sense of inherent worth, or of duties of respect based on the dignity of personhood, must be subordinated to "quality of life" measures—to predictable satisfactions. All animals are equal; but no two lives are of equal value.[65]

3. *Singer's consequentialism, allied to his metaphysics of suffering, makes some humans mere means to others' ends, mere carriers of consequences, as long as they suffer no pain.* Humans are no longer ends in themselves as in Christianity and Immanuel Kant's secularized Christian philosophy. Singer wants to move beyond Jesus and Kant but takes us behind them, to Stoic and pagan ethics.[66]

Nonrational humans (and also animals) become mere tools of Singer's preference utilitarian principle. He proclaims nothing wrong with killing those whose lives "no-one has a preference to protect" and whose parents decide their parental, and consequently society's, happiness will increase if they kill them and have other children. The (born or unborn) child's right to life is not in the kind of creature they are

---

[63]Tim Chappell, "In Defence of Speciesism," in *Human Lives: Critical Essays on Consequentialist Ethics,* ed. David S. Oderberg and Jacqueline A. Laing (London: Macmillan, 1997), p. 99.
[64]Daniels, "Utilitarianism Undermines," p. 19.
[65]Stephen Buckle, "Peter Singer's Ethics," *Bioethics Outlook,* 12, no. 3 (September 2001): 2-3.
[66]Singer, *How Are We to Live?* pp. 179-93.

but in their parents' mind or preferences. This denies our most basic moral intuitions about the intrinsic value of human life, evident in our abhorrence of parents who abuse or kill their children and our displeasure with those who smoke, drink or do drugs in pregnancy. Singer's reasoning "makes it difficult to justify a plausible response to child abuse."[67]

Singer describes "the end never justifies the means" as a "simplistic formula." He claims that it "is easily breached," for example in everyday trivial lies to save people's feelings. How much more for important issues like animal liberation![68] But Singer misses the point of such trivial lies. They are trivial compared with the absoluteness of the end involved, the inviolability of the human person—the very end he loses sight of and that the means must accord with.

"The ends justifying the means" can justify many things on Singer's view: animal liberationists' theft,[69] possible violence,[70] research on living embryos at any time prior

---

[67]Grant Gillett, "Young Human Beings: Metaphysics and Ethics," in *Human Lives: Critical Essays on Consequentialist Ethics*, ed. David S. Oderberg and Jacqueline A. Laing (London: Macmillan, 1997), p. 126. I would add that Singer's more recent advocacy of consenting sex between humans and animals would, if applied consistently, be likely to justify child sexual abuse as similarly consensual and nonharmful. Richard J. Neuhaus rightly asks "why, in the absence of *clear* consent on the animal's part, such intercourse is not a form of rape" ("Curious Encounter," p. 3, emphasis added).

[68]Singer, *Practical Ethics*, p. 292.

[69]Richard Egan ("Herod's Propaganda Chief," *News Weekly*, October 21, 1995, p. 14) writes of "a series of burglaries, arson, vandalism (of researchers' homes as well as offices and laboratories), bomb threats, harassment of blind people using guide dogs, contamination of food products and release of animals with infectious diseases carried out by the Animal Liberation Front and similar groups in the United States, Britain and elsewhere since 1976. . . . Singer supports ALF tactics in *Practical Ethics* 2nd ed., ch. 11 "Ends and Means," esp. 309: "because they treated sentient creatures as mere things to be treated as research tools . . . to stop such experiments is seen as a desirable goal and if breaking in to Genarelli's laboratory and stealing his videotapes was the only way to achieve it, then such action was justified." Earlier Singer said, "After more than a century, . . . militant opponents of uncontrolled experimentation can plausibly claim that legal means have been tried and have failed" (*Practical Ethics*, 1979, p. 188). Singer sees such methods as ways of informing the democratic majority (193).

[70]More seriously, Singer justifies violence in certain cases, though each case is different and thus subject to no general rules or prohibitions. Nonviolent civil disobedience is justifiable as a last resort, but Singer's naiveté about human nature opens the door too wide. His purely consequentialist constraints against violence, equating acts and omissions, thus holding the nonviolent responsible for violence they omit to prevent by violence, are like a finger in a dyke against the tide of violence. Singer claims that ALF members have damaged property used against animals "but they avoid violent acts against any animal, human or nonhuman. There seems no risk that by their tactics they will harden themselves to the use of violence against people (or other animals)" (*Practical Ethics*, 1979, p. 199; cf. 2nd ed., pp. 307-13). The record shows, however, that some groups have become hardened, violating researchers and their families' privacy and engaging in life-endangering acts such as car-bombing. Special legislation has been enacted in the United Kingdom, and at Cambridge alone, where I write this, police protection of researchers and their facilities cost over one million pounds annually, funds diverted from other needs. This shows the extraordinary

to the fetus's alleged ability to feel pain—that is, eighteen weeks[71]—wholesale abortion, declaring open season for a month on even mildly disabled newborns,[72] and possible experimental use of brain-damaged humans.[73] Many other morally unthinkable acts could also be justified on consequentialist grounds.

The justification of patently unjust acts such as torture in order to gain vital information has always been the Achilles' heel of utilitarianism. It is no less so of Singer's preference utilitarianism. This is alarming in the wake of post-September 11, 2001, calls for the use of torture on terrorists or suspected terrorists.[74] Once the genie of ends-justifying-means consequentialism is let out of the bottle of basic moral constraints, it cannot be put back in, despite Singer's confidence about our ability to control it.

4. *In the name of universal equality of interest/desire, Singer attacks speciesism— the automatic discounting of the desires of animals compared to humans.* Singer writes:

> Taken in itself . . . membership of the human species is not morally relevant. Other creatures on our planet also have interests. We have always assumed that we are justified in overriding their interests, but this bald assumption is simply species-selfishness. . . . Once we agree that race is not, in itself, morally significant, how can species be?[75]

---

naiveté of Singer's view that the means don't develop a momentum of their own. Further, while Singer deplores animal rights activists' mailing scientists razor blades, he does so only for strategic, utilitarian reasons. "It risks serious damage to the movement" (not to mention the scientists!) and risks being "seen simply as crazy terrorists trying to force their views on other people." Instead the movement's strength is its strong moral stand and case (Singer, "Only Human," p. 35). Without supporting all animal experiments or denying a place for civil disobedience, nonutilitarians can argue that some acts, such as cruelty to animals and the above violent acts against humans, are simply wrong.

[71]Singer, *Practical Ethics*, pp. 164-65. I say "alleged" because many researchers date fetal sentience much earlier than eighteen weeks. Peter McCullagh of the John Curtin School of Medical Research at the Australian National University, Canberra, concludes from "anatomical examination" and "observed foetal responses" that "the first trimester foetus has started to acquire sentient capacity perhaps as early as 6 weeks, certainly by 9 to 10 weeks of gestation" (quoted in Egan, "Herod's Propaganda Chief," p. 15).

[72]Singer, *Practical Ethics*, pp. 183-91, on the replaceability of mildly disabled (e.g., hemophiliac) infants on total utility grounds by analogy with the replaceability society practices with abortion. Egan cites the month figure (see *Rethinking Life and Death*, p. 217) but says, "Singer actually suggests 2-3 years of age as the logical cut-off point and implies that *any* infant could be ethically disposed of in this manner provided that there were not others eager to adopt such a child" ("Herod's Propaganda Chief," p. 15).

[73]Singer, "Only Human," p. 35.

[74]See <www.nytimes.com/2001/11/05/business/media/05TORT.html>.

[75]Peter Singer, "Ethics and the New Animal Liberation Movement," in *In Defence of Animals*, ed. Peter Singer (Oxford: Blackwell, 1985), p. 4.

To unpack this, we should note that Singer's regular refrain "in itself" in his attacks on speciesism hints that species may be deeply morally significant not just "in itself" but "more richly as an indicator of other features that are morally relevant." In fact, Singer distinguishes between the irrelevance of facts about species to the question of equal *consideration* of their interests and their relevance to equal *treatment* of those with interests.[76]

> It does not mean that animals have the same rights as you and I have. Animal liberationists do not minimize the obvious differences between most members of our species and members of other species. The rights to vote, freedom of speech, freedom of worship—none of these can apply to other animals. Similarly, what harms humans may cause much less harm, or even no harm at all, to some animals.[77]

Tony Coady comments that

> in Singer's own ethics . . . we have to consider every being in the universe, we have to turn our moral eye upon them, but how we judge and act will be determined by what we make of what sort of beings they are. At this point the trumpet call that species membership *in itself* is not relevant has begun to appear more like a gentle touch on the clavichord. Those of us still impressed by the moral pre-eminence of human beings may be excused for not hearing it.[78]

Singer's prophetic attack on the cruelty of modern intensive factory farming and much laboratory research is well taken. But in blaming Christianity for speciesism he falls for a form of genetic fallacy. His reasoning can be summarized thus:

> Christian (and some humanist) perspectives about the special nature of humanity have been dominant in Western culture.
> Modern Western culture is cruel to animals.
> Therefore this cruelty is due to the Christian philosophy of humanity's specialness.

This mistake is motivated by Singer's animus toward Christianity, not Christianity's animus toward animals. Animal cruelty is more simply explained first "from greed," second "from megalomaniac scientism. . . . We need to . . . reassert the very traditional value that cruelty to animals is wrong—indeed, the very appeal of Singer's work lies in the power of this traditional value, rather than in his 'new ethic.'"[79]

Ironically, Singer's stress on sentience and not species has itself been critiqued as a form of discrimination. It reduces not-yet or previously rational humans to the level

---

[76]Tony Coady, "Morality and Species," *Res Publica* 8, no. 2 (1999): 10.
[77]Singer, "Ethics and the New Animal Liberation Movement," p. 6.
[78]Coady, "Morality and Species," p. 10.
[79]Buckle, "Peter Singer's Ethics," p. 12.

of other sentient creatures because of its fixation on the capacity to suffer. Yet while this capacity to suffer is possibly a *sufficient* ground for moral significance—that is, we should seek to minimize pain—it is not a *necessary* one. Though beech trees feel no pain, they may be morally significant; because of what they are created to be, they shouldn't be chopped down indiscriminately.[80]

The beech tree example and Singer's indifference toward the intrinsic worth of nonsuffering creatures show that he is on his own grounds "sentientist," making moral discriminations on the basis of kind. Also, his sentientism in the context of ecophilosophy sits uneasily with his personism in the context of human bioethics. He was, after all, director of the Centre for *Human* Bioethics. If we should confine ourselves to arguments on the basis of sentience in the case of non-human interests, why is the same not true of human interests? . . . By demonstrating that he is pre-pared to distinguish between non-human interests and human interests, Singer acknowledges that there is some morally significant distinction between humans (qua type) and non-humans."[81]

"It is surely a ground-floor moral fact that if we are trying to work out how to respond to another being, we need to know what kind of being it is."[82] We need to know its nature to determine the distinctive conditions of flourishing or its opposite for that sort of being or species, to be aided or avoided respectively. So different treat-ments are morally appropriate to different species. Thus "the criterion of flourishing or well-being or its opposite *supersedes* the criterion of pleasure or its opposite because it *subsumes* it."[83] Pleasure as opposed to pain is part of flourishing but not the whole.

Further, each species has its "ecological niche," but humans, as "(reverent) regu-lator[s]" of ecological niches, are the only ones who can balance inevitable conflicts. This ability gives us a unique "moral status, right and role" as the only "scientific ani-mal" whose duty is to promote the natural world's well-being and flourishing overall, including humans, not just individual species' well-being."[84] This neo-Aristotelian philosophical view, of the flourishing of species according to their kinds and ends *(teloi)*, is a larger, deeper and more holistic understanding of human and species'

---

[80]Chappell, "In Defence of Speciesism," p. 98.

[81]Jacqueline A. Laing, "Innocence and Consequentialism: Inconsistency, Equivocation and Contra-diction in the Philosophy of Peter Singer," in *Human Lives: Critical Essays on Consequentialist Bioethics*, ed. David S. Oderberg and Jacqueline A. Laing (London: Macmillan, 1997), pp. 208-9.

[82]Coady, "Morality and Species," p. 10.

[83]Chappell, "In Defence of Speciesism," p. 100.

[84]Ibid., pp. 101-2, 107. Chappell illustrates the difference between humans and other creatures by arguing that we can cull deer because they cannot self-regulate their reproduction as rational humans can.

ends and interests/needs than Singer's "matter-of-fact" or "superficial" view of present, primarily sentient desires.[85] An Aristotelian teleological (purpose- or goal-oriented) ethic backs up the biblical view of the connection between human dominion and the flourishing of creation in our mutual end in God's kingdom.

Therefore Damon Linker perceptively sees an irony in Singer's advocacy of animal "rights" at the expense of human rights.

> It is a curious fact that in virtually all of human history, only in liberal democracies—societies founded on the recognition of the innate dignity of all members of the human race—have animals enjoyed certain minimum protections codified in our own country in the Animal Welfare Act. It is a no less curious fact that these same liberal democracies have become infected with a corrosive self-doubt, giving rise in some circles to . . . antihuman enthusiasms. . . . Can anyone really doubt that, were the misanthropic agenda of the animal rights movement actually to succeed, the result would be an *increase* in man's inhumanity, to man and animal alike? In the end, fostering our age-old "prejudice" in favor of human dignity may be the best thing we can do for animals, not to mention ourselves. . . . Until the day when a single animal stands up and, led by a love of justice and a sense of self-worth, insists that the world recognize and respect its dignity, all the philosophical gyrations of the activists will remain so much sophistry.[86]

Singer draws an analogy between racism and speciesism,[87] expressed in his rhetorical question: "If we assert that to have rights one must be a member of the human race, and that is all there is to it, then what are we to say to the racist who contends that to have rights you have to be a member of the Caucasian race, and that is all there is to it?"[88]

But the analogy has more rhetorical than logical force. The answer is that racism has been rejected on other grounds than Singer's equality of consideration principle, most commonly on the basis that racists reject our commonness of species or common humanity. Singer may reply that they were philosophically wrong to do so. "There is nothing about being human that can ground such a critique. But this can't be right, since there are all sorts of things about being human which form the bases for moral judgment and critique."[89] Examples include the capacities to suffer, love, grieve, be free, live by one's values. Some of these are uniquely human and contribute to distinctively human achievements.

---

[85]Coady, "Morality and Species," p. 11.
[86]Damon Linker in *Commentary*, quoted by Richard John Neuhaus, "The Public Square," *First Things*, August/September 2001, pp. 92-93.
[87]See Singer, *Practical Ethics*, pp. 55-62.
[88]Singer, "Ethics and the New Animal Liberation Movement," p. 4.
[89]Coady, "Morality and Species," p. 10.

Human beings have, for instance, achieved a developed understanding of their world through science, literature, philosophy, history and (some of us think) theology against which the purported successes of Washoe [the great ape] and his brethren pale into insignificance. And, as has often been remarked, we are the only species considering whether we should reform our attitudes and practices towards other species as a matter of principle. Although there are precursors and intimations of morality in other species, we are the only species considering who are capable of genuinely moral behaviour, both for good or ill, for nobility and, far too often, for wickedness.[90]

In sum, Singer has achieved much for animal welfare, but his argument against speciesism is specious and dangerous, not only to humans, as we shall see next, but to the flourishing of creation/nature as a whole.

5. *Singer wrongly personalizes some animals, like chimpanzees or pigs, and depersonalizes some humans, such as unborn children and newborns.* It is Singer's "guess" that "the pig is more self-aware, particularly if the infant has a brain disease and has no capacity to see itself as self-aware." "The pig [therefore] has the greater claim" to life. This leads him to say, "Pigs are highly intelligent animals. . . . Are we turning persons into bacon?"[91] Singer argues elsewhere that

> whatever criteria [for the right to life or having a valuable life or personhood] we choose . . . we will have to admit that they do not follow precisely the boundary of our own species. . . . There will surely be some nonhuman animals whose lives, by any standard, are more valuable than the lives of some humans. A chimpanzee, a dog, or pig, for instance, will have a higher degree of self-awareness and a greater capacity for meaningful relations with others than a severely retarded infant or someone in a state of advanced senility.[92]

Singer ranks animals (including humans) on a sliding scale of self-awareness. He normally ranks adult human persons higher than pigs and pigs higher than lizards.[93]

---

[90]Ibid. Cf. Williams, *Ethics and the Limits of Philosophy*, pp. 118-19: "Before we get to the question about how to treat animals we need to recognise the nature of the question implies the difference between humans and other animals. This is why speciesism is falsely modelled on racism and sexism, which really are prejudices. To suppose that there is an ineliminable white or male understanding of the world, and to think that the only choice is whether blacks or women should benefit from 'our' (white, male) practices or be harmed by them: this is already to be prejudiced. But in the case of human relations to animals, the analogues to such thoughts are simply correct."

[91]Quoted in Egan, "Herod's Propaganda Chief," p. 14. Cf. Singer, *Practical Ethics*, chap. 5, in more philosophical form.

[92]Singer, *Animal Liberation*, p. 19.

[93]Peter Singer, "Animals and the Value of Life," in *Matters of Life and Death: New Introductory Essays in Moral Philosophy*, ed. Tom Regan (New York: Random House, 1980), pp. 243-44.

"Somehow, . . . for Singer, the greater interest human beings have in living connects to the greater value human lives have (or normally have)." He cannot satisfactorily explain why. But a biblically based and intuitively recognized "relationship morality" can. Even if human beings are not the only persons, they are the preeminent examples of personal, relational presence we enter or experience in everyday ethical life. "We do not experience animals as persons" in themselves but by analogy to human persons. "As animals are like human persons, so they have an inherent value like that possessed by human persons." So pigs or chimpanzees which are more like humans would have a similar, though not the same inherent value as humans. Lower animals like lizards, and plants and inanimate nature, have a lesser, though not negligible, intrinsic value.

Further, different values lead to different obligations. "The closer animals are to human persons in their character and capacities, the more our obligations toward them will be like the obligations we have toward human persons by virtue of the person/person relationship." Still, "the responsibility we have toward a human infant is greater than that we have toward a fully grown higher nonhuman animal. . . . Our relationship to a human infant is the person/person relationship, while we have only an analogous relationship to even more developed nonhuman animals."[94] Relational morality can thus explain the basic moral intuition behind Singer's view of the differing moral values of various animals. This intuition of a *qualitative*, not just quantitative, difference between humans and even higher animals is summed up splendidly by Singer's utilitarian forebear John Stuart Mill: "It is better [morally?] to be a human being dissatisfied than a pig satisfied."[95]

Sadly, Singer follows Bentham's cruder utilitarian claim that "a full-grown horse or dog is beyond comparison a more rational, as well as a more conversable animal than an infant of a day or a week or even a month old." But as Tony Coady jokes, "The mind boggles at the conversations Bentham was prone to have with horses and dogs, but he appears, on the basis of this passage, to be in Dr. Dolittle's class."[96]

Moreover, without denying the need to treat pigs humanely or foreclosing debate on the issue of vegetarianism,[97] we must note that Singer's claims or guesses for the rationality, linguistic ability and personhood of pigs and chimps are controversial, to say the least. Jane Goodall, an expert on the great apes, whom Singer cites concern-

---

[94]James Kellenberger, *Relationship Morality* (University Park: Pennsylvania State University Press, 1995), pp. 363-76; I owe this section to Kellenberger.
[95]John Stuart Mill, *Utilitarianism*, ed. Mary Warnock (London: Collins/Fontana: 1962), p. 260.
[96]Coady, "Morality and Species," p. 11, quoting Bentham without source.
[97]See Stephen H. Webb, *Good Eating* (Grand Rapids, Mich.: Brazos, 2001).

ing their self-awareness,[98] still recognizes substantial differences between humans and apes.

> Man is aware of himself in a very different way to the dawning awareness of the chimpanzee. . . . Man's awareness of Self supersedes the primitive awareness of a fleshly body. . . . Man demands an explanation of the mystery of his being and the wonder of the world around him and the cosmos above him. . . . [A] chimpanzee can recognize himself in a mirror. But what if a chimpanzee wept tears of joy when he heard Bach thundering from a cathedral organ?[99]

Empirically, the story Singer cites of Washoe the chimp's using sign language as a form of self-awareness[100] has been questioned in basic psychology texts, as Brian Scarlett notes. He proposes Lloyd Morgan's psychological corollary of Occam's Razor stressing simplicity and economy of explanation: "In no case may we interpret an action as the outcome of a higher psychical function if it can be interpreted as the outcome of one which stands lower in the psychological scale."[101] Brian Scarlett cites a considerable body of criticism of "the ape language hypothesis." We can compare the nectar location of bees based on sophisticated data transfer. Should Singer then argue for equality for bees with humans? But all the bees do is transfer information. "They do not question, argue, make jokes, wonder whether it all matters." Neither does Washoe the ape. Yet this does not stop Singer from including a whole, eccentric section on "Common Themes in Primate Ethics"—from chimpanzees to Jesus—in his anthology *Ethics*.[102]

Ironically again, for one set against discrimination, Singer's argument for infanticide, based on newborn humans' not beating chimps and pigs to the title *person*, exchanges one "ism," speciesism, for another, variously labeled "adultism," "personism" and "I.Q.ism."[103] Young and old ends of the human spectrum are "excluded from the range of a stern and parochial myopic focus on the middle years of life." Singer's "denigration of human infants" is based on their lack of self-consciousness

---

[98]Singer, *Practical Ethics*, pp. 116-17.

[99]Jane van Lawick-Goodall, in her significantly named *In the Shadow of Man* (Boston: Houghton Mifflin, 1971), p. 251.

[100]Singer, *Practical Ethics*, pp. 111-15.

[101]Lloyd Morgan, quoted by Brian Scarlett, "The Moral Uniqueness of the Human Animal," in *Human Lives: Critical Essays on Consequentialist Bioethics*, ed. David S. Oderberg and Jacqueline A. Laing (London: Macmillan, 1997), pp. 97-99.

[102]Peter Singer, ed., *Ethics* (Oxford: Oxford University Press, 1994), part 1B.

[103]For it is only adult preferences that in practice count. See Jenny Teichman, "What Is Sacred?" *Quadrant*, May 1994, p. 20, and Jenny Teichman, "Humanism and Personism: The False Philosophy of Peter Singer," *Quadrant*, December 1992. Personism is the claim that a human has a right to life only as she or he shows certain characteristics of a "person" like rationality and self-consciousness. For "I.Q.ism" see Chappell, "In Defence of Speciesism," p. 98.

over time and a too easy dismissal of the moral significance of potential. This is not only logically but intuitively and empirically suspect. Psychologists confirm parents' intuitive knowledge that infants are much more aware than often assumed. They make predictions and act on them, experience a range of emotions, are sociable and are insatiable imitators. Also, despite Singer's claim that "differences in potential do not justify any difference in treatment," we kill baby tiger snakes on playgrounds because they are potentially poisonous to children.[104]

Singer's "moral actualism . . . values that which is actual and not that which is potential." Yet he is mainly an actualist against young human beings' right to life. Singer's argument against the significance of their potentiality confuses their humanhood and their personhood.[105] Young or unborn babies are *actually*, not just potentially, humans (unlike sperm and ova). They may not yet be rational persons with political rights, only potentially so, but they do have value and a right to life, and potentially other rights. Therefore humans "should give moral preference to the immature human person over the mature animal."[106]

Singer himself uses arguments from potentiality to support his own favorite causes and to distinguish his advocacy of infanticide or euthanasia for the allegedly nonrational from treatment of those who merely sleep or are anesthetized but have the potential to return to rational personhood. That Singer argues so hard "that 'euthanasia' might be the best thing for 'defective infants' indicates precisely that he considers the *potentiality* of non-disabled infants to develop in the *ordinary* way to be of moral significance. . . . Accordingly, there is no need to suppose that unborn humans are for moral purposes just like snails, a favorite personist contention designed to erode respect for the immature."[107]

---

[104]Scarlett, "Moral Uniqueness," pp. 89-92.

[105]Laing, "Innocence and Consequentialism," pp. 204-7. Singer's argument against the significance of potentiality for fetal or embryonic life is in *Practical Ethics*, pp. 152-63.

[106]Coady ("Morality and Species," p. 11) contrasts three interpretations of "the significance of species characteristics":

1. Global: gives moral significance to all members of a species because of species characteristics whether the member possesses the characteristics or not

2. Partial: bestows moral significance to all species members possessing species characteristics "actually or potentially or . . . retrospectively . . . [or by] connection with other individuals of the kind"

3. Particular: only accords moral significance to species members "who actually possess the characteristics [e.g., consciousness] at the time of consideration"

    Most people hold to 1 and 2; Singer seems to hold to 3.

[107]Laing, "Innocence and Consequentialism," pp. 204-7, citing Singer, "On Being Silenced in Germany," the appendix to *Practical Ethics*, pp. 354-56. The factory floor quality-control language of "defective infants," used in the first edition (1979, p. 132) was toned down in the second edition to "disabled" (1993, p. 183). It confuses humans and machines.

More colloquially and theologically, we can say that Singer makes personhood a special prize, not a humanly universal gift:

> The "species *Homo sapien*" is not an exclusive enough club for the Singers. Beyond "mere membership" you need a sort of Gold American Express card which shows you have attained the required physical development, moral maturity, high net worth, . . . or whatever other criterion the arbiters may choose.[108]

Ironically, as Bishop Rowan Williams notes:

> It is now far easier and more fashionable to defend the moral otherness of animals, or even of the inanimate environment, than to persuade people of the appropriateness of defending unborn humans . . . although there is intense *clinical* pressure to identify the foetus as a quasi-child whose welfare the mother is obliged to foster. The *reductio ad absurdum* of would-be legal definitions of foetal rights only serves to pinpoint the bizarre confusion British and American society tolerates in this area, where the defenders of veal calves and rainforests seem to find no problem with the moral invisibility of embryonic humans.[109]

To heap irony upon irony, Singer's non-speciesist world and use of "person" for pigs reminds us again of George Orwell's totalitarian *Animal Farm*, where in the name of an abstract equality the pigs became indistinguishable from the humans, proclaiming, "Four legs good, two legs better," and "All animals are equal, but some are more equal than others."[110] Singer's linguistic gymnastics are also reminiscent of the "newspeak" of Orwell's 1984, where ordinary terms acquired extraordinary meanings.[111] Rather than raising animals to the level of human persons as he claims, Singer lowers humans to their level by linguistic subterfuge.[112] Our uneasy question won't go away: "who will guard the guardians" or arbiters of personhood or a life worth living?

Historical experience warns us against the guardians. German protests against Singer were partly based on the "similarities between Singer's position on euthanasia and the . . . ideas of the eugenics movement." These were

---

[108]Charles Moore, "Protecting the Weakest Is Fundamental to the Moral Order of Society," *News Weekly*, October 21, 1995, p. 15.

[109]Rowan Williams, *Lost Icons: Reflections on Cultural Bereavement* (Edinburgh: T & T Clark, 2000), p. 46.

[110]George Orwell, *Animal Farm* (Harmondsworth, U.K.: Penguin, 1951), pp. 114, 120.

[111]George Orwell, 1984 (Harmondsworth, U.K.: Penguin, 1954), p. 7.

[112]Laing, "Innocence and Consequentialism," p. 219, quotes and then denies Singer's claim (*Practical Ethics*, p. 347) due to his "personist assumptions." Unlike some other views of animal rights, "Singer is *not* merely extending our ordinary concern for humans to animals. He is asking us to disregard our common humanity in any decision making about the vulnerable, the very young and the disabled."

that handicapped people are not persons in the full and usual sense, and that this lessens their claim to life. Critics warn that, once we accept that some human beings are separable from the rest via mere stipulative definitions (of "person" or "human being") dependent on certain background theories, then we are on a dangerous road, since then all sorts of criteria for segregating groups of people can be developed. Why would some definitions be more justified than others, if we can reach no agreement about the underlying frameworks (something standard in a pluralistic society)?[113]

The parallel between Singerite and Nazi policies is often dismissed due to the irony that the Jewish Singer himself lost family members to Hitler. Also, unlike Hitler, neither Singer nor euthanasia supporters are necessarily racist. But the eugenics movement for genetic purity was wider than just the Germans; between the two world wars it was widespread in Western societies, including my own Australia, where it was used to justify the separation of Aboriginal children from their families. In Germany the Nazi euthanasia policy "was 'racial' at this early stage only in the sense of aiming at creating a healthy population—an apparently worthy goal" like that of our own society, which can similarly slip into a form of "health fascism."[114]

In addition, some have noted that while Singer fights "speciesism," or discrimination against animals, he forgets the discrimination disabled people face, and even worse, supports it through his views. "The only alternative, they stress, is a formal principle of equality extended to all human beings, as is common in democratic societies."[115]

Viewed as mere functions, or mere sensate vehicles of pleasure over pain, we are all—conscious or not, with preferences or not—replaceable. There is no room for

---

[113]Herlinde Pauer-Studer, "Peter Singer on Euthanasia," *The Monist* 76, no. 2 (April 1993): 150.

[114]Almond, *Exploring Ethics*, p. 161. She notes the Christmas party at which staff celebrated their thousandth euthanasia. The Nazi philosophy was that some lives were unworthy of life. They tried to eradicate retarded children. This made it easier to move on to a hated race of people. Once you allow certain people to decide to kill on quality-of-life grounds, you have clambered onto a slippery slope where it is very difficult to apply a brake. Singerian Jonathan Glover (lecture at the Murdoch Institute, Royal Melbourne Children's Hospital, July 18, 2000) argues against the Nazi analogy by claiming that today's eugenics involves the choice of one or another fetus's being born for the sake of the child's own well-being, whereas Nazism focused on population elimination. Glover claims that the compassion (against Nietzsche) and individual autonomy (against the Nazi group perspective) and equality of respect involved in contemporary screening programs for Down syndrome, for example, make them very different from the Nazi program. Yet despite today's alleged compassion, the paternalism of parents and doctors, and the genetic screening system's coercion toward abortion, like Nazism combine to ensure that a whole class of people is being effectively eliminated. Cf. Michael Burleigh, *Death and Deliverance: "Euthanasia" in Germany, 1908-1945* (Cambridge: Cambridge University Press, 1994), p. 298, on the likeness between Singer's and Nazi intellectuals' redefinitions of personhood and analogies between some humans and nonhumans. See also 342 n. 30 for his view of Singer as a dangerous political rhetorician rather than a humane philosopher.

[115]Pauer-Studer, "Peter Singer on Euthanasia," p. 150.

complacency, as in Singer's claim to German disabled protestors that they would not now, having graduated to have preferences for life, fall under his executioner's ax.[116] On the basis of history they realized that Singer's philosophy is a fundamental attack on their worth and that of many others, even if they fortuitously happen to be alive with preferences for life now. They did not succumb to the sheer insensitivity of Singer's appeal to individualistic selfishness to set aside their connection to other disabled humans.[117] As the great German pastor Martin Niemöller memorably said: "First they came for the socialists, and I did not speak out—because I was not a socialist. Then they came for the trade unionists, and I did not speak out—because I was not a trade unionist. Then they came for the Jews, and I did not speak out— because I was not a Jew. Then they came for me—and there was no one left to speak for me."[118]

6. *Singer displays a very male form of ecological rationalism or "moral Thatcherism."*[119] He has strange bedfellows among economic rationalists with whom he often disagrees. One of them says, "Since he starts from the very same rationalist social calculus . . . there is no difference between his Benthamite calculus of social choice and that of the driest economist. . . . Modern economists . . . are simply Singer's philosophical cousins. But he takes his Benthamism far beyond the social sphere, by extending it to non-humans."[120] The fact that an economic rationalist sees him as a fellow traveler should set off alarm bells for Singer, his supporters and his opponents. As one critic said: "Singer is a Green candidate, and will in that guise argue against . . . economic rationalism; yet in another sphere [euthanasia] he will be arguing for the 'rationality' of death."[121] It shows the same paradoxical dominance of instrumental, calculative reason in Singer (or the means of reason over the ends of human life and relationship) that lies at the root of many of our ecological and social problems about which he is correctly concerned.

Consequentialist cost-benefit language is the native language of technologists, economists and policymakers. In bioethics this market language of measurable economic rationalism has changed patients to "customers" or "bed occupants." It is a dangerously dehumanizing language that challenges the integrity of the medical

---

[116]Singer, *Practical Ethics*, p. 345, in appendix "On Being Silenced in Germany."

[117]Coady, "Morality and Species," p. 12.

[118]Quoted by Franklin H. Littell, foreword to *Exile in the Fatherland: Martin Niemöller's Letters from Moabit Prison*, ed. Hubert G. Locke (Grand Rapids, Mich.: Eerdmans, 1986), p. viii.

[119]Scarlett, "Moral Uniqueness," p. 92, ironically after the former British prime minister, economic rationalist "Iron Lady" Margaret Thatcher. The American equivalent would be Reaganomics.

[120]Padraic McGuinness, "Senate Could Gain Benefits from the Fringe with Singer," *The Age*, February 14, 1996, p. A15.

[121]Michael Jorgensen, letter to *The Age*, October 26, 1996, letters page.

profession and its distinctive language of care.[122] Consequentialists have always been influenced by the pseudo-scientific quest for measurable morality, or a pleasure calculus, "or the increasingly popular 'qalys' (quality-assisted life years)" used to make life-and-death decisions. This runs "contrary to the Aristotelian dictum that ethics is only as precise as the subject matter allows and therefore contains more imprecision than, say, mathematics."[123]

Feminists such as Carol Gilligan and Nel Noddings[124] have questioned the universal validity of Singer's rather abstract male form of moral reasoning compared with more personal, relational and female forms of ethical responsibility. They advocate a warm ethics of care, intuition and feeling rather than cold consequences, and equal consideration of the interests of all sentient creatures. A feminist lecturer in social ecology aptly responds to Singer's advocacy of infanticide:

> I think [the newborn infant] does have a consciousness. Singer's position is clearly that of an arch-masculinist, one which somehow misses out on the personal, emotional and social. These are dry decisions he takes about the nature of life, whereas any woman who has been pregnant or been through an abortion has a completely different perspective on what it means to create life.[125]

Singer in turn accuses both Noddings and Gilligan of sexist stereotypes. (Thatcher was a woman, after all!). He claims, rather weakly, that evidence shows women are more universal and long-term in their ethical thinking than men.[126] I would not defend all of Gilligan's and Noddings's arguments.[127] However, Singer does not succeed in deflecting their basic point that abstract rational and utilitarian ethical theories are far from universally valid, at least for 50 percent of the human race. He admits that his "broader perspective must be able to recognize the central place that personal relationships have in human ethical life."[128] However, this is always a concession, not a passion of his own ethics, which therefore misses

---

[122]See Hans Reinders, "Why It Matters to Care About 'Care,'" *Zadok Papers* S117 (Autumn 2002).

[123]Introduction to *Human Lives: Critical Essays on Consequentialist Bioethics*, ed. David S. Oderberg and Jacqueline A. Laing (London: Macmillan, 1997), pp. 2-3.

[124]Carol Gilligan, *In a Different Voice: Psychological Theory and Women's Development* (Cambridge, Mass.: Harvard University Press, 1982); Noddings affirms a more female caring perspective of personal relationships with pets carrying obligations for the human party (*Caring*, pp. 153-59).

[125]Quoted in Leser, "Man in the Black Plastic Shoes," p. 57.

[126]Singer merely cites rough observations of David Suzuki and membership calculations from the environmental and animal liberation movements (*How Are We to Live?* pp. 177-78).

[127]For example, Noddings is wrong in denying our obligations toward animals whether they are our personal pets or not. She does, though, acknowledge the importance of not causing animals pain or treating them as mere means for humans (*Caring*, pp. 150, 158; see Kellenberger, *Relationship Morality*, pp. 375-76).

[128]Noddings, *Caring*, pp. 150, 158.

what is central in human existence and ethics.

7. *Singer is inconsistent in his treatment of moral intuitions. He seeks sometimes to undermine them, for example in relation to infanticide, and at other times to use them, for example against animal cruelty.* Singer claims the higher ground of reason in contemplating infanticide: "We should put aside feelings based on the small, helpless and—sometimes—cute appearance of human infants. . . . If we can put aside these emotionally moving but strictly irrelevant aspects of the killing of a baby we can see that the grounds for not killing persons do not apply to newborn infants."[129] His words trivialize profoundly positive human and parental emotions, the associated experiences of pregnancy and birth, and our instinctive reactions to them. These are basic to understanding the value of human life.[130]

The refrain of "putting aside feelings" or basic intuitions recurs in Singer's writings, as if he is afraid of them. This illustrates the way "consequentialism . . . obscures the habits of the heart or interpersonal perception and disposition that fuel moral judgment. . . . Consequentialism may lead us in a dangerous direction because it systematically devalues certain deep intuitions, such as those involved in the care and nurture of children . . . of fundamental significance in the constitution of a moral agent."[131] Noddings agrees: "We cannot accept an ethic that depends upon a definition of personhood if that definition diminishes our obligation to human infants. An ethic that forces us to classify human infants with rats and pigs is unsettling."[132] Contrary to Singer, James Kellenberger shows that unsettling intuitions can have good reasons behind them: "The basis for Noddings' intuition . . . is that humans, including infants, are persons, while rats and pigs are not."[133]

This objection to Singer's abstract rationalism does not entail an endorsement of postmodern irrationalism or subjectivism. Reason is important, but not all-important. "Rationality requires us to attend to facts about human nature (and other natures) and . . . it involves our dispositions, needs and emotions." "He quotes somewhere the Nazi, Göring, as saying 'I think with my blood,' and opposes rationality to this. But the moral emotions like sympathy, resentment, indignation, and compassion, are important to rationality and ethics." Again, the abuse of emotions does not deny their use. "Reason can also be abused; indeed it is arguable that many of the

---

[129]Singer, *Practical Ethics*, pp. 170-71.
[130]Coady, "Morality and Species," p. 12. Singer's inability to account for such "reactive attitudes," as P. F. Strawson discusses in *Freedom and Resentment and Other Essays* (London: Methuen, 1974), is critical.
[131]Gillett, "Young Human Beings," p. 126.
[132]Noddings, *Caring*, pp. 153-59.
[133]Kellenberger, *Relationship Morality*, p. 375.

Nazis were much more in thrall to their reason via a twisted and malicious ideology than they were to emotions. Himmler . . . writes somewhere of the difficulty he had in overcoming emotions like pity and compassion in favour of stern Nazi duties."[134] Singer deplores such "rigid moral fanaticism" but defines it as Kantian duty for duty's sake, not recognizing a similar danger in his own view. He wants an ethic "that builds on, instead of turning away from, our own nature as social beings,"[135] but his form of utilitarianism is unable to deliver this.

Raimond Gaita sees in Singer "an impoverished understanding of reason and its relation to feeling, of the distinction between knowledge of the head and knowledge of the heart."[136] Humankind does not live by head alone. C. S. Lewis diagnosed the Singerian problem in his essay "Men Without Chests": "It is not excess of thought but defect of fertile and generous emotion that marks them out. Their heads are no bigger than the ordinary: it is the atrophy of the chest beneath that makes them seem so."[137]

Singer is very honest about his anti-initiative strategy in one essay:

> Unfortunately, when a doctrine is very deeply embedded in people's moral intuitions, it is sometimes necessary to do more than refute the doctrine in order to convince people that it is false. . . . So the following historical excursion is intended to be a kind of softening-up operation on your intuitions, to persuade you that the doctrine of the sanctity of human life is a legacy of attitudes and beliefs that were once widespread, but which few people now would try to defend.[138]

Singer's softening-up operation is really an encouragement for people to harden their hearts and "by their wickedness suppress the truth" (Rom 1:18). Basic moral intuitions regarding such things as the intrinsic value of all human beings are not irrational but prerational, reflecting created and social reality, as I argued earlier concerning the yuck factor.[139]

---

[134]Coady, "Morality and Species," 12. Adolf Eichmann took a similar view (Singer, *How Are We to Live?* pp. 185-86).

[135]Singer, *How Are We to Live?* pp. 185-86.

[136]Raimond Gaita, "On the Sanctity of Human Life," *Quadrant*, April 1995, pp. 53-54.

[137]In C. S. Lewis, *The Abolition of Man* (1943; Oxford: Fount, 1978), p. 19.

[138]Peter Singer, "Unsanctifying Life," in *Ethical Issues Relating to Life and Death*, ed. John Ladd (New York: Oxford University Press, 1979), pp. 55-56. Contrast Hans S. Reinders, "Debunking the Sanctity of Life," chap. 2 of "Should We Prevent Handicapped Lives? Reflections on the Future of Disabled People in Liberal Society," unpublished manuscript, n. 7.

[139]Appeal to intuition is often suspect because of its subjective and metaphysical connotations, i.e., "immediate evidence of objective values." But many philosophers use *intuition* to refer to basic moral convictions forming the common basis of a society (therefore nonsubjective) which are internalized through socialization and which moral theories reflect. In this I believe there is often an echo of God's creation order. See Pauer-Studer, "Peter Singer on Euthanasia," p. 156 n. 40.

Singer is in a minority, with R. M. Hare his teacher, in rejecting the common idea that intuitions or "considered moral judgments can serve as 'the data' which moral theory is supposed to systematize. According to Singer, we should follow moral principles wherever they lead." Yet "it seems implausible either that principles should always defer to intuitions or that intuitions should always defer to principles."[140] Both are needed.

Paradoxically, Singer's two-level (critical and intuitive) form of utilitarian moral reasoning, following Hare, is an attempt to incorporate the intuitive in everyday decisions. Singer writes that our conventional intuitive principles built up from centuries of accrued experience—such as that honesty is the best policy—lead in the long term to the best consequences. This intuitive level is rather like "percentage tennis," which pays off most of the time, compared to the critical level or exceptional "freak shot." "In real life we usually cannot foresee all the complexities of our choices. It is simply not practical to try to calculate the consequences, in advance, of every choice we make." However, Singer's analogy is damaging to his theory, for if the critical level is like a "freak shot," for exceptional circumstances or players, why should we use it in everyday life? It creates two contradictory utilitarian principles, an everyday and an exceptional, elite one. The critical level is left to elite thinkers, like Singer, who can cope with "complicated issues."[141] Yet we saw earlier that actual complexity, such as in his mother's case, may drive him back to a more conventional action. In the end, utilitarianism's alleged practicality, crucial to its justification, is parasitic upon conventional, intuitive morality.

Rather than suggesting that Singer lacks all emotion, "as if some of the fuses marked 'emotion' have burned out in his brain,"[142] let me qualify my earlier comments by suggesting that he is driven by and does appeal to compassion or intuition, but inconsistently, for some animals, not others; for unborn or newborn humans sometimes and not other times.

Robert C. Solomon argues that there is another "compassionate Peter Singer" who is "often at odds" with the "champion of reason [and] hard-headed utilitarian weighing up harms and benefits." Singer agrees with David Hume that "sympathy" or compassion often declines with genetic distance from kin. Singer's aim is that the circle of compassion, "reciprocal altruism" or kindness, expand beyond kin

---

[140]Dale Jamieson, "Singer and the Practical Ethics Movement," in *Singer and His Critics*, ed. Dale Jamieson (Oxford: Blackwell, 1999), p. 8.
[141]Singer, *Practical Ethics*, pp. 92-93. For my critique see Laing, "Innocence and Consequentialism," p. 217.
[142]Macdonald, *Sunday Magazine*, p. 15.

and our own kind or species.[43]

But Solomon warns that impersonal reason can lose connection with the tacit, personal dimension that motivates ethical concern. We perceive others as feeling creatures not first because of rational principles but because of our "cultivated and expanded emotional awareness." Hardheartedness therefore is unnatural and requires the defenses of an ideological "pathology of theory" to distance ourselves from our emotional responses.[44] Solomon rightly notes that "utilitarianism and overly abstract calculations of the 'greatest good for the greatest number' can too easily serve as rationalizations for the most unethical practices and behavior. . . . Thinking about the 'greatest good for the greatest number'—even apart from the infinity-grabbing polemics of the philosophers—can too easily dull one's sensibilities."[45]

Solomon believes, "despite, as well as because of [Singer's] arguments," that an "ethics of emotion," not practical reason or theory, is primary in Singer. For Solomon "ethics is first of all a matter of emotion, to be cultivated from our natural inclinations of fellow feeling ('kinship') and moulded into a durable state of character." This is shown by the effectiveness of the photos of suffering animals in *Animal Liberation* for gathering supporters rather than "the ethereally controversial utilitarian attack on 'speciesism.'"

Solomon, however, rightly compares the use of unmistakably babylike photos of fetuses by antiabortionists.[46] Here I (not Solomon) note Singer's inconsistency, his constricted compassion, for animals but not for aborted humans. Singer's arguments against sentimentality regarding babies simply attempt to distance us from the intuitive force of recognizing the face of a human and its infinite demand.[47] As Rowan Williams states: if "moral otherness" depends on a form of quality control, a catego-

---

[43]See Singer's programmatic statement of his "expanding circle" in "Ethics and Animal Liberation," pp. 9-10. However, Holmes Rolston III argues that while some animals engage in mutual bonding and grooming as a kind of "I'll scratch your back, you scratch mine" (my terms), only humans love others for their own sakes and are able, though not always willing, to act as good Samaritans. "Naturalized" sociobiology neglects these unique capacities (Rolston, *Genes, Genesis and God: Values and their Origins in Natural and Human History*, Gifford Lectures 1997-1998 [New York: Cambridge University Press, 1999], pp. 222, 248, 252-56). While Singer partly attempts to stretch sociobiology beyond such theories as Richard Dawkins's "selfish gene," he remains somewhat stuck within its logic.

[44]Solomon, "Peter Singer's Expanding Circle," pp. 72-73, 76-77.

[45]Ibid., pp. 76-78.

[46]Ibid., pp. 82-83. Williams (*Lost Icons*, p. 45 n. 11) notes that the angry reactions against suggestions that women considering abortion see photos of an unborn child at their child's stage, or that such photos be published in the U.K. paper *The New Statesman*, show awareness of the power of "animal recognition."

[47]Emmanuel Lévinas, *Totality and Infinity: An Essay on Exteriority* (Pittsburgh, Penn.: Duquesne University Press, 1969), pp. 185-219.

rizing and counting up of rational or biological characteristics, it will inevitably be counterintuitive. Against Singer's counting of people as persons or moral others only if they are independent and share our interests, Williams sets "the significance of sheer instinctive recognition, 'animal' recognition we could almost say, in responding to something as a moral other."

Singer's questioning of this "animal" recognition is itself highly questionable, even on his own grounds of our affinity with animals. This recognition, not a rarefied, rationalist definition, rests on a recognition of our animal and ecological dependence on others along a spectrum at different stages of life, in or out of the womb, but at no point is there a clear "transition from one *kind* of life to another."[48]

Yet even Singer cannot ignore this intuitive recognition, in his mother's case, or in the case he examines of the possibility that we "grow human beings for use as spare parts in transplant surgery." Singer rightly urges caution here, for this "would do violence to our basic attitude of care and protection for infant human beings." Yet he is caught on the horns of a dilemma between his intuitive and critical levels. "If our basic attitude of care and protection matters morally even where non-persons [non-self-conscious beings on Singer's view] are concerned, then they matter where the lives of the embryonic, the unborn, the disabled, the suffering, comatose and elderly are at issue. It is, after all, precisely this kind of argument that is often relied on to demonstrate the wrongness of killing vulnerable people."[49]

And yet such counterintuitive killing is just what the critical, total utilitarian level of Singer's theory justifies. Singer justifies infanticide by challenging the arbitrary line of birth that distinguishes this from the wholesale abortion that our society practices.[50] The main difference would seem to be "out of sight, out of mind": we don't have to see the face of the aborted. Because Singer has a remnant of recognition of this intuition, he recommends an even more arbitrary cutoff point of one month for decisions regarding infanticide, so that the parents don't get too attached to their child. A far less arbitrary genetic and biological line is found when we work back from our birth intuitions into the womb to conception as the point where there is an onus of protection of the unborn.

---

[48]Williams, *Lost Icons*, pp. 42-43, 45 n. 11, drawing on Fergus Kerr (*Theology After Wittgenstein* [Oxford: Oxford University Press, 1986], pp. 176-77) who says, "Paradoxically enough, the more animal we remember ourselves to be [that is, the more we move away from defining ourselves as autonomous reasoners first and foremost—Williams], the weightier the theological objections to abortion and embryo experimentation [and euthanasia] might become." Cf. Oliver O'Donovan, *The Christian and the Unborn Child* (Bramcote, Nottinghamshire, U.K.: Grove, 1973), chap. 2, "Recognising the Human Face."

[49]Laing, "Innocence and Consequentialism," pp. 212-13.

[50]Singer, *Practical Ethics*, pp. 169-74.

In an increasingly postmodern society suspicious of rationalism or overly simple consistency, the appeal to people's basic moral intuitions is not without force. This is not to say that those intuitions are sufficient, just that they are necessary. An appropriate strategy for Christians in liberal and pluralistic postmodern cultures is to connect their Christian convictions concerning sanctity of life with those universal, creation-based and socially based intuitions. Otherwise the Creator's design for the flourishing of mutually dependent human lives from womb to tomb may be marginalized as mere ecclesiastical etiquette.

8. *Singer's strategy is to marginalize Christians (and representatives of other religions) from public rational debate and stereotype them as yesterday's people overtaken by the inevitable progress of reason.* Such "chronological snobbery" (C. S. Lewis) can readily rebound against its practitioners. The former Anglican archbishop of Melbourne, Keith Rayner, recently reflected upon the former premier of Victoria, Jeff Kennett, whose policies he sometimes opposed. Kennett dismissed the church's objections to gambling by describing them as "yesterday's people." The archbishop noted that "he is now yesterday's Premier," having lost an election.[51] To confuse the later with the better or more truthful involves a category mistake. Claims of inevitable progress that leaves religion in its wake are also disputable on rational and empirical grounds. We might note the turning of the tide against "inevitable secularization" theories[52] and against attempts to legalize euthanasia in some Western countries (the United States, the United Kingdom and Australia), and the 97 percent who rejected Singer in the 1996 Australian Senate elections.

Singer's anti-Christian secularism represents the nadir of Enlightenment humanism, ending in an antihuman naturalism. Singer is also almost the last Enlightenment or modern man—as Dale Jamieson says, "at his core Singer is an Enlightenment progressive."[53] Yet claims of unbiased scientific objectivity and unlimited progress are increasingly questioned.

"Singer chooses to ignore the psychological and social influences of his background, preferring to believe that his philosophy sprang from logic alone." He misses the postmodern irony in his old office poster "Knowledge is power, use it."[54] Postmodernists like Michel Foucault, for all their extremes, have demonstrated that knowledge is not disinterested but is socially and politically constructed, justifying

---

[51]Archbishop Keith Rayner, speech on receiving an honorary doctorate of Griffith University, Queensland, April 6, 2001, reported in *The Melbourne Anglican*, May 2001, p. 17.

[52]See John Squires, "Secularisation and Fundamentalism," *Values*, Spring 2001, pp. 1-5, for a useful survey.

[53]In Jamieson, "Singer and the Practical Ethics Movement," p. 14.

[54]Leser, "Man in the Black Plastic Shoes," pp. 54-56; yet Leser misses the irony.

one's particular position in the world and projecting it onto a universal screen as pure rationality or "the way things are."[155]

The greatest of American theologians, Jonathan Edwards, stood with one foot in the Augustinian tradition of "faith seeking understanding" and one in the Enlightenment. He argued that "all reason is *disposed*, that is, it is the embodied reasoning of some finite, historically located, human self which desires and loves, hates and loathes—and just so, *inclines* thought."[156] Rather than operating from some Olympian height with a privileged universal perspective, Singer stands in time and space in the Viennese and Oxford tradition of analytical philosophy, known as logical positivism, dominant between the two world wars, which rejected the meaningfulness or possibility of empirical verification of religious language. It is now largely discredited as one of the last gasps of overconfident modernity.[157] Singer is also very much a child of the 1960s with its sexual revolution and its antiwar and early ecological movements.

Singer's regular Enlightenment refrain is that through reason and cooperation we can deal with the problems facing humanity and creation, particularly those afflicting the weak and vulnerable, by promoting altruism. I do not question Singer's motives, merely the realism of his reading of history, both natural and cultural. He again prefers an abstract, speculative theory of the development of altruism to a historical explanation near to hand taking account of the role of Christianity in promoting it.[158] Singer resists Marxist utopianism with his own allegedly more realistic and

---

[155]Michel Foucault, *Power/Knowledge*, ed. Colin Gordon (New York: Pantheon, 1980). Note that this is not necessarily the same as total relativism or a denial of truth.

[156]Paul R. Hinlicky's summary in his review essay on Gerald R. McDermott, *Jonathan Edwards Confronts the Gods: Christian Theology, Enlightenment Religion and Non-Christian Faiths* (New York: Oxford University Press, 2000), in *Pro Ecclesia* 10, no. 3 (Summer 2001): 369.

[157]On the social location of the Viennese school see Stephen Toulmin, *Cosmopolis: The Hidden Agenda of Modernity* (Glencoe, Ill.: Free Press, 1990), pp. 84, 151, 157. Singer's teacher R. M. Hare was strongly influenced by it, and Singer is "a grand-child of Vienna."

[158]See Peter Singer, *A Darwinian Left: Politics, Evolution and Cooperation* (London: Weidenfeld & Nicolson, 1999), esp. pp. 60-62. Singer sees Darwinist views of self-interested human nature and genes as a useful reality check on abstract leftist ideals. But post-1960s Darwinism tracks the previously neglected "role of co-operation in improving an organism's prospects of survival and reproductive success" (p. 19). However, as Andrew Cameron comments (in his significantly titled review article "The Politics of Peace: Two Political Theologies," *Kategoria* 20 [Summer 2001]: 23-36), "perhaps we could ask whether this new move in evolutionary theory had less to do with the evidence of the fossil record than with the present-day existence of altruism and social co-operation demanding explanation in Darwinian terms. . . . If so, this would make it less a discovery than a supposition; and a supposition that might admit of other explanation. It is interesting, for example, that Singer's prime example of the phenomenon of altruism . . . are the high rates of blood and bone marrow donation in the UK [see *Darwinian Left*, p. 57]." Singer wants to understand why this happens so that we can foster further altruism. "But in this enquiry, apparently it is inadmissible that

modest but ultimately utopian Darwinian-left advocacy of cooperation between human and nonhuman animals. Singer's focus on self-awareness now includes self-awareness of our evolution and ability to engage in genetic manipulation toward a new age of universal animal altruism.[159] Given the historical record, however, especially of the twentieth century with its world wars, nuclear bombs and Chernobyl, and the natural record "red in tooth and claw," it is little more than a leap of faith. Perhaps Singer should read George Orwell's prescient critique of an earlier left utopia, appropriately entitled *Animal Farm*.

Many of Singer's critics wonder at his naive faith in systematic reason. He was quite surprised when *Animal Liberation* didn't win the world over to vegetarianism.[160] He is described as a neat systematizer influenced by his teacher Hare, one of the most systematic of contemporary thinkers. But the problem for such rationalists is the nonrationality of the world—the fact that, as Hare admitted, we're not "archangels."[161]

Singer's utopian faith in scientific reason and creaturely cooperation and his antagonism to Christianity, based on a mythical war between it and science, are easily illustrated. He makes a breathtaking, unjustified generalization that "once we admit that Darwin was right when he argued that human ethics evolved from the social instincts that we inherited from our non-human ancestors, we can put aside the hypothesis of a divine origin for ethics."[162] This assumes (along with fundamentalist Christians) that Darwinians must be anti-Christian and Christians must oppose Darwinian evolution. It is logically (given the possibility of theistic evolution) and empirically (given that there are many theistic evolutionists, including many scien-

---

the self-identity of the UK has until recently remained substantially Christian, and that high rates of charity overall there are deeply rooted in the strong Christian social conscience of at least the Victorians [the same could be said of the United States or Australia]. In Singer's closed universe, this 'understanding' of altruism is, apparently, an evolutionary one, or nothing" (pp. 31-32).

[159]Singer agrees with the anarchist Mikhail Bakhunin's criticism of Marx's naiveté about human nature and its lust for power (*Darwinian Left*, p. 4) and with recent history's verdict against Communism. However, toward the end this is naively forgotten in favor of rational altruism. "Only a little reflection" and awareness of the warmth of cooperation as opposed to competition will bring people out of their genetic and "economic self-interest" (*Darwinian Left*, pp. 45-46, 42). Quoting Richard Dawkins, Singer sees that although "we are built as gene machines we have the power to turn against our creators." Having reached Hegel's "End of History" as a "state of Absolute Knowledge," including knowledge of our own evolution, we can now direct evolution toward a new age of altruism and freedom (ibid., p. 63). Like a gnostic, Singer assumes that sin is ignorance and mere knowledge will overcome our captivity to sin. This is not science but what John Milbank calls "atheology" (Cameron, "Politics of Peace," p. 34).

[160]Gruen, "Must Utilitarians Be Impartial?" p. 129.

[161]R. M. Hare, *Moral Thinking* (Oxford: Clarendon, 1981), p. 44.

[162]Singer, introduction to *Ethics*, ed. Peter Singer (Oxford: Oxford University Press, 1994), p. 6.

tists) mistaken.[163] It is also a massive jump from the more strict scientific sense of Darwinism to social or ethical Darwinism; such a jump in fact is a form of the famous naturalistic fallacy (making *is* equal to *ought*, or *description* equal to *prescription*).

Compare Singer's overenthusiasm for education as the long-term solution to terrorism. In a series of logical leaps, Singer claims that such education would counter fundamentalism of all forms (Islamic and Christian). Fundamentalism is equated with belief in heavenly rewards—"about the only thing that could make it rational to fly into a building, killing yourself along with everyone else." Bible reading and faith are dismissed as "irrational beliefs" without argument, merely by association with fundamentalist literalism.[164] Singer also seems blind to the fact that his own fundamentalist philosophy that denies the intrinsic dignity and sanctity of individual lives could be just as easily responsible for the evil events of September 11, 2001, as was a peculiar version of Islamic fundamentalism.

These are examples of Singer's illiberal liberalism and antireligious rationalism. Singer's preference utilitarianism parades as liberal, seeking to maximize people's autonomous choices. But he uses liberalism to cover over the totalitarian implications of his utilitarianism and to banish the main alternative, Christianity, from the public realm of reason. Singer uses John Stuart Mill's liberalism as the soft, appealingly thin edge of his philosophical wedge, catering to our individualistic "culture of choice."[165] This justifies such practices as abortion, infanticide and voluntary euthanasia. However, like Mill, he is more utilitarian, even totalitarian (total utility being paramount), than liberal. Their "one very simple principle" that others' liberty can be constrained only for self-protection requires that everyone agree with their rational conclusions, thus ending political deliberation about social order. John Paul II describes this "thinly disguised totalitarianism," or liberalism against life, as due to "divorcing democracy from truth."[166]

As Hans Reinders notes, in banishing believers' distinctive language from the public realm,[167] Singer and Helga Kuhse use a kind of royal plural including them-

---

[163]See Michael Ruse, *Can a Darwinian Be a Christian?* (New York: Cambridge University Press, 2001).

[164]Peter Singer, "The Secret to Beating Fundamentalism," *The Age*, October 11, 2001, opinion page.

[165]Sally Blakeney, "The Brave New World of Peter Singer," *The Australian Weekend Review*, September 28-29, 1996, Features, p. 28. See Williams's perceptive comments in *Lost Icons*, chap. 1, "Childhood and Choice," questioning this culture.

[166]See Roger Kimball, *Experiments Against Reality* (Chicago: Ivan R. Dee, 2000), and John Paul II, *Centesimus Annus*, quoted in Richard John Neuhaus, "The Public Square," *First Things*, January 2001, p. 71.

[167]Helga Kuhse and Peter Singer, *Should the Baby Live? The Problem of Handicapped Infants* (Oxford: Oxford University Press, 1985), p. 117—this is characteristic of their argument.

selves and "liberal believers" as an assumed moral consensus in Western society. This covers "the question-begging nature of their argument" and excludes alternative arguments of sanctity-of-life supporters from the community of liberal rational thinkers like themselves. It is a serious if not fatal drawback, given their constant appeal to reason.

In effect, they are preaching to the converted, those who share the royal plural with them. Such a "consensus" is empirically questionable. Singer and Kuhse's argument against the sanctity of life can be paraphrased thus: "We—the authors of this book and the reader who shares our views—take X to be morally justified because it follows from what we—the authors . . . and the reader who shares our views—have already accepted as morally justified." Singer (and Kuhse) makes the classic modern liberal mistake of universalizing his alleged rationality as that of everyone—"we"— and making voiceless and invisible anyone who disagrees.[168]

In the well-known joke, Tonto and the Lone Ranger find themselves surrounded by twenty thousand Sioux Indians. The Lone Ranger asks, "What do you think we ought to do, Tonto?"

Tonto replies, "What do you mean *we*, paleface?" Many of us would reply similarly to Singer.

Singer's attempt to ban Christian reasons from public moral debate because not everyone in a pluralistic society can share them is inconsistent. First, it applies to all other views too. Moral positions are rational in terms of consistency with their internal premises and moral and nonmoral beliefs and convictions.[169]

Second, Singer's attempted censorship of Christians is inconsistent with his recognition that debate about different foundations for morality is unfinished. If so, no view can make exclusive or privileged claims to rationality as Singer regularly does, or try to ban other theological and moral views like a secular sanctity-of-life view as irrational. "The truth about moral reasoning is that it is governed by 'local rationalities.' Even if some of the locations are more crowded than others, this fact does not provide anyone with a title upon which 'we' together with 'many of us' could claim the right to occupy all of the universe of moral rationality."[170]

[168]Reinders, "Debunking the Sanctity of Life," pp. 10-11, citing Stanley Hauerwas, *After Christendom* (Nashville: Abingdon, 1991), p. 133, for the Tonto story.

[169]Alasdair MacIntyre, *After Virtue: A Study in Moral Theory*, 2nd ed. (London: Duckworth, 1985), pp. 6-12.

[170]Reinders, "Debunking the Sanctity of Life," p. 14. This is illustrated by the patronizing reactions of Singer to his German critics that "if the opponents only knew how to reason" they would agree with him. This is problematic when the contested situation of applied ethics is examined. It assumes we should apply rational principles to pressing social problems, but "there is no agreement among philosophers as to the underlying principles. In a way we have the situation that the

Third, Singer is, in effect, doing the same thing to Christians and other critics that he protests German and Princeton protestors have done or want done to him— silence free speech. This tendency toward exclusion fits with Singer's tendency to define some out of the community of rational personhood. Today it is the unborn, the disabled, the nonconscious aged, the Christians as a "deviant tradition"; who knows who it will be tomorrow?[71]

9. *Singer's preeminence in practical ethics is an expression of utilitarianism's strategic retreat or movement sideways into practical ethics after its metaphysical and moral inadequacies in philosophical ethics were widely recognized.* These include its inability to recognize the intrinsic wrongness of certain actions and the importance of motivation and personal, active agency in assigning responsibility.[72] Singer relies on Hare's and

---

'endless debates' of philosophers on normative ethical principles find a continuation on the level where they ought to be 'applied.' . . . Hence reference to rationality alone is not sufficient to decide these issues" (Pauer-Studer, "Singer on Euthanasia," p. 151).

   Raimond Gaita agrees. Singerians are often lauded for their logical consistency, no matter how unpalatable to the morally squeamish. "But they did not reach their conclusions gritting their teeth as reason relentlessly compelled them to go somewhere they desperately did not want to go. Nobody is in that way compelled by arguments about anything remotely interesting in ethics. Firstly, because all arguments in ethics have so many unclarities and depend on so many controversial premises. Secondly, . . . [if] Singer's arguments for infanticide are now accepted as deserving of serious consideration it is not just because of the logical power of the argument. It is because changes in the culture have disposed us to accept a conclusion that only thirty years ago discredited any argument that led to it, however logically powerful the argument might have appeared. Why hasn't Peter, who prides himself on thinking about thinking, taken more seriously the concept of a corrupted sensibility?" Further, acceptance of Singer's arguments represent not a victory of reason but "our turning away from our obligations to others when they conflict with our self-interest." Quoted in Sally Blakeny, "The Brave New World of Peter Singer," *The Australian Weekend Review*, September 28-29, 1996, Features, pp. 3-4.

[71]Reinders, "Debunking the Sanctity of Life," pp. 15-17.

[72]Jeffrey Stout (*Ethics After Babel: The Languages of Morals and Their Discontents* [Boston: Beacon, 1988], p. 297) describes consequentialism as "one of two major forms of optimistic modernism in ethical theory, recently come upon hard times" and "a machine for practical reason to live in." See also Bernard Williams, "A Critique of Utilitarianism," in *Utilitarianism: For and Against*, ed. J. J. C. Smart and Bernard Williams (Cambridge: Cambridge University Press, 1973). Williams's critique of Smart's type of act utilitarianism highlights a fatal flaw in utilitarianism generally. If consequences trump other moral considerations such as moral agency, motivation or character, then it will often be right to do the prima facie wrong. Williams presents two examples where utilitarianism/consequentialism pushes us to act in ways that violate our intuitive moral feelings. In both cases, if a person does not do a certain evil, someone else will, with far worse consequences. In one example, Pedro, a soldier, will kill twenty innocents unless Jim, a tourist, shoots one, thus setting the nineteen others free. For the utilitarian or consequentialist, if Jim refuses to shoot, his omission is as bad consequentially as if he shot the nineteen himself. Williams shows that utilitarianism is confused about Jim's (or any individual's) personal responsibility and completely inadequate concerning personal integrity. It makes all the difference in the world to his character whether he shoots. He shows that our core convictions, attitudes and personal projects do not fit utilitarianism.

others' inadequate answers and uses the urgency of being practical to cover over utilitarianism's fundamental ontological, anthropological and ethical flaws.

Catholic philosopher Charles Taylor shows how general morality involves, first, "strong evaluations" that some things are of supreme worth and, second, an "ontology of the human" involving fundamental claims about human nature and worth. These are best understood not in terms of human autonomy (self-rule) but as an objective recognition of a transcendent order of reality. Because we cannot suspend our ethical evaluations in a morally neutral midair position,

> we need an explicit moral ontology based on a description and assessment of human nature and the nature of the world. In the past this has usually been based on theistic claims. We are in the unfortunate position today that most of the secular moral ontologies belie the claims they make, in that their theories of human nature are at odds with the ethic they propose. Thus, in the case of utilitarianism, it has "a reductive ontology and a moral impetus, which are hard to combine."[73]

10. *Singer, more than anyone, sees how high the stakes are in the debate between consequentialism and Christianity.* He is in some ways like the great anti-Christian philosopher Friedrich Nietzsche, who in the nineteenth century condemned the novelist George Eliot and other Victorian moralists as "English flatheads" for trying to hold to Christian morality without Christian belief. Singer also agrees with Alasdair MacIntyre that Western reverence for individual lives as ends in themselves is a secularized form of Christian morality, which makes little sense as isolated fragments or moral formulas without the overarching theological framework or theory that grounds them.[74]

In some ways similarly, Quaker philosopher Elton Trueblood aptly describes our age as "a cut-flower civilization." Cut flowers look good for a while in a vase but are doomed because they have no sustenance or roots. Trueblood adds: "It is impossible to sustain certain elements of human dignity, once these have been severed from their cultural roots."[75] These Christian roots ironically sustain even Singer's intui-

---

R. M. Hare ("Loyalty and Evil Desires," in *Moral Thinking* [Oxford: Oxford University Press, 1981]), Singer's Oxford supervisor, responds to Williams by distinguishing "intuitive level" and "critical level" moral thinking, but we have already seen the contradiction between these two utilitarian principles.

[73]Charles Taylor, *Sources of the Self* (Cambridge: Cambridge University Press, 1989), p. 337.

[74]See Alasdair MacIntyre's "disquieting suggestion" that our current moral situation is like that after a violent antiscientific coup that, having destroyed all laboratories, has left us with only scientific fragments or formulas, which we uncomprehendingly quote against each other, without the theories that make sense of them (*After Virtue*, pp. 1-3). But also see Stout, *Ethics after Babel*, for a more optimistic view of the possibilities of moral agreement across traditions.

[75]D. Elton Trueblood, *A Place to Stand* (New York: Harper & Row, 1969), p. 14.

tive-level utilitarianism, by preventing the full consequences of its critical level, consequentialism, from being foreseen or felt.

Singer is right that his real enemy is Christianity. In his *Spectator* article entitled "Killing Babies Isn't Always Wrong," he writes: "Pope John Paul II proclaims that the widespread acceptance of abortion is a mortal threat to the traditional moral order. . . . I sometimes think that he and I at least share the virtue of seeing clearly what is at stake in the debate." Singerians advocate infanticide in order to re-create the stern philosophies of the pre-Christian world when babies—especially females, regarded as the property of their fathers—were left on garbage dumps. (In later generations Christians rescued and cared for these abandoned children.) "We must stoically resign ourselves, Singer argues, to an unredeemed and overpopulated world in which we have to kill useless and unwanted human beings." "Singer . . . sees clearly (as Nietzsche did before) that the Judeo-Christian prohibition against baby-killing is a tattered, incoherent, and indefensible ethical remnant when divorced from Judeo-Christian religious belief."[76]

Singer is correct that current debates about life issues reflect a choice between worldviews—secular utilitarian/consequentialist or Christian. However, at the risk of having a bet each way, I will claim not that *only* a Christian view can support the sanctity of human life, persons and relationships, but that it *best* supports it. Though Christians advocate a specifically Christian narrative ethic, we need not see this as necessarily in total opposition to a rational ethic based on universally recognizable principles, rules and virtues. Rather the two can work in tandem, as they often do in Scripture, given that God is Creator as well as Redeemer, as evidenced in Genesis, the wisdom literature, and such New Testament passages as Acts 17 and Romans 1—2.[77] Fortunately many, on seeing how high the stakes are, such as the sacrifice of the young and old, intuitively reject them, though not necessarily knowing why.

As Jean Bethke Elshtain argues against indiscriminate advocates of genetic engineering like Singer, "it is *our* ethics. Ethical reflection belongs to all of us—all those agitated radio callers—and it is the fears and apprehension of ordinary citizens that

---

[76]J. Bottum, "Facing Up to Infanticide," *First Things*, February 1996, pp. 41-44.
[77]Cf. Stanley Rudman, *Concepts of "Person" and Christian Ethics* (Cambridge: Cambridge University Press, 1997), p. 25, and Robert Gascoigne, *The Public Forum and Christian Ethics* (Cambridge: Cambridge University Press, 2001), for similar perspectives, and in Gascoigne's case a view in chap. 2 that Scripture itself provides a basis for "mediating principles" (or a form of natural law) between biblical revelation and human personal and communal experience. Protestants call this "general revelation" or "common grace." Contrast Stanley Hauerwas, *With the Grain of the Universe: The Church's Witness and Natural Theology* (Grand Rapids, Mich.: Brazos, 2001).

should be paid close and respectful attention."[78] We must make common cause with "all those agitated radio-callers" as cobelligerents, without being literally belligerent. And we must share with them good creation-based and Christian reasons for their moral intuitions.

Richard Neuhaus negotiates a nuanced way between mere commonsense or yuck-factor ethics based on common grace and the need for special, biblical revelation.

> The Yuck Factor may be an intelligently informed intuition that anticipates the disastrous consequences in what we human beings can do to ourselves. . . . Against the Yuck Factor playing much of a role in defending the *humanum*, however, is Raskolnikov's [the redeemed murderer of Dostoyevsky's *Crime and Punishment*] despairing cry, "Man gets used to anything—the beast!" We must hope that Raskolnikov will turn out to be wrong about that.'[79]

In Christ, he will be.

Conclusion

In this chapter I have argued, first, that our moral intuitions against infanticide, bestiality and the like are not to be easily rejected. The yuck factor, set within a balanced anthropology and ethic of reason and emotion, reflecting our personal and relational nature, is often a helpful warning against unwarranted ethical innovations such as Singer's. The yuck factor needs very strong reasons to be overturned, stronger than Singer has so far come up with.

Second, Singer's utilitarianism fails its own test of practicality. It leads to a split between critical utilitarian theory which prioritizes universal utility and our primary, personal and intuitive moral obligations and motivations. That Singer has only begun to appreciate this in the tragic case of his mother shows the naiveté and unlivable nature of his ethical theory.

Third, Singer's utilitarianism is reductionistic in its rationalism. It is unable to do justice to the nature of care, female rationality, persons and God's creation and is inconsistent in its use of intuition for the sake of animals but not newborn or unborn humans. For such reasons Singer's theory needs to be radically rethought.

---

[78]Jean Bethke Elshtain, "To Clone or Not to Clone," in *Clones and Clones: Facts and Fantasies About Human Cloning*, ed. Martha C. Nussbaum and Cass R. Sunstein (New York: W. W. Norton, 1998), pp. 184-85.
[79]Neuhaus, "Public Square," pp. 70-71.

2

Singer, Preference Utilitarianism & Infanticide

A N D R E W   S L O A N E

Peter Singer is a widely published and controversial philosopher and ethicist.[1] His views on animal liberation and biomedical ethics have become prominent in both philosophical literature and the media. His views on infanticide, while not enjoying the prominence in the media of, say, his position on voluntary euthanasia, constitute a serious challenge to "traditional" morality, and need to be addressed by those, like me, who endorse traditional views.[2] For his belief that defective newborns do not have a right to life, and so can be painlessly killed in certain circumstances, conflicts with the traditional commitment to infants as powerless people who must be protected and treated with respect, whether they are defective or not.

In this paper I will engage Peter Singer's ethical theory, preference utilitarianism, by way of his views on infanticide. In doing so I will explore the theoretical context of his views on infanticide and the relationship between his general ethical theory and his views on infanticide. For as I hope to demonstrate, Singer's conclusions on the morality of infanticide are an application of his theory to this specific issue.

---

[1]This is evident in Singer's editing A *Companion to Ethics* (Oxford: Blackwell, 1991) and writing the article on ethics in the *Encyclopaedia Britannica* CD 97 (Chicago: Encyclopaedia Britannica, 1997).
[2]The term "traditional morality" in this paper functions as a shorthand expression for various moral theories that accept traditional Western notions of the value of human life. It includes various kinds of Jewish, Islamic, Christian and nonreligious moral theories which differ from each other in important respects. My argument does not depend on their having crucial common features, except for their endorsement of the objective nature of morality. Given that I am an evangelical Christian ethicist, most of the examples will be drawn from recent work in evangelical ethics. The general arguments are, however, broadly applicable to other "traditional" moral theories.

In the first section I will briefly outline his stance on infanticide and his arguments in favor of the practice. The next section outlines preference utilitarianism and seeks to demonstrate the connections between his views on the ethics of infanticide and his general ethical theory, arguing that the former is an articulation of the latter with reference to a particular ethical issue.

In the third section I outline the arguments Singer adduces in favor of preference utilitarianism, before noting some crucial problems with the theory. I will seek to show that his arguments in favor of infanticide depend on the cogency of his theory; that preference utilitarianism suffers from fatal philosophical flaws which justify its rejection; that therefore his views on infanticide should be rejected. This, in turn, means that those who accept the traditional view—that infants, defective or not, are to be treated as persons rather than painlessly killed—are entitled to do so, despite Singer's claims to the contrary.

Singer and Infanticide

A case for Singer. I open this discussion with a case, for it is in real cases that we see clearly the implications of ethical theories. Ethics is ultimately about people and their problems, not just abstract theology or philosophy. The case I will use is one that Peter Singer uses in his discussion of infanticide, one in which he believes infanticide was clearly justified.

John Pearson was born on June 28, 1980. He had Down syndrome but no other defect. Down syndrome is a chromosomal abnormality associated with particular physical and intellectual abnormalities. People born with this abnormality normally have a reduced IQ, a characteristic physical appearance,[3] a high incidence of congenital heart disease, and a greater than average risk of developing certain infections and malignancies. However, despite their reduced life expectancy and "quality of life," such people do not suffer from the condition per se. John's parents, on discovering that he had Down syndrome, decided that they did not want him, and so those responsible for his care sedated him, gave him water "on demand only" and provided him with "nursing care" only. The aim of this treatment was to ensure he did not survive. He died three days later (July 1, 1980).[4]

Singer believes that not only was it right that John Pearson should die, all things considered, but his parents should have had the option of openly and painlessly kill-

---

[3]Down syndrome includes such features as short stature, so-called mongoloid facial appearance and a single palmar crease.

[4]Helga Kuhse and Peter Singer, *Should the Baby Live? The Problem of Handicapped Infants* (Oxford: Oxford University Press, 1985), pp. 1-3; Peter Singer, *Rethinking Life and Death: The Collapse of Our Traditional Ethics* (Melbourne: Text, 1994), p. 121.

ing him by, say, a lethal injection, as should others in similar circumstances.[5] He recognizes that this view evokes horror and revulsion in many people and that it conflicts with many of our deep-seated moral intuitions. However, far from leading him away from his conclusions, he believes that we should reject such feelings and intuitions as unjustified vestiges of a crumbling ethical tradition.[6]

Singer's case for infanticide. Why does Peter Singer believe that in a case such as this, infanticide—killing a newborn human baby—is ethically justified? There are two main reasons: (1) such an infant is not a person, and so painlessly killing her[7] is not wrong; (2) the consequences of killing that infant may be better than the consequences of not killing her, and so infanticide is a permissible, or even the right, action.

Singer's first line of argument for infanticide is that the normal reasons that count against (painlessly) killing persons do not apply to infants. He claims that a human infant has no inherent value that makes killing her wrong, for the traditional notions of the sanctity of (human) life that justify the wrongness of such an action are untenable. Singer argues this on two grounds: (1) the principle cannot be justified by recourse to rational argument, indeed such doctrines "collapse as soon as they are questioned";[8] and (2) it leads to unacceptable consequences when applied to difficult practical cases.[9] What does make killing wrong, he argues, is not that the entity that is killed is a human being but that such an entity is a *person*, human or otherwise.[10] To be a *person* an entity must be rational, self-conscious, aware of its own existence over time, able to communicate and so on.[11] Infants, like fetuses, do not have such capacities and so are not persons.[12] They should not be made to suffer, for

---

[5]This is the argument of Kuhse and Singer in *Should the Baby Live?* and is specifically endorsed by Peter Singer in *Practical Ethics*, 2nd ed. (Cambridge: Cambridge University Press, 1993), pp. 169-174, 181-91; *Rethinking Life and Death*, pp. 128-29.

[6]Singer, *Practical Ethics*, 170-71; Kuhse and Singer, *Should the Baby Live?* pp. 96-39; Singer, *Rethinking Life and Death*, pp. 1-6, 210-17.

[7]Singer and many other writers regularly use the impersonal pronoun *it* in reference to neonates. Such linguistic usage both reflects, and subtly reinforces, their view that such entities are not persons. I do not share that belief, and so I will refer to neonates using personal pronouns.

[8]Singer, *Practical Ethics*, p. 175, cf. 55-61, 72-78, 88-89, 150, 172-73; *Rethinking Life and Death*, pp. 159-83; Kuhse and Singer, 111—129.

[9]Singer, *Practical Ethics*, 176—178, 180; *Rethinking Life and Death*, 9—158; Kuhse and Singer, *Should the Baby Live?* pp. 18—54. Parallel to this claim is the one that other healthy cultures practice infanticide without horrendous social consequences, and hence ours is a "deviant tradition." See esp. Kuhse and Singer, *Should the Baby Live?* pp. 98-117; Singer, *Practical Ethics*, pp. 172-73; *Rethinking Life and Death*, pp. 129-30. I believe that all these claims can be defeated; demonstrating this, however, lies outside the scope of this paper.

[10]Singer, *Practical Ethics*, 83-100; Kuhse and Singer, *Should the Baby Live?* pp. 129-32.

[11]Singer, *Practical Ethics*, pp. 83-95; Kuhse and Singer, *Should the Baby Live?* pp. 131-32.

[12]Singer, *Practical Ethics*, pp. 169-70; *Rethinking Life and Death*, p. 210; Kuhse and Singer, *Should the Baby Live?* pp. 132-33.

that would violate what interests they do have, but they can be killed, so long as that is done painlessly.

Further, within Singer's ethical theory there are two main types of argument against killing persons, neither of which, he claims, counts against infanticide. The first is *indirect*: A policy of killing persons would generate anxiety in living persons, for they would themselves be potentially threatened by it.[13] But an infant is not able to understand the policy and so cannot feel threatened by it; "once we are old enough to comprehend the policy, we are too old to be threatened by it."[14] The second is *direct*: Persons have preferences oriented toward their future life, including the desire to go on living. Killing a person thwarts those preferences and so is wrong.[15] An infant, however, has no understanding of herself as existing over time and so can have no future-oriented preferences that killing her would thwart.[16]

Singer's second line of argument is that the consequences of killing a defective newborn may outweigh those of her surviving. Given that the normal reasons for the wrongness of killing persons do not apply to the killing of infants, the only grounds on which the question "should the baby live?" can be answered are consequentialist ones.[17] Now, it is not normally the case that the consequences of killing a normal healthy infant outweigh those of letting her live: her birth is usually a happy occasion for her parents; the quality of her life is likely to be good; if her parents do not want her, others in the community will. Hence killing a normal, healthy baby is wrong, but only because of the deleterious consequences of the action.[18] These arguments do not normally apply to severely handicapped infants, and so killing them may not be wrong. But again the considerations that make it wrong to kill a normal infant, but not wrong to kill a handicapped infant, are not due to the normal infant's having

---

[13]Singer, *Practical Ethics*, pp. 92-94.
[14]Ibid., p. 171; cf. Kuhse and Singer, *Should the Baby Live?* p. 138.
[15]Singer, *Practical Ethics*, pp. 94-95.
[16]Ibid., p. 171; Kuhse and Singer, *Should the Baby Live?* p. 132. He also refers to arguments he does not directly endorse as a preference utilitarian: a right to life that depends on "the capacity to want to go on living," or on the ability to see oneself as a "continuing mental subject," and respect for autonomy, in which killing a being is wrong if it goes against that being's clear choice. A human infant does not have the requisite capacities, and so the principle or right in question does not apply. For this, see Singer, *Practical Ethics*, pp. 95-100, 171, and Michael Tooley, "Abortion and Infanticide," in *Applied Ethics*, ed. Peter Singer (Oxford: Oxford University Press, 1986), pp. 57-85. In the former section Singer rejects autonomy as relevant to the level of crucial moral thinking but accepts it at the intuitive level. For this distinction, see below.
[17]Singer, *Practical Ethics*, pp. 182-84; Kuhse and Singer, *Should the Baby Live?* pp. 135, 140-71. The form of the question is of course taken from the title of Kuhse and Singer, *Should the Baby Live? The Problem of Handicapped Infants*.
[18]Singer, *Practical Ethics*, p. 182; Kuhse and Singer, *Should the Baby Live?* p. 135.

a right to life that the disabled one has not, but to the consequences of the action.[19] What are these considerations?

The first consideration is the consequences that killing the child will have on her parents. Singer states, "Parents may, with good reason, regret that a disabled child was ever born. In that event the effect that the death of the child will have on its [sic] parents can be a reason for, rather than against killing it."[20]

He does acknowledge that "some parents may want even the most gravely disabled infant to live as long as possible, and this desire would then be a reason against killing the infant."[21] However, the contrary desire counts in favor of killing the child, for the child threatens the future happiness of the parents and the family. Thus they are entitled to painlessly kill the child given their preference that she not live and the deleterious consequences of her doing so.[22]

The second consideration is what decision is in the best interests of the infant?[23] Singer assumes for the sake of the argument that the parents do not want the child and that it is unlikely that anyone else will either, thus making only the infant's interests relevant to the case.[24] He states:

> Infants are sentient beings who are neither rational nor self-conscious. So if we turn to consider the infants in themselves, independently of the attitudes of their parents, since their species is not relevant to their moral status, the principles that govern the wrongness of killing non-human animals who are sentient but not rational or self-conscious must apply here too. . . . Hence the quality of life that the infant can be expected to have is important.[25]

He argues that if "the life of an infant will be so miserable as not to be worth living," then all forms of preference utilitarianism would suggest that "it is better that the child should be helped to die without further suffering."[26] Such would be the case, for instance, for an infant with a severe case of spina bifida requiring multiple operations with commensurate suffering, but for whom such surgery would not overcome the paralysis, incontinence and intellectual disability associated with the condition.[27]

---

[19]Singer, *Practical Ethics*, p. 182.
[20]Ibid., p. 183. In Kuhse and Singer, *Should the Baby Live?* pp. 146-55, he extends this to the interests of the family as a whole, including siblings.
[21]Singer, *Practical Ethics*, p. 183.
[22]Ibid.
[23]Ibid.; Kuhse and Singer, *Should the Baby Live?* pp. 140-46.
[24]Singer, *Practical Ethics*, p. 183.
[25]Ibid., pp. 183-84.
[26]Ibid., p. 184; cf. Singer, *Rethinking Life and Death*, pp. 211-12; Kuhse and Singer, *Should the Baby Live?* p. 140-46.
[27]Singer, *Practical Ethics*, p. 184.

However, more marginal cases exist, in which the "total" and "prior existence" versions of utilitarianism diverge, cases in which an infant has "disabilities that make the child's life prospects significantly less promising than those of a normal child, but not so bleak as to make the child's life not worth living".[28] In such a case, say of hemophilia, the child's life is likely "to contain a positive balance of happiness over misery."[29] One version of preference utilitarianism, the "prior existence view," would see it as wrong to kill the infant even if his parents do not want him to live, for his death would rob him of this positive balance of pleasure and so would be wrong.[30] The other version, the "total" version, would see it as right to kill him if his death would mean that his parents would have another child whom they would not otherwise have, and that child were not similarly disabled.[31]

Central to this argument is the claim that infants, as sentient beings but not persons, are *replaceable*: it is not the life of the disabled child that matters but the quality of the life of the person which would result from the decision.[32] Thus the decision is to reject one potential life in favor of another: what justifies the decision is the claim that the loss of one life is outweighed by the conception of another, better life.[33]

No, it is not entirely clear which of these views Singer adopts. He recognizes problems with both the "total" and "prior existence" views,[34] but on balance it seems to me that he adopts the replaceability thesis, at least with respect to infanticide.[35]

---

[28]Ibid.

[29]Ibid., p. 185.

[30]Ibid.

[31]Ibid., pp. 185-90. It has been suggested to me that "total utilitarianism" is not a *version* of preference utilitarianism but an alternative to it; only the prior existence view is a version of it. Strictly speaking, this may be true in the literature, although I am not convinced that this is necessarily the case. Both versions are applicable to all accounts of utilitarianism, for they merely describe the scope of the entities whose benefit is being appraised. The impersonal nature of the total view is not in contrast with Singer's theory, as I will discuss below. In the preface to the second edition of *Practical Ethics* he notes that he has "dropped the suggestion . . . that one might try to combine the 'total' and 'prior existence' versions of utilitarianism, applying the former to sentient beings who are not self-conscious and the latter to those who are. I now think that preference utilitarianism is able to draw a sufficiently sharp distinction between these two categories to enable us to apply one version of utilitarianism to all sentient beings" (ibid., pp. x-xi).

[32]Ibid., pp. 186-88.

[33]Ibid., p. 188. He specifically argues for the replaceability of fetuses and extends it to infants.

[34]Ibid., pp. 119-31.

[35]See ibid., pp. 185-90, where he endorses the view and recognizes many advantages in seeing infants as replaceable, particularly with respect to the diagnosis of certain congenital abnormalities that are difficult or risky to detect *in utero*. Allowing the child to be born and then killing it may have clear advantages over *in utero* diagnosis and early abortion (ibid., pp. 189-90). He is more clearly in favor of the replaceability thesis in Kuhse and Singer, *Should the Baby Live?* pp. 155-61, and in Singer,

When these considerations are added to questions about the interests of the family and of society, the case for infanticide is stronger in such instances.[36]

Many of Singer's specific arguments in favor of infanticide are dubious at best.[37] However, my purpose in this paper is not to analyze the independent cogency of his specific arguments but to identify the relationship between them and his preference utilitarian theory. Indeed to analyze the specific arguments without reference to their place in his theory is mistaken, as Singer's arguments in favor of infanticide all reflect, and depend on, his general ethical theory. Thus I presented his views on infanticide largely as a window on his ethical theory. Hence I will leave the specific criticisms of his view of infanticide to one side and turn to the exposition of Singer's theory, preference utilitarianism, showing how it leads directly to his views on infanticide.

Singer's Theory: Preference Utilitarianism

Peter Singer's ethical theory can be stated quite simply: "Whatever action satisfies more preferences, adjusted according to the strength of the preferences, that is the action I ought to take."[38] This can be put in terms of a criterion of ethical action:

An action is right if it maximally furthers the interests of those affected by it.

This theory, however, entails a number of other important claims:

☐ the interests of all beings who have demonstrable interests should be considered, regardless of species[39]

☐ no interests (or the interests of no affected party) have more weight than any oth-

---

Rethinking Life and Death, he seems to have surrendered all his reservations (pp. 213-17). I think that the explanation for this, and his comment in the preface to the second edition of *Practical Ethics* (pp. x—xi), is that Singer has incorporated the replaceability thesis into his preference utilitarianism by way of two metaphors—the "moral ledger" and "life's uncertain voyage"—thus making the distinction between "prior existence" and "total" versions of utilitarianism otiose for his purposes (*Practical Ethics*, pp. 128-31).

[36]Kuhse and Singer, *Should the Baby Live?* pp. 146-55, 161-71.

[37]For specific counter-arguments, see Herlinde Pauer-Studer, "Peter Singer on Euthanasia," *The Monist* 76, no. 2 (April 1993): 135-57; Suzanne Uniacke and H. J. McCloskey, "Peter Singer and Non-voluntary Euthanasia: Tripping Down the Slippery Slope," *Journal of Applied Philosophy* 9, no. 2 (1992): 203-19; Raimond Gaita, "Some Questions for Peter Singer's Admirers," *Bioethics Outlook* 6, no. 4 (December 1995): 1—4; W. A. Landman, "The Morality of Killing and Causing Suffering: Reasons for Rejecting Peter Singer's Pluralistic Consequentialism," *South African Journal of Philosophy* 9, no. 4 (1990): 159-71; Michael Lockwood, "Singer on Killing and the Preference for Life," *Inquiry* 22 (1979): 157-70. For Singer's response to Pauer-Studer, see Peter Singer and Helga Kuhse, "More on Euthanasia: A Response to Pauer-Studer," *The Monist* 76, no. 2 (April 1993): 158-74.

[38]Peter Singer, *The Expanding Circle: Ethics and Sociobiology* (Oxford: Clarendon, 1981), p. 101.

[39]Singer, *Practical Ethics*, pp. 21, 57-62, 72-78; *Expanding Circle*, pp. 101, 119-21.

ers—that is, an interest is not more important than another just because it is *my* interest (the principle of universalizability)[40]

☐ only entities who have demonstrable interests can be factored into the ethical calculus, regardless of their species[41]

These ideas need to be dealt with in detail with reference to Singer's views on infanticide.

Now there are a number of general observations to be made before I show how this theory leads to his conclusions on infanticide. First, Singer's is a *consequentialist* theory: the moral value of an action (or disposition) lies in its historical effects and in them alone.[42] There is no transcendent value or goal to which actions (or dispositions) ought to head or to which they should conform.[43] There is nothing about an action (or disposition) which has intrinsic moral value; indeed important principles such as autonomy and rights are reducible to consequences.[44] This can be seen clearly in his views on infanticide in which consequences alone are relevant to the moral calculus. More specifically, it is a utilitarian theory, in that it aims at maximizing the nonmoral goods and minimizing the nonmoral evils of all affected by a decision.[45] For Singer the nonmoral goods to be sought are the *interests*, or *preferences*, of sentient beings,[46] and the nonmoral evils to be avoided are the *frustration* or *thwarting* of such interests or preferences.[47] Again, this is clearly illustrated in his case for infanticide: if the parents of a disabled child desire her to live, then that counts as a reason against killing her; if they do not desire the child to live, then that counts as a reason for killing her.[48]

Second, his theory operates at two levels: one in which general (not absolute) rules operate, the other in which they do not. The first of these is what he calls, following R. M. Hare, "the everyday intuitive level."[49] At this level we should

---

[40]Singer, *Practical Ethics*, pp. 10-11, 21.

[41]Ibid., pp. 67-68; *Expanding Circle*, pp. 122-24.

[42]Singer, *Practical Ethics*, p. 3.

[43]Ibid., pp. 3, 7-8.

[44]Ibid., pp. 95-100. In context of this discussion of the ethics of killing, he glosses autonomy in terms of a person's preferences and says that "rights" language is at best a shorthand expression for more fundamental moral considerations—namely preferences.

[45]Ibid., pp. 3, 13.

[46]These preferences are defined rather broadly as anything that such a being desires, unless that desire conflicts with another desire of that being (ibid., p. 13). While, strictly speaking, there is a difference between interests and preferences (for which see R. E. Goodin, "Utility and the Good," in *A Companion to Ethics*, ed. Peter Singer [Oxford: Blackwell, 1991], pp. 241-48), Singer uses the terms interchangeably.

[47]Singer, *Practical Ethics*, p. 13; *Expanding Circle*, p. 101.

[48]Singer, *Practical Ethics*, p. 183.

[49]Ibid., pp. x, 92-95; *Expanding Circle*, pp. 148-75.

operate according to established moral rules, seeing them as guidelines that, on the whole, will maximally further the interests of all those concerned. The reason we should do so is that we do not normally have the time and access to the amount of information, objectivity and foresight needed to make a considered judgment in each specific case.[50] In general, then, we should follow those rules that society has established because, on the whole, they "maximize the preferences" of all concerned.

However, when we are thinking philosophically we operate at the more reflective, critical level: we are consciously assessing such rules to see whether and in what circumstances they do, on balance, further the interests of those concerned.[51] At times this may dictate to us that we change the rules or break one in a specific circumstance, given that we are assured that it will maximize utility.[52] Thus preference utilitarianism, as expounded by Singer, is a careful synthesis of rule (more strictly, general) and act utilitarianism.[53] This, again, is illustrated in his views on infanticide: most of his discussion operates at the critical level; however, he acknowledges the social utility (intuitive level) of "granting" infants the right to life from birth, or perhaps a week or a month after birth.[54]

So what are the implications of this theory, and how does this relate to Singer's views on infanticide? Let me restate the preference utilitarian criterion of ethics in light of what I have just said:

> A rule should be adopted, or an action performed, if it maximally furthers the interests of those affected by it.

The first point to emphasize is that, according to Singer, all affected entities who have interests to consider should be "factored in" to the ethical calculus.[55] This means that parochial ethics that limit the focus of ethical decisions to those within our group, be that group a family, tribe, nation or species, are in error.[56] If a being as

[50]Singer, *Practical Ethics*, pp. 92-94; *Expanding Circle*, pp. 163-64; cf. R. M. Hare, "Universal Prescriptivism," in *A Companion to Ethics*, ed. Peter Singer (Oxford: Blackwell, 1991), pp. 461-62.

[51]Singer, *Practical Ethics*, pp. x, 92; *Expanding Circle*, pp. 152-67; Hare, "Universal Prescriptivism," p. 461.

[52]Singer, *Expanding Circle*, p. 167. For a detailed presentation of this, see R. M. Hare, *Moral Thinking: Its Levels, Method and Point* (Oxford: Oxford University Press, 1981), esp. pp. 25-28, 40-64.

[53]For a helpful description of these forms of utilitarianism, see W. K. Frankena, *Ethics*, 2nd ed. (Englewood Cliffs,, N.J.: Prentice-Hall, 1973), pp. 34-43.

[54]The "critical level" is seen in Singer, *Practical Ethics*, pp. 169-72, 181-91; the "intuitive level" is seen in ibid., pp. 172, 190; *Rethinking Life and Death*, p. 217; Kuhse and Singer, *Should the Baby Live?* pp. 193-96.

[55]Singer, *Practical Ethics*, pp. 21, 57-62, 72-78; *Expanding Circle*, pp. 101, 119-21.

[56]Singer, *Expanding Circle*, pp. 119-21.

such is to have an interest, then its interests must be considered, and weighed purely on the strength of the interest, not the entity's membership in a particular group or species.[57] Hence Singer's celebrated views on animal liberation and "speciesism." However, it must be noted that for beings who have interests, only the interests they do have are to be included in ethical decisions and given equal weight in them. Thus the interests of a normal human being are more wide-ranging than those of a fish or a mouse, and so have greater influence on ethical decisions.[58] And so "it is only when we are comparing similar interests—of which the interest in avoiding pain is the most important example—that the principle of equal consideration of interests demands we give equal weight to the interests of the human and the mouse."[59]

This brings us to a second important point. Only those beings who have an interest that can be affected are to have their interests considered when an ethical decision is being made. Thus any being that is not *sentient*, capable of experiencing pleasure and pain, has no *ethical* value: it has no interests to consider. Rocks, trees, microorganisms and so on have no value *in themselves* in ethical terms, for they are not sentient. The way a decision affects them has ethical value only if that, in turn, has an impact on those beings that *are* capable of experiencing pleasure and pain (so, for example, rain-forest loss is important because of its impact on sentient beings).[60]

But, further, only those sentient beings that are persons—that is, capable of reason and communication of some sort and conscious of themselves as existing over

---

[57]Singer, *Practical Ethics*, pp. 16-82; *Expanding Circle*, p. 120. This claim, of course, depends on a prior demonstration that the differences between human persons and nonhuman animals are differences of *degree* (of sentience, self-consciousness and so on), not of *kind* (being or not being created in the image of God), for which see Singer, *Practical Ethics*, chap. 3. This aspect of his theory, while very important, lies beyond the scope of this paper, and so I will not explore it any further here.

[58]Singer, *Practical Ethics*, pp. 57-61; cf. *Expanding Circle*, pp. 120-21.

[59]Singer, *Expanding Circle*, p. 121. This seems a puzzling claim to me, for I doubt that there are *any* cases in which a mouse's and a person's interests are comparable. Let us suppose that a mouse and a person could be similarly injured by an action, that such injury has no long-term effects and that it causes no anxieties and so on which may adversely affect the life of the person. I admit these are all rather implausible suppositions, but let us suppose them nonetheless. Just because one is a person and the other a mouse, they will have *different experiences of suffering*, and these differences will be such as to make their experiences incommensurable. For a person, according to Singer's own notion of what it means to be a person, is rational, aware of herself as a being existing over time, will have a range of beliefs, values and so on, all of which will influence how she experiences the injury. Hence there are no circumstances in which the interests of a mouse and a person are similar. This, it seems to me, is an important flaw in Singer's theory. I expect, however, that it is amenable to suitable articulation, and so I will not pursue it further here.

[60]Singer, *Practical Ethics*, pp. 264-88.

time—have any valid claim to a "right to life."[61] For while sentient beings with no such awareness clearly have interests in avoiding suffering and experiencing enjoyment, they can have no interest in their continued existence, for they are not aware of it.[62] This holds regardless of the species of the entity: hence Singer's argument against the "right to life" of infants.[63]

It is this claim that has the clearest impact on Singer's views on infanticide. For, he claims, human infants, while clearly sentient in that they can experience pleasure and pain, are not *persons*, for they are not rational, are unable to communicate and have no sense of themselves as existing over time.[64] Thus while it is wrong, on preference utilitarian grounds, to cause an infant to suffer, it is not wrong to kill an infant. Indeed in light of the preferences of the infant's parents not to rear, say, a disabled child, it may be permissible, even right, to kill the infant.[65]

The Justification of Preference Utilitarianism

Singer's case for preference utilitarianism. Now, it seems to me that Singer's views on infanticide are justified in terms of his ethical theory; they are a reasonable, consistent and coherent application of his views to an important area of practical ethics. But why should we believe Singer's account of ethics? He presents a number of arguments for the adoption of preference utilitarianism. His basic line of argument in justifying his view is as follows. Moral, or "ought," statements are prescriptions and nothing but prescriptions.[66] Inherent to the logic of such statements is universalizability.[67] This, when coupled with the associated assertion that there are no "facts of the matter" to which moral statements conform or refer, means that we are left with universal prescriptivism, which in turn either entails or is most consistent with preference utilitarianism.[68]

So the claim that ethical statements are not objective is a crucial one. If there is

---

[61]For Singer "right to life" is in quotation marks, for he does not believe that rights language is particularly helpful, nor does it comport well with his preference utilitarian theory. Thus the language of rights is useful only as a moderately inaccurate short-hand way of asserting other ethical values. See ibid., p. 96.

[62]Ibid., pp. 90-101.

[63]This argument is spelled out in detail above.

[64]Singer, *Practical Ethics*, pp. 182, 188.

[65]Ibid., pp. 169-74.

[66]Ibid., pp. 7-8; Peter Singer, "Reasoning Towards Utlitarianism,"in *Hare and Critics*, ed. D. Seanor and N. Fotion (Oxford: Clarendon, 1988), pp. 147, 149-51.

[67]Singer, *Practical Ethics*, pp. 10-12; *Expanding Circle*, pp. 100-103, 111-24; "Reasoning," pp. 149, 152-59; Peter Singer, *How Are We to Live? Ethics in an Age of Self-Interest* (Melbourne: Text, 1993), pp. 173-75.

[68]Singer, *Practical Ethics*, pp. 11-15; *Expanding Circle*, pp. 100-24; "Reasoning," pp. 147-59.

an objective realm of moral facts, then universal prescriptivism falls; indeed if a plausible account can be given of the logic of such objective moral claims, then it falls. For a central reason for adopting prescriptivism is that there is no coherent account of descriptivism.[69] So why does Singer believe that there is no objective "moral order," that "morals are not part of the fabric of the world"?[70] There are a number of strings to his skeptical bow.

The first directly follows J. L. Mackie's rejection of the objectivity of moral "facts" residing in some feature of the universe. Mackie sees assertions of the objectivity of moral statements as *ontological* rather than *linguistic* claims; that is, they claim to tell us something about how the world is, not just about how humans characteristically, or ideally, use language in moral discourse.[71] However, for such claims to be true, two further claims must follow: (1) that there are entities "out there" of a purely moral sort, hence different from all other entities we experience, and (2) that we have a faculty or means of perception by which we can come to know such entities, and which is similarly different from our other faculties.[72] Mackie proceeds to argue that no coherent account of such entities, or the moral faculties required to get in touch with them so as to derive moral knowledge from them, has been, or can be, presented. There is something "odd" or "queer" about such claims, and this queerness shows that they are false.[73] While this argument is arrayed against the "more extreme" theories of the objective status of moral claims, such as Platonic forms or pure intuitionism, he claims that other objectivist ethical theories simply mask the same features.[74] This argument is bolstered, Mackie believes, by a more cogent account of the objectifying qualities of moral dis-

---

[69]Singer, *Practical Ethics*, pp. 11-15; *Expanding Circle*, pp. 100-124; "Reasoning," pp. 147-59. Cf. Hare, "Universal Prescriptivism," pp. 451-63.

[70]The quote is from J. L. Mackie, *Ethics: Inventing Right and Wrong* (Harmondsworth, U.K.: Penguin, 1977), p. 15, whom Singer cites in support of his claim: Singer, *Practical Ethics*, pp. 7-8; *Expanding Circle*, pp. 106-10; "Reasoning," pp. 151-52.

[71]Mackie, *Ethics*, pp. 19-22, *pace* R. M. Hare, who argues that there is no true *philosophical* difference between subjectivist and objectivist moral claims (for which see, e.g., Hare, "Universal Prescriptivism," pp. 451-63).

[72]Mackie, *Ethics*, p. 38. Cf. Singer, *Expanding Circle*, p. 105; "Reasoning," p. 151.

[73]Mackie, *Ethics*, pp. 38-42. Cf. Singer, *Expanding Circle*, p. 107; "Reasoning," pp. 151-52. It must be noted that Singer follows Hare rather than Mackie in concluding that such accounts are *incoherent* rather than *false*.

[74]Mackie, *Ethics*, pp. 40-41. Note that Singer's citation of Mackie applies the criticisms he levels against extreme versions to all objectivist theories (Singer, *Expanding Circle*, p. 107; "Reasoning," p. 151). As we shall see, this is a crucial flaw in his argument against objectivist ethics—particularly in light of his caveat that it applies to all *nontheistic* objectivist views. However, the issues of his characterization of Christian theories and the cogency of his anti-Christian arguments, as important as they are, must be left to one side as beyond the scope of this paper.

course[75]—a claim Singer endorses, as we shall now see.

Singer presents a detailed account of the development of human morality in line with recent work in sociobiology. He sees the origin of ethical action in the altruistic behavior of many species.[76] Such altruism has, he believes, a genetic basis: once the genes coding for altruistic behavior (kin and reciprocal altruism) are established in a given social group, then such behavior has positive survival value for the bearers of those genes.[77] Human ethical systems are products of this genetic altruism's being paired with the cultural development of ethical systems by particular communities. The genetic component explains the commonalities of ethical systems; enculturation explains the differences between them.[78] Cultures themselves may be of evolutionary value, since a particular culture, and associated ethical code, may, on balance, enhance the survival of individuals within it.[79] This, he claims, does not establish the *normative value* of such ethical systems: far from it, it may undermine them by providing a sufficient explanation for the development of what are claimed to be universal moral facts or intuitions.[80] The logic of ethical reasoning grows out of this evolutionary development of human ethics.[81]

Such a (critically modified) sociobiological account of the development of ethics enables us to see it as a mode of human reasoning that arose out of limited, biologically based altruism, thereby seriously impugning the objective standing of moral claims.[82]

> So ethics loses its air of mystery. Its principles are not laws written up in heaven. Nor are they absolute truths about the universe, known by intuition. The principles of ethics come from our own nature as social, reasoning beings. . . . The fact that our ethical judgments are not dictated to us by an external authority does not mean that any ethical judgment is as good as any other. Ethical reasoning points the way to an assessment of ethical judgments from an objective point of view.[83]

---

[75]Mackie, *Ethics*, p. 42.

[76]Singer, *Expanding Circle*, pp. 3-53; *How Are We to Live?* pp. 84-105, 129-53.

[77]Singer, *Expanding Circle*, pp. 3-23; *How Are We to Live?* pp. 129-53. It is worth noting two things here, which Singer acknowledges. First, such a theory explains the survival value of an established genetic trait; it does not and cannot explain how it could get established in the face of group selfishness, for initially altruistic behavior would be detrimental to the survival of individuals within such a group, as Singer specifically acknowledges (*How Are We to Live?* p. 140). Second, such altruistic behavior has value, not necessarily for individual bearers of the genes, for it may well disadvantage them as individuals, but for the survival of the genes via the increased chance of the survival of the bearers of the genes *as a group* and passing on of the genes to future generations.

[78]Singer, *Expanding Circle*, pp. 24-32.

[79]Ibid., pp. 52-53; *How Are We to Live?* pp. 101-5.

[80]Singer, *Expanding Circle*, pp. 71-72, cf. 74-86.

[81]Ibid., pp. 87-124, and see below.

[82]Ibid., p. 149.

[83]Ibid.

To this claim, that moral judgments can be objectively assessed, and the way that justifies preference utilitarianism over other theories, we will now turn.

Having established, he believes, the incoherence and superfluity of objectivist accounts, Singer then claims that universal prescriptivism, and hence preference utilitarianism, necessarily follow.

> The rejection of descriptivism eliminates many possibilities [for the reconstruction of our moral concepts]. As long as this rejection stands, no reconstruction will allow us to support moral ideals by claiming that they are objectively true. On what basis, then, shall we assert our moral judgments? It seems our moral judgments will have to obtain their content from our own preferences, universalized. Nothing else can sneak in, because the only way in which it could sneak in would be by some claim that it is some kind of essential moral truth. In the absence of any coherent sense for such claims, they can only be treated as expressions of preferences.[84]

To see how this works, we need to understand the rationality of ethical assertions in Singer's theory and how that relates to the social evolution of ethical systems.

Singer argues, as we have seen, that ethical systems arise out of biological and cultural processes. Genetically based altruism, when added to a person's ability to make judgments, use language, be aware of the self over time and so on, gives rise to ethical systems.[85] In such a system justification entails giving a response to demands for reasons for one's actions—reasons whose validity will be acknowledged by all members of the group, thereby giving it at least the semblance of impartial reasoning.[86] Such reasoning, he argues, gives rise to a line of development of ethical systems from animal reciprocity, to customary morality and then to critical-reflective morality, with increasing application of reasoning at each stage.[87]

It is worth noting here that despite his (critical) acceptance of sociobiology, Singer rejects the claim frequently associated with it that we are genetically selfish beings and that all ethics is merely disguised (genetic) selfishness.[88] Indeed he claims that since the rise of ethical systems we are "moved" toward greater consistency within our ethical theories, and between them and our actions, by the psychological phenomenon of "cognitive dissonance" and the drive toward "dissonance reduction."[89] It is in relation to this social development of moral reasoning that the logic of moral assertions operates.

---

[84]Singer, "Reasoning," p. 154.
[85]Singer, *Expanding Circle*, p. 90.
[86]Ibid., p. 93; *How Are We to Live?* p. 174.
[87]Singer, *Expanding Circle*, pp. 94-100.
[88]Ibid., pp. 125-47; cf. *How Are We to Live?* pp. 84-105.
[89]Singer, *Expanding Circle*, pp. 141-47.

Given that there are no ethical "facts," the *meaning* of ethical statements cannot be referential, for there is nothing "out there" to which they refer.[90] Indeed assertions of moral ideals become themselves no more than expressions of preferences.[91] Does this entail that there is no meaning to ethical statements, no rationality to moral discourse? No.[92] For what we are left with after the abolition of objectivity are prescriptions: all moral ideals, assertions, laws and so on are logically equivalent to "thou shalt" or "thou shalt not." By their very nature these prescriptions, or "ought" statements (as opposed to commands), are universalizable; indeed logically they are universalized expressions of preferences.[93] Hence if they are to be asserted meaningfully at all, they must be taken to apply to all relevantly similar circumstances, no matter who is involved.[94]

It is interesting that Singer seems on some occasions to assert that this universalizability of prescriptions is *logically necessary* and on others that it is *socially necessary*.[95] I think what he means is that while the development of human reason is a social and cultural phenomenon largely related to getting on in society, the process of reason it gives rise to transcends that social and cultural context. If it is rational, it is eternal and objective, transcending human social pragmatism. That, at least, seems to be the force of his statement that "there is *something* in ethics which is eternal and universal, not dependent on the existence of human beings or other creatures with preferences. The process of reasoning we have been discussing is eternal and universal."[96]

When this essential, logical feature of moral discourse is added to the existence of preferences or interests that moral assertions reflect, the result is universal prescriptivism, which in turn justifies preference utilitarianism.[97] For there are no substantive moral facts (except perhaps universalizability as the definition of a moral claim);[98]

---

[90]Ibid., pp. 105-11; "Reasoning," p. 154.

[91]Singer, "Reasoning," pp. 150-51, 154.

[92]Singer, *Practical Ethics*, pp. 7-8; "Reasoning," pp. 152-59.

[93]Singer, *Practical Ethics*, p. 10.

[94]Ibid., pp. 10-12. Singer acknowledges his dependence on the arguments of R. M. Hare, for which see, e.g., "Universal Prescriptivism," pp. 451-63; *Moral Thinking*, esp. pp. 65-116, 206-28.

[95]For the former, see Singer, *Expanding Circle*, 93-100; for the latter, see *Expanding Circle*, 105-6; "Reasoning," pp. 149, 154-59. For what seems to me to be a confusion of the two, see *Practical Ethics*, p. 10. A similar charge is made against Singer in W. A. Rottschaefer and D. L. Martinsen, "Singer, Sociobiology and Values: Pure Reason Versus Empirical Reason," *Zygon* 19, no. 2 (June 1984): 159-70. They make the charge in order to justify sociobiological ethics, which is, of course, substantially different from my purposes here.

[96]Singer, *Expanding Circle*, pp. 105-6.

[97]Singer, *Practical Ethics*, pp. 12-15; *Expanding Circle*, pp. 100-101, 106, 109, 118-21; "Reasoning," pp. 154, 157-59. Cf. Hare, "Universal Prescriptivism," pp. 460-62.

[98]Singer, "Reasoning," pp. 155-56, hints at this as a moral "fact of the matter" when he talks of it as

there are only people's preferences.[99] But for these preferences to be moral at all, they need to be universal in scope.[100] This, then, means that all preferences must be taken into account, regardless of whose preferences they are.[101] Hence preference utilitarianism.

The case against Singer's preference utilitarianism. Before I turn to crucial flaws in Singer's theory, let me acknowledge some of its positive features. First, it is a (relatively) consistent theory which articulates well the philosophical viewpoint with which he operates. Second, he effectively exposes some of the intellectual and practical flaws in rigidly absolutist versions of sanctity-of-life ethics and some of the inconsistent maneuvers proponents of such views must make to deal with difficult and conflicted situations. Third, he reminds us that we need to consider the consequences of our actions and policies if we are to do justice to the realities of personal existence.

However, there are a number of flaws in Singer's preference utilitarianism and the reasons he adduces as to why it should be adopted. Let me note in passing that the following discussion does not directly address whether Singer is entitled to his theory; rather it aims to demonstrate that exponents of traditional moral theories are entitled to reject it. So too it may be the case that some of these criticisms are less than persuasive to Singer and others who accept preference utilitarianism. That does not mean that the criticisms are unsound; it is a reflection of my task. For my purpose in this paper is to address the challenge Singer has presented to the traditional rejection of infanticide. However, some of the problems I identify are such that Singer and other exponents of preference utilitarianism need to address them to be entitled to hold the theory. Indeed if the criticisms of preference utilitarianism are sound, then they may undermine his arguments on other ethical issues such as voluntary euthanasia. Again, however, these are secondary concerns, as my primary aim is to demonstrate that Singer's arguments do not lead to the final collapse of traditional morality, and that therefore we are entitled to reject Singer's theory and his views on infanticide. Furthermore, what follows is not comprehensive: much of the discussion refers to other works which demonstrate my claims, and there are no doubt other arguments which could be advanced. To address these issues is beyond the scope of this paper. Let me turn, then, to some specific criticisms of preference utilitarianism.

---

being a substantive decision to talk about some questions rather than others, a decision that largely determines his prescriptivist, and hence preference utilitarian, conclusions.

[99]Singer, *Expanding Circle*, pp. 105-11; "Reasoning," pp. 150-51, 154.

[100]Singer, *Practical Ethics*, pp. 10-12; *Expanding Circle*, p. 100. In these passages the status of "universalizability" as an absolute moral principle along with its apparent intuitive nature is clear.

[101]Singer, *Practical Ethics*, pp. 13-14; *Expanding Circle*, pp. 100-102, 119-21; "Reasoning," pp. 155-59.

First, Singer's account of the sociobiological development of ethics in human communities is highly speculative and at times may justify the existence of an objective moral order, the very thing he seeks to undermine. On numerous occasions he relies on possibilities and suppositions, at times with no factual support, but then treats his account as sufficiently well grounded as to provide a more cogent explanation of human morality than its rivals.[102] At a crucial point in the development of altruism, its getting established in a particular biological community, he has no explanatory mechanism—even a hypothetical one.[103] While he demonstrates its survival value *once established* in a particular biological community, he cannot explain how it could gain the necessary foothold in the face of the short-term value of selfish behavior.

It seems to me that the existence of an objective moral order, with which such behavior coheres, provides the required explanation.[104] Moral order is composed of generic and teleologically ordered relationships between entities. These objective patterns of relationship determine the moral status of an agent's character, actions and consequences. If there is such a moral order, the development of altruistic behavior and its generic correlatives can be seen as an expression of objective moral order and as corresponding to that order. This then accounts for the emergence of moral behavior such as altruism, for it corresponds to this moral order, enables the organism to interact meaningfully with it and contributes to its flourishing.[105] Such a pattern of behavior, then, is of survival value for the organisms and groups that express it, just because it enables them to live in a manner consistent with moral reality.

Thus belief in an objective moral order fills in a gap in Singer's explanation of the development of morality.[106] Of course Singer cannot endorse an explanation such as

---

[102]See, e.g., Singer, *Expanding Circle*, pp. 3-23, 33-41, 52-53. Throughout these pages Singer is heavily dependent on conditionals, such as *may, might* and *can*, in outlining the evolutionary development of altruism (and hence the starting point for ethical systems). However, he then treats such suppositions as a sufficient *factual* basis for his further theorizing, thus hiding the essentially hypothetical nature of his case.

[103]See Singer, *Expanding Circle*, chap. 1, "The Origins of Altruism."

[104]In this discussion I am indebted to Oliver O'Donovan's treatment of moral order in *Resurrection and Moral Order: An Outline for Evangelical Ethics* (Leicester, U.K.: Inter-Varsity Press, 1986), pp. 31-52.

[105]I am not here claiming that there is a Platonic world of moral substances to which we gain access by means of specific moral faculties. Rather I am claiming that the world as it is exhibits patterns of relationships that can best be explained in moral categories and that such explanations comport with states of affairs in the world. Furthermore, the emergence of such moral traits may still have an evolutionary explanation, without vitiating the reality of moral order. Such traits would be analogous to sight, for instance, which provides an organism with the ability to respond to the objective reality of light and its effects on other entities.

[106]This means that sociobiological accounts of the development of human morality need not be in conflict with Christian and other objectivist moral theories.

the one I have outlined here, for that would defeat the purpose of his study, which is to discount claims that such an objective moral order exists.

Second, his account of and arguments against Christian ontology and the ontological grounding of Christian morality are at different times specious, misleading, question-begging, irrelevant or just wrong.[107] This is particularly apparent in his discussion of Jesus and his ethic.[108] Nor do Singer's arguments against objectivism (or descriptivism) deal directly with Christian ethics or any other theistic ethical system, for he first rather casually dismisses theistic belief systems and then directs his critique against nontheistic objective accounts of morality.

Indeed Christian ethics provides coherent accounts of the existence and nature of an objective moral order that correspond to the available data at least as well as, and I believe better than, its rivals.[109] Thus theistic ethical systems are much more robust than Singer claims and survive his attempts to undermine them. This, in turn, means that those who hold to theistic ethical theories are entitled to do so.

Third, while he uses a notion of reason and its deliverances that is clearly community transcendent, even hypostasized, he asserts that reason is a human product, developed in, by and for communities. How, then, can it transcend space and time in the way he describes? One way it could do so would be if there were a being who transcends space and time in the requisite manner and who engages in such a practice. For if, as Singer correctly acknowledges, reason is essentially a *practice* in which persons engage, then it can transcend the particularities of persons and their communities in the way Singer's argument requires only if it is "transcendentally" practiced. There is, then, no transcendent entity *Reason* but only persons who engage in the practice (or practices) of reasoning.

Now, I believe that there is such a being in whom the transcendence of reason can be grounded—namely God—and that God's rationality is universal and eternal (at least in a loose sense), for he is universal and eternal. I do not believe that our rationality has those qualities, for it is situated in particular cultural and historical

---

[107]See, e.g., his formulation of and arguments against the divine command theory: Singer, *Practical Ethics*, pp. 3-4; Kuhse and Singer, *Should the Baby Live?* p. 126. They ignore recent discussion of divine command theories and defense of the theory against the Euthyphro objection by reference to the consistent character of the one who commands. For an articulation of such a theory, see R. J. Mouw, *The God Who Commands* (Notre Dame, Ind.: University of Notre Dame Press, 1990).

[108]For this, see Anna Wierzbicka, "Peter Singer and Christian Ethics," *Quadrant*, April 1997, pp. 28-29.

[109]I cannot explore this issue in any more detail here. For examples of such systems which justify my assertions, see O'Donovan, *Resurrection and Moral Order*; C. S. Layman, *The Shape of the Good: Christian Reflections of the Foundation of Ethics* (Notre Dame, Ind.: University of Notre Dame Press, 1991); and for a brisfer account, Arthur F. Holmes, *Ethics: Approaching Moral Decisions* (Leicester, U.K.: Inter-Varsity Press, 1984).

contexts and is practiced by fallible persons. However, I do believe that our thinking can be rational, in a defeasible sense, for the contextual nature of rationality does not entail relativism.[110]

This line of reasoning, of course, cannot be adopted by Singer, for he specifically rejects all theistic metaphysical and ethical theories. He needs, then, to provide another account of how human reasoning can be universal and eternal without reference to a transcendent entity such as God.

If the human practice of reason is to provide ethics with its objective, universal grounding, then human reason must be in some way universal and eternal. But if reason is a human practice, devised in, by and for particular communities, it is essentially situated; it can be practiced in a universal and eternal manner only if it is able to transcend its particularity in such a way as to grant it universal and eternal validity. It is important to note here that reasoning must not only transcend its tradition-specificity, something it is clearly capable of doing; it must do so in such a way as to make its deliverances universal and eternal. Limited transcendence across the boundaries of communities and traditions is not adequate for Singer's purposes; his argument for the universal nature of morality holds only if moral reasoning can be shown to be transferable across *all* such boundaries and in such a way as to make it universal and eternal. This is a crucial problem, for if reason is defeasible and context specific, rather than universal and eternal, then Singer has no reason to expand the ethical circle beyond particular contexts, let alone across species lines. So while I think Singer is right to assert that reason can be universal and eternal, this holds only for a transcendent being, God, not for finite beings such as humans. Thus Singer has no grounds, ontological or epistemological, for believing it to be true of human reasoning.

Other crucial questions remain unanswered in Singer's view of universal rationality. Is there an ideal realm of "logic" or "reason" in which it resides and from which it is instantiated from time to time? If so, what is that realm like? How do we have access to it? How are its universal and eternal qualities transferred to our particular and time-bound thinking? Surely such a conception falls prey to his own "argument from queerness" against the existence of an objective realm of moral "facts."[111] The problematic nature of Singer's account of reason infects his ethical theory as a

---

[110]Again, this cannot be explored in detail here. For brief accounts of such a situated notion of rationality, see K. J. Clark, *Return to Reason* (Grand Rapids, Mich.: Eerdmans, 1990); D. L. Wolfe, *Epistemology: The Justification of Belief* (Downers Grove, Ill.: InterVarsity Press, 1982); Nicholas Wolterstorff, *Reason Within the Bounds of Religion*, 2nd ed. (Grand Rapids, Mich.: Eerdmans, 1984).

[111]Singer, *Expanding Circle*, p. 107; "Reasoning," pp. 151-52.

whole, for, as I shall shortly argue, these flaws in his notion of moral rationality undermine a central tenet of preference utilitarianism.

The fourth problem with preference utilitarianism is a flaw in all utilitarian theories: the question of justice. The argument can be put quite simply. According to utilitarian criteria, an action or rules is right if, on balance, it is in the best interests of all those affected by it (maximum utility). But slavery and other forms of injustice may lead to maximum utility, even from a universal point of view; therefore such oppression, if it does in fact maximize utility, is right.[12] If this is so, then it counts against utilitarianism rather than for a particular form of oppression. We generally believe, for good reason, that such oppression is wrong, regardless of its positive results.[13] Such beliefs are, in general, the product of key ethical intuitions. While we may not be able to fully articulate these intuitions or provide clear and cogent arguments in their favor, we come to believe that certain things are wrong—and we may be justified in so believing.

Now this is not to say that moral intuitions are pristine, indubitable foundations for ethical reflection. They are influenced by culture, environment and traditions of moral discourse and may be mistaken. However, this does not mean in itself that such intuitions are insignificant or worthless—any more than the culture-specific nature of reasoning means that there is no such thing as rationality. As is the case with our beliefs in general, they are innocent until proven guilty rather than guilty until proven innocent.[14] Thus unless there are grounds for the rejection of such intuitions, we are justified in rejecting utilitarian theories just because they conflict with those justified moral intuitions.

Hare and Singer both reject the claim that intuitions play an important role in ethical reflection, and indeed argue that they should be rejected if they conflict with their ethical calculus.[15] However, I do not believe we can just dismiss such intui-

---

[12]Hare accepts this "criticism" but believes that it shows the superiority of his position; for in such a case that unjust system is *right*, and its injustice is irrelevant, or overwhelmed by consequentialist considerations. See *Moral Thinking*, pp. 164-68. It is to be noted, however, that he believes such posited "worlds" to be unlikely and that (relative) egalitarianism can be justified on strictly consequentialist lines. Cf. Singer, *How Are We to Live?* pp. 149-51.

[13]For this argument, regarding utilitarian theories in general, see Frankena, *Ethics*, pp. 37-39, 42-43; Layman, *Shape of the Good*, pp. 73-74; for its specific application to Singer, see Landman, "Morality of Killing," p. 168. This argument can be formulated to cover both act and rule utilitarian theories, and it certainly covers Singer's two-level theory. For if it could be shown that such a systematic injustice would maximize utility, then it must become the rule by which we operate at the intuitive level. For an excellent narrative presentation of this problem at the level of social policy, see Ursula K. LeGuin's short story "The Ones Who Walk Away from Omelas," in *The Wind's Twelve Quarters* (St. Albans, U.K.: Granada, 1978), pp. 112-20.

[14]For the justification of such a theory or rationality, see Clark, *Return to Reason*; Wolfe, *Epistemology*; Wolterstorff, *Reason Within the Bounds of Religion*.

[15]Hare, *Moral Thinking*, p. 166; Singer and Kuhse, "More on Euthanasia," 172-73.

tions. Certainly they need to be examined, but it may well be that even if we cannot articulate them fully, such intuitions capture something we must not ignore in moral thinking.[116]

Indeed this raises a fifth problem with Singer's theory: it rejects central moral intuitions and their relational implications. An example of this is his exclusion of all emotional concerns, and related intuitions concerning the value of human infants, from the ethics of infanticide.[117] Now it is true that emotions can obscure or compli-cate ethical issues unnecessarily: but equally they can bring to light important ethi-cal issues. Would Singer claim that his views on animals, for instance, are unrelated to his feelings on the matter? Emotions, such as indignation and sympathy, and related intuitions feature heavily in his discussion of animal liberation.[118] Such emo-tions are an important, if fallible, guide to the presence of core ethical intuitions.[119] As I said earlier, not all intuitions can be articulated and justified in full. However, that does not mean that allowing them to influence our moral theorizing is irratio-nal, as Singer suggests. For even in science, the "paradigm" of Western rationality, tacit knowledge and intuitions play a crucial role.[120] To dismiss these moral intui-tions in such a cavalier fashion is a flaw in Singer's ethical theory.[121]

It is ironic that he does so, for it seems to me that Singer's case paradoxically, even inconsistently depends on just such an intuition: that universalizability is the defin-ing quality of ethical statements and hence is inherent to the logic of ethical dis-course. I believe that he is right in taking universalizability as crucial to ethical reasoning, in a limited sense at least. But this principle is not grounded in the inher-ent *logic* of ethical discourse, as can be demonstrated from Singer's own arguments. He switches from talking of it as inherent to the *logic* of ethics to its being grounded in the *social practice* of ethical discourse.[122] If Singer's arguments are to hold, then

---

[116]For a sophisticated articulation of such intuitions in ethics, see James Kellenberger, *Relationship Morality* (Philadelphia: University of Pennsylvania Press, 1995).

[117]Singer, *Practical Ethics*, pp. 170-71; cf. 76-77. It is interesting that he has to parody them in order to do so. Perhaps this is an indication of the weakness of his argument?

[118]See, for instance, Singer, *Practical Ethics*, pp. 65-68; *Rethinking Life and Death*, pp. 159-64, 172-83; cf. Pauer-Studer, "Peter Singer on Euthanasia," p. 137, for the same criticism.

[119]David van Gend, "On the Sanctity of Human Life," *Quadrant*, September 1995, pp. 57-58; Pauer-Studer, "Peter Singer on Euthanasia," p. 152; W. J. Prior, "Compassion: A Critique of Moral Ratio-nalism," *Philosophy and Theology* 2, no. 2 (Winter (1987): 173-91. Similar claims are made about linguistic usage and moral intuitions in Anna Wierzbicka, "The Language of Life and Death," *Quadrant*, July-August 1995: 21-25.

[120]For this, see the essays in Imre Lakatos and Alan Musgrave, eds., *Criticism and the Growth of Knowledge* (Cambridge: Cambridge University Press, 1970).

[121]Kellenberger, *Relationship Morality*, pp. 147-48, 353-76; Landman, "Morality of Killing," pp. 163-64, 166; Pauer-Studer, "Peter Singer on Euthanasia," p. 152; Prior, "Compassion," p. 180.

[122]The term "social practice" is drawn from the work of Alasdair MacIntyre, *After Virtue: A Study in*

reason and the logic of ethical discourse need to be eternal and universal.[123] However, as I argued earlier, if reason is an evolving social practice, as Singer himself acknowledges, how can its human expressions be universal and eternal?

Universalizability is, then, a principle situated within one particular tradition of moral rationality and hence is not necessarily universal; it cannot be transferred beyond the bounds of that tradition without good reason to do so.[124] There are two basic reasons that would warrant its transfer: (1) the principle of universalizability can be shown to be applicable to the logical structure or social practice of all other traditions of moral discourse; (2) the principle has objective status as a statement about ethical states of affairs. The former Singer has failed to demonstrate; indeed given the context specificity of moral discourse, it is hard to see how it could possibly be demonstrated. The latter has unacceptable consequences for Singer's preference utilitarianism, for if that principle stands, then why not others? Indeed if it stands as a substantive principle per se, then Singer's system falls, for this ethical principle at least refers to an objective moral order.

Singer cannot have it both ways. Either (1) there is an objective moral order, in which case universalizability may be a valid *substantive* ethical principle. But in this case other principles cannot be ruled out of court; indeed a case must be made against other principles arising from similar fundamental moral intuitions. Or (2) there is no such moral order, in which case the principle does not hold. But if the principle does not hold, then Singer's theory falls. Either way, Singer's theory falls.

This raises the final, central problem with Singer's theory. It is an impoverished, reductionistic theory. This can be seen in a number of areas. Singer not only claims that there is no objective moral order but also that ethics can be reduced to consequentialist analysis. As has just been shown, there is nothing about an action that is inherently right or wrong, even when our moral intuitions say there is: there is no true *deontological* component to ethics.[125] Nor does the character of the one performing the action have any ethical status, except in that it may influence this action or future actions: there is no true *aretaic* component to ethics.[126]

This, it seems to me, ignores two crucial components of ethical analysis, and does so on insufficient grounds. Singer's theory fails to consider the essentially relational

---

Moral Theory, 2nd ed. (Notre Dame, Ind.: University of Notre Dame Press, 1984), esp. pp. 187-90, 220-24, 274.

[123]Singer, *Expanding Circle*, pp. 105-6, and the argument above.

[124]For a good account of this socially situated nature of moral reasoning, see MacIntyre, *After Virtue*, and Alasdair MacIntyre, *Whose Justice? Which Rationality?* (London: Duckworth, 1987).

[125]See, e.g., Singer, *Practical Ethics*, pp. 324-25.

[126]See, e.g., ibid., pp. 323-24; and the criticism by Prior, "Compassion," pp. 188-90.

character of human, indeed all personal, life.[127] As persons we are beings-in-relation-
ships. The consequences of our actions are important constituents in the formation
of relationships, but they are not the only constituents. Thus inasmuch as Singer
reduces life to consequences, his theory does not do justice to the reality of human
life and is therefore flawed.[128]

A further area in which it is impoverished is the metaphysics of morality. This poverty is seen in two related issues: Singer's answer to the question "Why be moral?" and
his discussion of what gives meaning to human life. On the first question, he attempts
to steer a "middle course" between (1) the selfishness that characterizes contemporary
Western culture and (2) religious commitment.[129] He recognizes that most ethical
reflection has taken place in the context of a particular religious commitment and that
secular ethics is a "fledgling" exercise.[130] However, in light of the "collapse" of religious
ways of life, a nonreligious ethic is needed if we are to save the planet and ourselves
from the perils of selfishness.[131] Furthermore, an ethical life, he argues, is a life of self-
fulfillment rather than sheer self-sacrifice. The question "Why be moral?" then is
answered by its social, environmental and personal utility.

Regarding the second issue, he claims that the ethical standpoint itself gives
meaning to life, for once we adopt an ethical point of view we recognize the enor-
mity of the ethical tasks that lie before us. And that gives us something to live for.[132]
We all face a fundamental choice between living ethically and living unethically.[133]
On the basis of the *utility* of the ethical way of life, he argues that such a choice is
not irrational. He claims that a commitment to an ethical way of life gives us the per-
son-transcendent meaning we all look for: "An ethical life is one in which we identify ourselves with other, larger goals, thereby giving meaning to our lives."[134] While

---

[127]See, e.g., Singer, *Practical Ethics*, pp. 76-77, where he specifically rejects claims that our unique
relationship with others of our own species is of any ethical significance; and ibid., pp. 170-71,
where he claims that we should not allow sentiment (surely an important component of our relational interaction with other persons) any weight at all in ethical reflection. Only an impartial view
even qualifies as an ethical point of view. He claims "ethics does not demand that we eliminate
personal relationships and partial affections" (ibid., p. 76), but he does claim that assessing the
moral claims of those affected by our actions requires "some degree of independence from our
feelings for them" (p. 77). But how can such independence be achieved without effectively effac-
ing the relationship?

[128]For an articulation of a relational ethic, see Kellenberger, *Relationship Morality*. Further exploration of a relational theory of ethics must await another occasion.

[129]Singer, *How Are we to Live?* pp. vii-viii.

[130]Ibid., pp. 15-17.

[131]Ibid., pp. 10-12, 17-18, 22-54.

[132]Ibid., p. vii.

[133]Ibid., pp. 1-12.

[134]Ibid., p. 20; cf. pp. 207, 216.

there is no ultimate history-transcendent goal, there is a succession of immanent goals, which together give us enough to fill our lives with meaningful action.[135] The underlying idea is that simply being in the world entails an obligation to make it better, to reduce the amount of avoidable suffering in it.[136] Such a series of suffering-eliminating actions gives sufficient meaning to a person's life.[137]

There are many flaws in this account. It is circular, and in a way that vitiates Singer's claims. He argues against religious ethics on the grounds that it makes no sense outside a particular religious framework. But his own account of the meta-ethical justification of ethics relies on the very utilitarian viewpoint he seeks to justify. This is seen in the fact that he argues for the personal utility of his kind of commitment. But it is just that commitment to utility that he seeks to justify. Now, some "epistemic circles" are acceptable, but only within a theory of rationality that comports poorly with Singer's theory.[138] Broadly speaking, such circularity is warranted in the context of the articulation and justification of a person- and situation-specific belief system.[139] Singer's criticisms of other views are inconsistent with that kind of rationality; indeed his theory is founded on the claim that it provides an *objective* basis for ethics. A claim of that sort, grounded in a nonsituated theory of rationality, is undermined by this kind of circularity. For Singer's theory to gain the meta-ethical justification he is looking for, he needs to rely on a notion of rationality radically different from the one he espouses, one that would be inconsistent with his own ethical theory.

This problem is parasitic on another, more central one. Singer denies that there is any ultimate meaning to the universe and human life.[140] This means that if his ethical commitment is to be rational, rather than a nonrational "leap of (un)faith," he needs to provide reasons for it. For Singer, such reasons cannot lie in the inherent rightness of an ethical commitment, for that would rely on some kind of objective meaning or moral order that inheres in the universe. The existence of such an objective order would destroy his ethical theory. This, then, forces him to look elsewhere for a reason to be ethical. Given his understanding of the world and morality, there is only one place left to look: the interests of persons. Hence he is back where he started, having smuggled a commitment to furthering preferences, which is what he

---

[135]Singer, *Practical Ethics*, pp. 331-35; *How Are We to Live?* pp. 216-18, 231.

[136]Singer, *How Are We to Live?* pp. 221-23.

[137]Ibid., pp. 222-23.

[138]Singer, *Practical Ethics*, p. 316, where he notes that if the meta-ethical justification of ethics is a moral (I would add, quasi-moral) one, then it is viciously circular.

[139]See, for instance, Wolfe, *Epistemology*.

[140]Singer, *Practical Ethics*, p. 331.

is seeking to prove, into the premises of the argument. This may be unavoidable at this level of meta-ethical discourse; if so, that just proves the point made earlier, that this line of justification comports poorly with the structure and content of his theory. Indeed it suggests that his ethical theory, like all others, is an articulation of a particular worldview, or belief and behavior system, and that his theory, like all others—including those he rejects as viciously circular—finds whatever justification it has in that context alone.[141]

This means that we are left with the higher-level question, why be concerned with preferences? If ethics is about preferences, and the justification of the ethical point of view relies on those preferences (personal fulfillment, the alleviation of suffering), the question remains, why worry about that? If there is no ultimate meaning to our lives, those of others or the universe itself, why does it matter if we are less than perfectly fulfilled? Why does it matter whether human societies progress? And how can we determine that it is in fact *progress?*[142] Why does it matter whether animals suffer or the planet is destroyed as a biological system (at least in its current form)? Why do any of these things matter? How can Singer claim that it is "better" to live this way rather than that?

I suspect that, again, we come upon Singer's fundamental ethical intuitions. Many of them are sound; some are not. None of them have any real justification within the context of his theory or its attendant belief system. Paradoxically, many (but not all) of these intuitions can be justified in the context of belief systems, such as Christian ones, that affirm the objective nature of morality. But that is cold comfort for Singer.

So we come to the final reductionistic aspect of Singer's ethical theory. His clear rejection of any ultimate meaning to our lives leaves us with this impoverished, and ultimately inconsistent, commitment to particular ungrounded immanent values, which are supposed to give meaning to our lives. These values point us beyond ourselves to involvement in greater ethical tasks, a succession of which, he argues, will enable us to live meaningful lives. Apart from the question I raised earlier, why we should bother with those tasks, it seems clear to me that Singer's account of meaning is starkly reductionist. Rather than dealing with questions of why it all matters anyway, he tries to answer the question "How can we make it *seem to ourselves* that it all matters?" Meaning, then, far from being an explanatory category or a way of anchor-

---

[141]Detailed exposition of this point, and the related matter of Singer's underlying metaphysic and epistemology, is beyond the scope of this paper; this too must await another occasion.
[142]For clear claims that there is a right thing to do and that we have seen real ethical progress, see Singer, *How Are We to Live?* pp. 222-25; for a critique of them, see Wierzbicka, "Language of Life and Death," p. 28.

ing a life in a reality beyond itself, is reduced to a psychological state of feeling meaningful.[43] Of course Singer is left with nothing else once he has rejected all objective
meaning and value in the universe. But how satisfactory is that account? Is it enough
to say, "Regardless of the facts of the matter, I *feel* meaningful"? If so, how does that
escape meta-ethical relativism? The tendency for Singer's account to slide into relativism and even subjectivism at this point is well illustrated in his work.[44] It is, perhaps, best seen in the closing statement of *Practical Ethics*: "Those reflective enough
to ask the question we have been discussing in this chapter are also those most likely
to appreciate the reasons that can be offered for taking the ethical point of view."[45]
This statement indicates that only the adoption of the very point of view in question
can justify its adoption. Such circularity demonstrates that only in the context of a
personal commitment to this particular ethical point of view can his line of justification be valid. Indeed the way he articulates this point seems to leave him with meta-
ethical relativism, for he has no framework-transcendent argument for the adoption
of the ethical point of view. Again, this raises crucial problems for the "objectivity" of
his ethical theory.

Here we see another inconsistency in Singer's theory. I do not see how he can hold
to meta-ethical relativism without sliding into ethical relativism. For if his claims to
meta-ethical meaning and the justification of an ethical commitment are relativist,
even nonrational, then that relativism or nonrationality vitiates the nonrelativist and
rational status of his ethical theory. After all, if this is the best he can do in terms of
meta-ethical warrant, why should someone not adopt a radically different stance? And
how could such commitments be arbitrated in a nonsubjectivist manner? Ultimately
Singer, who is committed to the development of ethical ideas in the realm of public
discourse, is left without any account of what makes such discourse possible.[46] In all
these crucial respects, then, Singer's preference utilitarianism is inadequate and unsatisfactory and fails to undermine traditional moral theories. Thus exponents of traditional morality are entitled to reject preference utilitarianism.

Once Again: Singer and Infanticide
So what do these problems with preference utilitarianism mean for Singer's position

---

[43]For this see Singer, *Practical Ethics*, pp. 333-35; *How Are We to Live?* pp. 194-96, 221-22, 230-32, 235;
cf. the critique by Wierzbicka, "Language of Life and Death," pp. 29-30.
[44]See Singer, *How Are We to Live?* pp. ix–x, 163-64, re the "uplifting" nature of unselfish action,
despite the controverted nature of the ethics involved; pp. 167-70, 173-75, for the rationality of
nonethical ways of life; pp. 218-22, re the subjective motivation of ethical activists.
[45]Singer, *Practical Ethics*, p. 335.
[46]Michael Smith, "Back to Basics: A Review of *How Are We to Live?*" *Eureka Street* 4, no. 5 (June-
July 1994): 43-45; Wierzbicka, "Language of Life and Death," p. 28.

on infanticide? The cogency of Singer's stance on infanticide depends on the cogency of preference utilitarianism, for as we have seen each of his arguments against the wrongness of killing an infant and in favor of infanticide depends on his preference utilitarian position. Since the latter is unsound, so are the former. He has failed to defeat alternative views, especially those that advocate the existence of an objective moral order to which we must conform. This is a serious flaw, for it means that a crucial argument in favor of his theory is unsound. Furthermore his own theory and the justification he presents for it are not sound. This means that his views on infanticide are unjustified; for he has specifically excluded from his discussion any reference to the inherent value of infants or the inherent moral qualities of the act of infanticide. All that is left are the preference utilitarian arguments he presents in its favor, and if the theory itself is unjustified, then so are the arguments that rely on it. Thus we are entitled to reject Singer's preference utilitarianism and his support for the practice of infanticide as both unjustified and morally bankrupt, and we are entitled to continue to accept traditional moral theories and their rejection of this practice.

Let us return, for a moment, to the case with which we began. Infants like John Pearson should not be "allowed to die," nor should they be killed. In this case, and those like it, our normal moral intuitions and the feelings of horror they generate are justified. The fact that a child is unwanted and stands little chance of being adopted does not justify his death. Such reasons do not defeat the "traditional" view that as a human being he is of such value that both killing him *and* allowing him to die are inherently evil acts.

The horrific and counterintuitive nature of Singer's views on infanticide and their consistency with his overall theory show not that the "traditional ethic" and its intuitions should be abandoned but that preference utilitarianism should be rejected. Those like myself who endorse traditional morality and as a result are vehemently opposed to the practice of infanticide can continue to do so, knowing that Peter Singer's arguments, at least, do not constitute grounds for a rejection of traditional morality.[47]

[47]Previous versions of this paper were presented at the Centre of Applied Christian Ethics, Ridley College, Melbourne, and the Christian Philosophical Society. I would like to thank members of those groups, in particular Graham Cole, Gordon Preece, Derek Brookes and an anonymous reviewer for their helpful comments on earlier drafts of this paper.

3

Singer on Christianity

Characterized or Caricatured?

GRAHAM COLE

Peter Singer is one of Australia's leading thinkers and also one of our most controversial.[1] He made his philosophical reputation by defending the well-being of animals. Animal liberation is a concept he put on the ethical agenda, and although he
did not coin the term *speciesism* (human discrimination against other forms of life),
he more than anyone has secured its place in ethical discussion.[2] Singer has exer-
cised a very wide influence on ethical debate both by his writings and by his use of
other media. Animal liberation is not his only interest these days. He has also turned
his considerable intellect to moral issues concerning human conception, birth, life
and death as well as wider environmental concerns.

Singer has written no formal critique of Christianity per se. Yet in many of his
works a critique is to be found. The aim of this paper is to examine his criticisms of
Christianity's ideas. What are the criticisms? How well founded are they? Does he
accurately characterize the Christianity he critiques? Put another way, does he fairly

---

[1]A version of this paper was first published in *The Reformed Theological Review* 57, no. 2 (1998): 80-
90. Used by permission.
[2]For Singer's contribution see Lori Gruen, "Animals," in *A Companion to Ethics*, ed. Peter Singer
(Oxford: Blackwell, 1991), p. 343. As for *speciesism*, the term was coined by Oxford psychologist
Richard Ryder in 1970, as Singer himself noted in his famous review essay "Animal Liberation,"
New York Review Of Books, April 5, 1993, reprinted in *Ethics in Perspective*, ed. K. J. Stuhl and P. R.
Stuhl (New York: Random House, 1975), p. 227, and again in Peter Singer, *Rethinking Life and
Death* (Melbourne: Text, 1994), p. 173. Even so other writers persistently give Singer the honor. For
example, see I. S. Markham, "Questions People Ask: 8. Life After Death," *Expository Times* 107
(1995-1996): 165.

and accurately set out its defining characteristics? Or does he caricature a position with which he vehemently disagrees? That is to say, is his presentation of Christianity a distortion?

The answer to these questions is in two parts. The first part seeks to expound Singer's problems with God and Christianity. The second part then critiques the critique. The point of the exercise is not purely negative. There is much to learn from Singer, as this writer hopes to show—albeit not uncritically.

Singer Expounded

By way of introduction to this part of our discussion, it is worth noting something of Singer's own religious background. This background does not of course determine the truth or falsity of his arguments. To think so would be to fall into the genetic fallacy—assuming that the origins of a view determine its truth value. However, some knowledge of Singer's background may illuminate the development of his ideas.

Singer is the son of Jewish refugees from the Nazi Holocaust who fled Austria in 1938. Singer lost relatives in the Holocaust.[3] Singer himself was born in 1946 in Melbourne. His family were not practicing Jews. Singer himself says, "Not having had a religious background, I've never had a strong sense of the separation and superiority of human beings over the rest of the world."[4] The absence of religious background shows itself in Singer's works. For example, as the years have gone on he appears to have become more and more aware, at least in print, of the content of Christian theology on a range of issues and of the differences between liberal and conservative Christianity, Roman Catholic and other forms of Christianity.[5]

Although Singer has specific problems with Christian doctrines, his most fundamental problem with the Christian religion is that he disbelieves in the very existence of the Christian God: an omniscient, omnipotent and omnibenevolent Supreme Being. To this fundamental issue we now turn.

Singer on God. English-speaking philosophy of religion in the twentieth century had a major preoccupation with questions concerning the meaningfulness of religious language.[6] In recent years the debate has moved on to accent other matters, but the issue of whether religious language actually refers to any reality beyond itself

---

[3]"Singer, Peter," in *The Current Biography Yearbook 1991* (New York: H. W. Wilson, 1991), p. 525.
[4]As quoted in G. Haigh, "Peter's Principles," *The Australian*, November 3, 1994, p. 10.
[5]For an example see Sally Blakeney, "The Brave New World of Peter Singer," *Weekend Australian*, September 28-29, 1996, Weekend Review sec., p. 3, where Singer distinguishes between the views of Archbishop George Pell and Father Bill Uren, both of the Roman Catholic Church and with whom Singer disagrees.
[6]For a fine survey of the debates see Dan R. Stiver, *The Philosophy of Religious Language: Sign, Symbol and Story* (Oxford: Blackwell, 1996).

received an illuminating comment from Singer. "'Theology and Absolute Ethics,' wrote Frank Ramsey, a brilliant Cambridge philosopher who died in 1936 at the age of twenty-six, 'are two famous subjects which we have realised to have no real objects.'"[7] Singer went on to state that he shares Ramsey's view of theology and to a certain degree his view of ethics as well. Religious language about God is meaningless, as it is objectless and empirically unverifiable.[8]

The great reason for Singer's rejection of belief in God, however, has to do with the existence of evil in the world. Singer maintains that "there is unnecessary and indefensible evil in the world. Therefore the God of traditional Christian belief does not exist."[9] He is aware that many Christians appeal to a free-will defense of God's justice. On this view, evils spring from the misuse of the human will (what philosophers call the moral problem of evil). So Singer concentrates on what philosophers call the natural problem of evil: the suffering of people and animals at the hands of nature.

He is aware that his argument is not a knockdown one. He is self-consciously operating with a lesser standard of proof. But by this lesser standard, the evidence is against the existence of the Christian God. So he does not believe.[10] Although he does not spell out the implications of his stance, clearly *ex hypothesi* if there is no God there is no revelation from God. The Scriptures reduce to human artifacts. Christianity likewise reduces to a human project, and a largely unfortunate one in Singer's estimate, as we now shall see.

Singer on Christianity. For Peter Singer, as an animal liberationist and environmentalist, there are many sticking points in a Christian worldview, but none more problematical than the traditional Christian doctrine of creation. According to Singer our Western intellectual roots lie in ancient Greece and in the Judeo-Christian tradition, and neither is kind to those not of our species. In a number of his works Professor Singer quotes from the opening chapter of Genesis:

> And God said, Let us make man in our image, after our likeness: and let them have
> dominion over the fish of the sea, and over the fowl of the air, and over the cattle, and

---

[7]Peter Singer, *How Are We to Live?* (Melbourne: Text, 1993), p. 188.

[8]Ibid. The wider context of Singer's appeal to Ramsey is his reference to the contribution of the logical positivists, especially A. J. Ayer, to the question of the meaningfulness of ethical and religious language.

[9]See Peter Singer, "Is There a God? (Revisited)," *The Age*, February 14, 1994, opinion page, and the article in an earlier issue, Peter Singer, "Is There a God?" *The Age*, December 24, 1993, opinion page. In his second article Singer acknowledges the thoughtful reply of another professional philosopher, a Christian, Bruce Langtry of Melbourne University. Langtry argues that the success of a theodicy turns on whether we can be confident that God may have a morally sound reason for allowing evil, even if we are not privileged to know that reason.

[10]Ibid.

over all the earth, and over every creeping thing that creepeth upon the earth. So God created man in his own image, in the image of God created he him; male and female created he them.

And God blessed them and God said upon them, Be fruitful, and multiply, and replenish the earth, and subdue it; and have dominion over the fish of the sea and over the fowl of the air, and over every living thing that moveth upon the earth.[11]

Interestingly, the quotations are always from an archaic version that reinforces the impression of a statement from a remote past. The question, however, is what Singer makes of the Genesis material.

In *In Defence of Animals*, Singer maintains that "here is a myth to make human beings feel their supremacy and their power. Man alone is made in the image of God. Man alone is given dominion over all the animals and told to subdue the earth."[12] He is aware, however, that some Christians have accented the stewardship dimensions of the Genesis presentation rather than the dominion ones. Such Christians (such as St. Francis of Assisi) are kinder toward the environment and other species. But Singer forcefully states ("beyond dispute," he says) that the dominion view has been the "mainstream" one.[13]

The flood narrative of Genesis 9, for Singer, is indicative of what dominion means for the value of animal life. He argues that Christians have no justification for interpreting the language of dominion in benevolent terms given the example God sets by drowning "almost every animal on earth in order to punish human beings for their wickedness."[14] He concludes, "No wonder that people think the flooding of a single river valley is nothing worth worrying about."[15]

Singer's problem with the traditional reading of Genesis is a moral one. Here Genesis displays "species-selfishness."[16] Such speciesism is morally indefensible, as it privileges human beings without rational and moral justification and leads to cruelty

---

[11]The quotation has been taken from Peter Singer, *Practical Ethics*, 2nd ed. (Cambridge: Cambridge University Press, 1993), pp. 265-66. But also see Peter Singer, "Prologue: Ethics and the New Animal Liberation Movement," in *In Defence of Animals*, ed. Peter Singer (Oxford: Blackwell, 1985), p. 2 and *Rethinking Life and Death*, pp. 165-166. That Singer uses archaic Scripture versions is puzzling given that the volume he coedited with Tom Regan, *Animal Rights and Human Obligations*, 2nd ed. (Englewood Cliffs, N.J.: Prentice-Hall, 1989), pp. 1-3, quotes from a modern version. Moreover, some of the quotations are pro animal or plant welfare (e.g., Prov 12:10; 31:8; Rev 7:3). Perhaps Egan, rather than Singer, was responsible.

[12]Singer, "Prologue," pp. 2-3.

[13]Ibid., p. 3. Singer repeats the argument in a number of other places, including *Practical Ethics*, pp. 265-68, and *Rethinking Life and Death*, pp. 165-67.

[14]Singer, *Practical Ethics*, p. 266.

[15]Ibid.

[16]Singer, "Prologue," p. 4.

in practice. In Singer's moral universe, speciesism is morally akin to "the most blatant racism."[7]

For Singer, ideas have practical consequences. He cites key figures in early Christianity to support his point. According to one Gospel account, Jesus sent demons into a herd of pigs, making them drown in the sea. Jesus also cursed a fig tree. Augustine appealed to these incidents to teach that human beings have no duties to animals or plants. Aquinas embraced the Augustinian interpretation. Finally, the Roman Catholic Church made it official. Singer cites Pope Pius IX, a mid-nineteenth-century pope who refused permission for the Society for the Prevention of Cruelty to Animals to set up its organization in Rome on the grounds that this might imply that human beings have duties to lower animals.[18]

Another key figure in early Christianity whom Singer criticizes is the apostle Paul, whom he describes as among "the most influential Christian thinkers."[19] Singer points out that in Paul's discussion of an Old Testament command to rest one's ox on the sabbath the apostle asks rhetorically, "Doth God care for oxen?" and expects the answer to be negative. For Singer, this is Paul's application of the Genesis concept of human dominion over animal life and evidence that "Paul scornfully rejected the thought that God might care about the welfare of oxen."[20]

There is a further problem for Singer in the Genesis story because of the value it gives to human life. He describes the sanctity-of-life principle—that human life is sacred because we are in some way Godlike creatures—as "the standard Western doctrine."[21] He argues that in our day the sanctity-of-life principle needs to be replaced by a quality-of-life principle that does not privilege the human species.[22]

So then, Singer finds sticking points in the biblical teaching on both creation and anthropology. A further sticking point he locates in Christian expectations of the future, or eschatology. According to Singer, historically there has been "a specific theological motivation for the Christian insistence on the importance of species

---

[7]Ibid., p. 6.

[18]Ibid., p. 3, and also see Singer, *Rethinking Life and Death*, pp. 166-67. Singer's appeal to history appears highly tendentious. What he does not relate is that the SPCA, founded in 1824, had a Christian foundation. Arthur Broome, its chief architect, was committed to the extension of Christian compassion to suffering animals, as Andrew Linzey shows in his *Animal Theology* (London: SCM Press, 1994), p. 19. Linzey also shows that the first systematic defense of animal well-being was a theological one that antedated the concerns of Jeremy Bentham, whom Singer often refers to in his works. See Humphrey Primatt, *Dissertation on the Duty of Mercy and the Sin of Cruelty to Brute Animals* (London: T. Cadell, 1776).

[19]Singer, *Practical Ethics*, p. 266.

[20]Ibid., p. 267, and esp. Singer, "Prologue," p. 3.

[21]Singer, "Prologue," p. 8.

[22]Ibid., p. 8.

membership."[23] Christians believe that life born of human parents is "immortal and destined for an eternity of bliss or for everlasting torment."[24] Thus to kill a human being is to consign a human life to either heaven or hell. From the time of Jesus to the Enlightenment, Christian warnings of the danger of eternal punishment went unchallenged and thus made "a lasting impression on the Western mind."[25] But since the Enlightenment of the eighteenth century, the Christian view has faced challenge. Immanuel Kant prevailed over Jesus, and the Christian doctrine of the future no longer exercises hegemony over the Western mind.[26]

Singer does not believe in the Christian doctrine of the future, but importantly, he also does not believe in "the morality of self-interest" that he perceives in the Gospels' presentation of the teaching of Jesus.[27] This teaching he sums up as "obedience to God's command in order to avoid damnation."[28]

Singer's problem with Christianity on the ideational level is clear. The creation myths have been seminal in shaping a view in the West that human life is special because sacred and that animals and the environment are for human benefit since human beings have dominion over them.[29] This speciesism is further reinforced by the doctrine that human beings are immortal.[30] These views no longer prevail in Western society. The Enlightenment was the watershed, and now a new moral framework is needed in which sanctity-of-life arguments are replaced by quality-of-life arguments and in which no species qua species enjoys moral superiority over any other by appeal to species membership alone.

How then may a Christian thinker respond?

Evaluation

The caricature question. It is said that the English preacher Leslie Weatherhead was confronted on one occasion by an angry atheist who declared that he did not believe

[23]Singer, *Practical Ethics*, pp. 88-89.

[24]Ibid., p. 89.

[25]Singer, *How Are We to Live?* p. 181.

[26]Ibid., pp. 179-86. In Singer's view the debate has moved beyond Kant too.

[27]Ibid., p. 181.

[28]Ibid., p. 186.

[29]Singer, *Rethinking Life and Death*, p. 166. Interestingly, Singer's appeal to the history of Western ideas significantly omits, in places, the contribution of René Descartes, the founder of modern philosophy. Descartes, a seventeenth-century figure, argued that animals were machines without souls and were to be treated accordingly. Compare Singer's *Practical Ethics*, pp. 265-69 (reference omitted), and his *Rethinking Life and Death*, pp. 165-69 (reference present). See B. E. Rollins, *The Unheeded Cry* (Oxford: Oxford University Press, 1990), p. 169, who sees the rise of modern science as the key to modern animal abuse, and see O. R. Barclay, "Animal Rights: A Critique," *Science and Christian Belief* 4, no. 1 (April 1992): 55, for the significance of Descartes.

[30]Singer, *Rethinking Life and Death*, p. 166.

in God. Weatherhead replied: "Tell me about this God. I may not believe in Him either."

The question then is, has Singer characterized Christianity rightly? Or are we dealing with a distortion of Christian doctrines in his works? Some think so. Professor Anna Wierzbicka states quite categorically that Singer misrepresents the Judeo-Christian tradition in a book like *Rethinking Life and Death.*[31]

If Singer misrepresents the position he criticizes, then he can be accused of setting up an easy target. But how may caricature take place, if it has? The world of cartooning provides analogies here. Caricature happens when one or more features of a person become disproportionate for effect (e.g., a haughty member of high society whose nose becomes a peninsula). Or caricature takes place by omission (e.g., a politician depicted as so small of stature that only his voice is represented in the cartoon). A third way is by association (e.g., politicians represented as game hunters out to bag the poor).

The discussion needs some delimiting at this point to make it manageable. Since all traditions of Christianity take the Scriptures as foundational to their thinking, I will concentrate on Singer's criticisms of their content. Whether Singer caricatures the teaching of Aquinas may hold little interest for a Protestant, but whether he caricatures the teaching of Christ, as presented in Scripture, holds interest for all Christians.[32]

Our question now becomes several. Does Singer so emphasize some dimensions of Scripture as to caricature by disproportion? Does Singer so present biblical evidence that key elements are omitted? Does Singer link the believing of certain scriptural teachings with people or events that damn the Scriptures by association?

Take the biblical story of creation. There are good reasons for believing that Singer has caricatured the biblical content by omission. Consistently Singer appeals only to the Genesis 1 presentation of human beings as the image of God and exercisers of dominion. There is no balancing quotation from the Genesis 2 story of Adam as caretaker of God's paradise and of how God brings animals to Adam to provide him with companionship.

---

[31] Anna Wierzbicka, "The Language of Life and Death," *Quadrant,* July-August 1995, p. 22.
[32] Thomas Aquinas is a good example. One can ask to what degree his views of animal value were shaped by Scripture and to what degree by Aristotle, whom he called "the philosopher." Singer shows an awareness of Aquinas's debt to Aristotle ("Thomas Aquinas, whose life work was the melding of Christian theology with the thought of Aristotle") but not the significance of it for interpretation of the biblical evidence: that Aquinas in places reads Scripture through an Aristotelian grid. See Singer, *Practical Ethics,* p. 267.

Likewise with regard to the flood story that ends in Genesis 9, Singer is selective in his use of evidence. That animals were drowned becomes grounds for criticism of the presentation of God. There is no balancing appeal to the way God is presented as the preserver of species through the ark in Genesis 6—7.

Singer is on firmer ground when he points out the high value the Scriptures place on humanity. Jesus' sending the demons into the Gadarene swine is evidence. But Singer omits evidence that Jesus did value animal creation though he valued human life more highly. The issue is comparative value in a hierarchy of values. Jesus in the Gospels does teach that people matter more than property and more than sparrows and sheep. But nowhere does he teach that property or other animal life, or plant life for that matter, is without value.

A story of Jesus' healing a man in Luke 14:1-6 is instructive with regard to Jesus' attitude to animal suffering. While on his way to a Pharisee's house, Jesus heals a man with dropsy. It is the sabbath. He knows that his actions are under close scrutiny. So he asks, "Is it lawful to cure people on the Sabbath, or not?" There is silence from the watching Pharisees and lawyers. He then puts a key question to them: "If one of you has a child or an ox that has fallen into a well, will you not immediately pull it out on a sabbath day?" The force of the language expects the answer "We would."[33] That Jesus in his question juxtaposes a child at risk and an ox at risk should be noted. To use Singer's own metaphor, Jesus' circle of compassion is an expansive one.[34]

With regard to the future, Singer is right. Jesus does warn his hearers of the consequences of disobedience. The Sermon on the Mount provides a strong example. On the Last Day it is not those who have prophesied or cast out demons or done other works of power who will enter the kingdom, but those who did the Father's will. Those who have not are dismissed from Jesus' presence at the Last Judgment as evildoers (Mt 7:21-23). What Singer fails to cite is the evidence from the Gospels themselves that the motivation of disciples is complex and cannot be reduced to mere self-interest. In the Upper Room discourse in John's Gospel, Jesus predicates the disciples' obedience on their love for Him (Jn 14:15).

The other key figure from early Christianity whom Singer considers is the apostle Paul. Again, Singer's use of biblical evidence is highly tendentious. He makes no attempt to situate Paul's rhetorical question about whether God is concerned for an ox in the argument of the letter, which is not a discussion of an Old Testament com-

---

[33]The use of οὐκ not μή in the question found in Luke 14:5 implies "we would."

[34]See Singer, "Prologue," p. 9, for the notion, following W. E. H. Lecky, of the expanding circle of "benevolent affections."

mand.[35] Paul's argument in 1 Corinthians 9 is about the right of an apostle to be supported by the church, and the reference to the Old Testament is only a strand in a much more complex argument.

Singer fails to consider other Pauline passages. Particularly noteworthy is Paul's belief that God has a future for the created order that is cosmic in scope and not reducible to a concern for only human destiny. The return of Christ will mean liberation for the whole created order and not just human beings (Rom 8:18-25). Likewise, as recent theologians (such as Jürgen Moltmann) have seen, the reconciliation effected by Christ's death on the cross, as set out in Colossians 1:15-20, has implications for the created order, including animal life.[36] In both places we find Paul's endorsement of the value of creatures other than ourselves.

More examples could be given of the lack of balance in Singer's use of biblical evidence. This is caricature, not characterization. The means is the omission of balancing propositions or complete stories found in the text of Scripture. This one-sided use of Scripture is symptomatic of a systemic hermeneutical (or interpretative) mistake that pervades Singer's deployment of biblical evidence. He consistently fails to place a text in its immediate context, then in its argument, then in its book, then in the canon. Sadly, many a Christian reader of Scripture has done the same.

Learning from Singer

St. Augustine has proved to be one of Christianity's seminal thinkers. As he contemplated the fact that truths are to be found outside the Scriptures, he understood such truths as gifts of God's providence. He used the metaphor of "spoiling the Egyptians" as the way forward for Christians to think through what those outside the church have to teach us. Israel did not leave Egypt under Moses' leadership empty-handed but took with them some of the gold and silver of Egypt.[37] But first the dross.

Singer systematically misuses the biblical evidence through tendentious citation.

---

[35]Indeed Singer is very sloppy in his citation of sources. He writes that the quotation comes from *Corinthians* 9:9-10 (*sic; Practical Ethics*, p. 374). Singer does not help the uninformed reader know that the New Testament has two Corinthian letters and that the quotation comes from the first of them.

[36]Thus with regard to eschatology, which Singer sees as narrowly focused on human destiny, the biblical canvas is actually a broad one. It is not surprising then to find that as long ago as the eighteenth century John Wesley expected a future beyond physical death for animal life. See John Wesley, "The General Deliverance," in *Sermons on Several Occasions*, vol. 2 (London: Wesleyan Conference Office, 1874), quoted partly in Andrew Linzey and Tom Regan, eds., *Compassion for Animals* (London: SPCK, 1988), p. 84. As for Moltmann, see his *The Way of Jesus Christ* (London: SCM Press, 1990), pp. 254-56 and the discussion in Markham, "Questions People Ask," p. 168.

[37]See Augustine *On Christian Doctrine*, in *Augustine on Education*, ed. and trans. George Howie (Chicago: Henry Regnery, 1969), p. 364.

He thus demonstrates the need for a sound hermeneutic to uncover what Scripture is saying to our generation, by first recovering the meaning of the text in its original setting and then discerning its significance for our own. There is a negative lesson here, as Christians are prone to the same methodological problems of selective citation and hasty inference based on inadequate induction.

Positively, Singer has drawn Christians' attention to a neglected area: our environment and other creaturely life. C. S. Lewis suggested that ethics can be understood on analogy with a convoy of ships. Taking care of one's ship is the stuff of personal ethics. Being thoughtful in relating to other ships in the convoy is the theme of social ethics. Being clear as to the destination in mind is to be clear on the *summum bonum*, or supreme good.[38] Helpful as Lewis's analogy is—and he was a genius at finding the right metaphor or analogy—this analogy does not go far enough. There is also relationship to the sea and the life found in it—what these days we would term environmental ethics. The bracing criticisms of Singer should help Christians realise that the biblical picture is broader than simply God and the soul.[39]

Conclusions

As one might expect of an atheist, Peter Singer has many criticisms of the Christian's Scriptures, Christian history and the doctrines of its leading thinkers. In particular, he holds that Christianity has made speciesism part of the fabric of Western history with its teachings that human beings are in the image of God, that human life is sacred, that human beings have dominion over other species and that human beings are immortal. In his view none of these ideas can be justified in a post-Enlightenment world.

But as we have seen, in an area basic to Christian thought, the use of the biblical testimony, Singer caricatures the Christian position. To use the words of the Christian animal rights activist Andrew Linzey, Singer exhibits "a prosecuting zeal at the expense of the understanding."[40] He does so not by disproportion or association but by omission. We examined his use of the creation narrative, the flood narrative, the example and teaching of Jesus, and the teaching of St. Paul to reveal the lacunae. Singer's use of Scripture is tendentious as a result.

But even given the above, the Christian's engagement with Peter Singer need not

---

[38]C. S. Lewis, *Mere Christianity* (London: Fontana, 1958), p. 66.

[39]A substantial number of Christians have recognized the bigger picture, including C. S. Lewis, who was a vigorous opponent of vivisection. See Linzey, *Animal Theology*, especially the annotated guide to the literature, pp. 174-201.

[40]Ibid., p. 169.

be a wholly negative experience. From a moral point of view, the environment does matter, as does animal life. The Christian track record in these areas has been very unimpressive in places, as Singer correctly shows. What he does not see is that the very Scriptures he criticizes alone provide the necessary corrective for any one-sided Christianity that takes only God and the soul as matters of moral concern.

4

Human Beings—Species or Special?

A Critique of Peter Singer on Animals

LINDSAY WILSON

W hat place do animals have in God's creation? What are the limits to the way animals can be treated? What responsibilities do humans have toward animals? Do animals have rights that must not be infringed? These are some of the questions that confront modern men and women in thinking about the animal world.

In response to such questions, I hear many people suggest that Christian ethics should be focused instead on more contemporary issues like Third World debt, ethnic cleansing or genetic engineering. Can anything novel or worthwhile be said about animals, which have been around for thousands of years? Yet it is vital for us to think Christianly about animals, for several reasons.

First, our view of animals as part of creation has significant implications for our doctrine of humanity, as well as for a right understanding of human dominion (its nature, extent, purpose).

Second, there are important questions today about the ethical use of animals, in part focusing on what responsibilities humans have to God in our treatment of God's creation. While the physical environment is rightly prominent in this discussion, the interconnectedness of our planet means that we cannot ignore its living creatures. There are many unresolved issues in animal ethics, such as animal cloning, appropriate boundaries on the use of animals in research, the treatment of animals raised for food production (e.g., battery versus free-range chickens), vegetarianism, the place of zoos and the preservation of endangered species. These are all important issues.

Third, human responsibility for and treatment of animals is a neglected and underexplored area in ethics. It is missing from many ethics syllabi and textbooks, apparently not regarded by many in our society as a significant moral issue. Yet animals are significant in daily life, both by their presence and by their produce. There is an almost total absence of ethical debate, for example, on the common practice of keeping pets. If animals are such a part of daily life, we need to think Christianly about them.

What Singer Is Saying About Animals

Peter Singer is one leading thinker who has raised the profile of ethical reflections on the place of animals in our world. He has raised some questions that needed to be aired.

Singer dared to ask what was so special about the human species, accusing many in the Western world of "speciesism." This is a term first coined by Richard Ryder, but it has been popularized by Singer, who uses it to mean "the giving of preference to the interests of one species, usually the human species, over against other species." Parallel to racism and sexism, speciesism in Singer's view involves unfair discrimination, in this against nonhuman animals. In *Animal Liberation* he writes: "The core of this book is the claim that to discriminate against beings solely on account of their species is a form of prejudice, immoral and indefensible in the same way that discrimination on the basis of race is immoral and indefensible."[1]

One must not caricature Singer as a half-crazy animal lover. His expressed concern is not simply for animals but for justice. In *Animal Liberation* he states that he is not inordinately fond of dogs, cats or horses but merely wants them to be treated as independent sentient beings, not as means to human ends. He thinks it wrong to inflict needless suffering on another being even if of a different species, and he is morally opposed to arbitrary discrimination.[2] For Singer, then, the consideration of animal interests is a justice or equity issue.

All sentient beings (those with the capacity to suffer or to experience enjoyment or happiness), not only human beings, have interests that are of moral significance. Sentience, not humanity, is the proper boundary line between those who have morally significant interests and those who do not. Singer explicitly appeals to the eigh-

---

[1] Peter Singer, *Animal Liberation*, 2nd ed. (London: Jonathan Cape, 1990), p. 243.
[2] In the preface to the first edition of *Animal Liberation* (1975, p. ii), he writes, "The basic moral principle of equal consideration of interests is not arbitrarily restricted to members of our own species." Tony Coady, "Morality and Species," *Res Publica* 8 (1999): 9-10, comments that while this argument is rhetorically useful, it is persuasive only if "species membership is just as superficial a moral characteristic as race membership."

teenth-century English philosopher Jeremy Bentham, who suggests that one day
people may come to see that animals' interests may be included in the equation—
and that it makes sense to ask not whether they can reason or talk but whether they
can suffer (that is, it is suffering versus enjoying happiness that is crucial).[3] Singer
suggests that stones cannot suffer but animals can, and so their interests should be
taken into account. Thus sentience (Singer's shorthand term for the capacity to suffer or experience enjoyment or happiness) is the only defensible boundary of concern for the interests of others, since only a being who is capable of suffering and
experiencing enjoyment or happiness can have interests in any meaningful sense.[4]
Singer concedes that there are substantial differences between humans and other
animals, yet he argues that this self-evident truth "is no barrier to the case for extending the basic principle of equality to nonhuman animals."[5]

Self-conscious sentient beings (adult mammals such as pigs, dogs, horses, whales,
dolphins, cats, bears and seals, together with *most* humans) are persons[6] with preferences to be maximized, while all sentient beings (such as fish, birds, reptiles, young
mammals in general, young humans and severely retarded humans) have interests to
be promoted. The goal is the equal consideration of interests, without denying that
there are differences between most humans and other animals.[7] Singer agrees that
most humans are capable of foresight and planning in a way that nonhuman animals
are not. Yet this does not mean that the death of an animal who is not a person is of
no account; it is merely of less account.[8]

Such a view of preferences and interests precludes cruelty to all animals (since it
does not promote their interests) and normally precludes the killing of self-conscious
animals (since they have a preference for continued existence). This would rule out
many uses of animals in research experiments (those involving cruelty like the LD-
50 test and Draize test, those that are avoidable, and those against the preferences of

---

[3]Jeremy Bentham, *An Introduction to the Principles of Morals and Legislation* (1789), 17.4, note, in
The English Philosophers from Bacon to Mill, ed. E. A. Burtt (New York: Random House, 1939), p.
847.
[4]Peter Singer, *Practical Ethics*, 2nd ed. (Cambridge: Cambridge University Press, 1993), pp. 57-58.
[5]Peter Singer, "All Animals Are Equal," in *Animal Rights and Human Obligations*, ed. Tom Regan
and Peter Singer, 2nd ed. (Englewood Cliffs, N.J.: Prentice-Hall, 1989), p. 75.
[6]Singer, *Practical Ethics*, pp. 110-11. He explains what he means by "persons": "rational and self-conscious beings, aware of themselves as distinct entities with a past and a future."
[7]Singer, "All Animals Are Equal," p. 77, asserts that "the claim to equality does not depend on intelli-
gence, moral capacity, physical strength, or similar matters of fact. Equality is a moral ideal, not a
simple assertion of fact. There is no logically compelling reason for assuming that a factual difference in ability between two people justifies any difference in the amount of consideration we give
to satisfying their needs and interests."
[8]Singer, *Practical Ethics*, p. 275.

self-conscious animals) and would normally lead to vegetarianism (since animal flesh is unnecessary for adequate nutrition and is used only for trivial human reasons such as "they like the taste"). Singer argues that "killing animals for food (except when necessary for sheer survival) makes us think of them as objects we can use casually for our own nonessential purposes."[9] He points out that vegetarianism would increase the amount of grain available to feed others, reduce pollution, save water and energy, cease contributing to the clearing of forests, and save money (which could then be given to other causes). He concedes that some like the Inuit, living in an environment where they must kill animals or starve, might be able to justify the eating of animals.[10] He points out, however, that such is not the case in most industrialized societies.

Any use to which animals are put could be equally appropriate for humans who are not self-conscious (such as severely mentally retarded adults or even normal young infants). Singer suggests that if an experiment could be justified, human infants (perhaps orphans) or severely disabled humans would be in the same category as nonhuman animals, as they would not have any idea what was going to happen to them.[11]

What Singer Is Not Saying—the Animal Rights Alternative

Despite his obvious support for the interests of animals, Singer's views have been met with some unease and concern from other members of the "animal welfare" movement. They have pointed out that there are some problems of internal consistency, as well as some unattractive implications.

In particular, it is noted that Singer is deliberately not arguing that nonhuman animals have rights or intrinsic value. Indeed he rejects the idea of attributing intrinsic value to the rest of the animate and inanimate creation or to the preservation of species or ecosystems.[12] A number of participants in the animal welfare movement

---

[9]Singer, *Animal Liberation*, p. 229.
[10]Singer, *Practical Ethics*, p. 62.
[11]Ibid., pp. 59-60.
[12]Singer thinks that a sufficient case for safeguarding these can be based on the interests of sentient creatures, present and future, human and nonhuman. These interests are sufficient to establish that "at least in a society where no one needs to destroy wilderness in order to obtain food for survival or materials for shelter from the elements, the value of preserving the remaining significant areas of wilderness greatly exceeds the economic values gained by its destruction" (ibid., p. 284). His argument for an environmental ethic is thus based largely on the impact of any harm to the environment on future sentient beings. Thus any actions that are harmful to the environment are ethically dubious, and those that are unnecessarily harmful are clearly wrong (p. 285). He bases this on "consideration for the interests of all sentient creatures, including subsequent generations stretching into the far future" (p. 286). He asserts but does not justify that "it is accompanied by an aesthetic of

have criticized him for not moving in the direction of animal rights.[13] They claim that his theory is not coherent. Tom Regan, for example, suggests that Singer's equality principle cannot consistently be regarded as a moral principle by a utilitarian, since it would sometimes be in tension with the maximization of utility.[14] Evelyn Pluhar believes that Singer's utilitarianism fails to provide the protection for innocent life that most of us require in a moral theory.[15]

Singer's theory is not able to justify the protection of young mammals (and humans), since it does not overcome the problem of replaceability. The replaceability problem for utilitarians is that if they are concerned to maximize total utility, they are apparently committed to holding that present and future individuals are interchangeable in the right circumstances. Thus Pluhar has pointed out that classical utilitarianism would hold it right to raise, use and kill a sentient nonhuman if

1. the nonhuman would not otherwise have existed

2. the nonhuman has had a pleasurable life

3. the death of the nonhuman causes it no pain, fear or other disutility

4. those close to the nonhuman (e.g. mothers, mates) are not allowed to suffer as a result of its use and killing

5. the nonhuman is replaced at death by another nonhuman for whom conditions 1-4 apply[16]

Singer appears to have accepted this with regard to very young (whether an infant is "normal" or not) and severely mentally disabled humans, as well as many sentient nonhumans, if its overall utility is thereby increased.[17] If Singer were right,

---

appreciation for wild places and unspoiled nature" (p. 286). I can only assume that this can be justified by the future aesthetic pleasures of (probably) human beings. I think he ends up with a position that has little ground to argue for the preservation of species of plants and other nonsentient living beings, except that they may be of some value to future sentient beings.

[13]Singer's views have also been criticized by philosophers outside the animal welfare movement, such as R. G. Frey, who writes from a utilitarian viewpoint in *Rights, Killing and Suffering* (Oxford: Blackwell, 1983) in defense of meat eating. See also Peter Carruthers, *The Animals Issue* (Cambridge: Cambridge University Press, 1992), who argues that it is improper to weigh the suffering of animals against the suffering of humans.

[14]Tom Regan, *The Case for Animal Rights* (Berkeley: University of California Press, 1983), p. 211-18. On p. 231 Regan concludes that "neither those who seek a solid foundation for the obligation to be vegetarian nor those who seek a sound theory will find it in [Singer's] preference utilitarianism."

[15]A substantial critique of Singer is given in Evelyn B. Pluhar, *Beyond Prejudice: The Moral Significance of Human and Nonhuman Animals* (Durham. N.C.: Duke University Press, 1995), pp. 179-217.

[16]Ibid., p. 185.

[17]In ibid., p. 206, Pluhar refers to a revealing exchange between Singer and H. L. A. Hart. Hart pointed out (*New York Review of Books*, May 15, 1980, p. 31) that Singer's view would imply that the parent of an infant would be justified in killing it, provided no one else wanted to adopt it into a good home and they undertook to replace it by conceiving another child who would have a mar-

one could raise, kill and eat some animals (for example, infant mammals like calves and lambs) provided we allow them pleasant lives and painless, fearless deaths. Such an argument may not justify many current practices (such as hen batteries and veal calf pens) but could theoretically justify a wide range of treatments for nonhumans. It would even be permissible to breed, use and kill human infants, provided you replaced them with beings that were similar; indeed it would be obligatory to do so if the replacement would have a better life than the replacee![18] Singer has admitted that he has no satisfactory response to the replaceability problem[19] but argues that to move in the direction of rights (such as a right to life) entails greater problems.

Richard Wade echoes the reservations of many when he concludes that "Singer's beliefs in regard to human and animal natures do not ring true. His moral theory is unfair, unworkable and alarming."[20]

A Biblical Theology of Animals
Is there a Christian view of animals that is a more compelling alternative to Singer's? It has been rightly pointed out that the nineteenth-century animal welfare lobby was largely Christian and clearly predated the secular animal rights movement of the second half of the twentieth century.[21] Christian concern for animals is thus not simply a novelty or fad, another example of the church trying to imitate the latest fashion in contemporary culture.

A number of diverse ways forward have been proposed by Christian writers. Andrew Linzey has argued from a Christian animal rights perspective, while Wade proposes a natural law approach.[22] Others emphasize the place of human responsibil-

---

ginally happier life. Indeed parents who kill a normal infant and do not replace it because they do not want the burden of parenthood are *no more wrong* in preference utilitarian terms than a couple with the same motive who refuse to conceive a child in the first place. Singer replied to Hart ("Letter to the Editor," *New York Review of Books,* August 14, 1980, p. 53) fully accepting these implications for human infants, including the equivalence of killing and failing to conceive a child.

[18]Pluhar, *Beyond Prejudice,* p. 206, refers to Jonathan Swift's eighteenth-century satire proposing that poor Irish babies be bred, farmed and sold for food: "I have been assured by a very knowing American of my acquaintance in London, that a young, healthy child well nursed is at a year old a most delicious, nourishing, and wholesome food, whether stewed, roasted, baked, or boiled."

[19]Singer, *Animal Liberation,* p. 229: "I still have doubts about this issue." For an insightful discussion and evaluation of how Singer seeks to address this question, see Pluhar, *Beyond Prejudice,* pp. 190-211.

[20]Richard Wade, "Towards a Christian Ethic of Animals," *Pacifica* 13 (2000): 212.

[21]J. A. Sargent, *Animal Rights and Wrongs* (London: Hodder & Stoughton, 1996), p. 182.

[22]See, for example, Andrew Linzey, *Animal Theology* (London: SCM Press, 1994), and his many other works; Wade, "Towards a Christian Ethic," pp. 202-12.

ity rather than animal rights.[23] In the present essay I intend to outline a biblical theological perspective, before returning to critique Singer from this vantage point.[24]

Biblical theology is an approach that aims to examine the unfolding teaching of the Bible as it is progressively revealed. The Bible has much to say about animals. In the Old Testament, for example, the only book that makes no reference to animals is Ruth.[25]

The animal creation is arranged according to kinds (Gen 1:20-25), which reflects God's delight in the diversity of the animal world. Distinctions are made between different types of creatures, and this is part of what God called good or "in accordance with his plan." In the ideal picture of the opening chapter of the Bible, diversity of species is valued by God.

The creation account (Gen 1—2) describes humans as both like and unlike the animals. They are like the animals in being creatures, not the Creator, yet are unlike the other creatures in that a distinct formula is used and the human species alone are made in the image of God (Gen 1:28), which involves responsible dominion over God's creation.[26] Naming the animals (Gen 2:19) also implies authority over them.[27] In Genesis 2:7, the man is made from the dust of the ground (like the rest of creation), but God breathes the breath of life into him (unlike the rest of creation).

The human need for companionship is not met by the animals, but only through the creation of a fellow human being (Gen 2:19-23), one fashioned from his rib or side, a metaphor for coming from the very stuff of which he was made.[28] In God's ordering of his creation, there appears to be a deeper level of companionship possible between two human beings than between a human being and an animal.

---

[23]For example, Richard Griffiths, *The Human Use of Animals*, Grove Booklet on Ethics 46 (Bramcote, U.K.: Grove, 1982), or, more briefly, Richard Higginson, *Dilemmas* (London: Hodder & Stoughton, 1988), pp. 218-23.

[24]The closest to this approach is probably Sargent, *Animal Rights and Wrongs*, who surveys the biblical material in depth but does not trace the progressive teaching of the Bible as it unfolds.

[25]Griffiths, *Human Use of Animals*, p. 6. A comprehensive account of the place of animals in everyday life in Old Testament times is given in Oded Borowski, *Every Living Thing: Daily Use of Animals in Ancient Israel* (Walnut Creek, Calif.: Altamira, 1998).

[26]There is, of course, great theological debate over the meaning of the concept "the image of God," but the context seems to imply at least a relational aspect (Gen 1:27) and a dominion aspect (Gen 1:28). As Griffiths notes, dominion here implies not only authority but also responsibility (*Human Use of Animals*, p. 9).

[27]G. J. Wenham, *Genesis 1-15*, Word Biblical Commentary (Waco, Tex.: Word, 1987), p. 68; contra J. H. Eaton, *The Circle of Creation* (London: SCM Press, 1995), pp. 7-8, who proposes that in naming each animal the man recognizes them as friends and companions.

[28]V. P. Hamilton points out that the word *side*, commonly translated as "rib," refers everywhere else in the Old Testament to the side of an object. The sense here is probably that the woman was made from an undesignated part of the man's body (*The Book of Genesis Chapters 1-17*, New International Commentary on the Old Testament [Grand Rapids, Mich.: Eerdmans, 1990], p. 178).

The animals appear to be victims in the flood—for not only are humans wiped out but also animals and creeping things and birds (Gen 6:7). But the taking of two of each animal into the ark means that the created distinctions or "kinds" of Genesis 1 are preserved after the flood (Gen 6:19-20). The seven pairs of clean animals (Gen 7:2-3) enable later sacrifices to be offered without endangering these species. God's will after the flood is still that the animals multiply fruitfully (Gen 8:17, 19).

The Fall in Genesis 3 seems to spoil all relationships and also human dominion. The ground is now cursed (Gen 3:17). Human beings are still to exercise dominion (Gen 9), but their dominion will be marred by sin. Death is present in the animal world, for in Genesis 3:21 God makes garments for Adam and Eve from skins, which presupposes that animals have died, and in Genesis 4 Abel offers an animal sacrifice.[29]

After the flood, Genesis 9:8-17 speaks of a covenant between God and every living creature, not just humans. However, Genesis 9:13 immediately describes the covenant as between God and the earth, so this promise goes beyond extending God's blessings to the animal world. The covenant of Genesis 9 may well be a limited covenant or oath-based, sign-sealed promise not to destroy all flesh again, rather than a relational covenant like the later Abrahamic, Sinai or Davidic expressions of the covenant.

What is clear after the flood is that animals can be eaten by humans (Gen 9:3-6). A distinction is drawn between killing animals for food (Gen 9:3) and killing a human being (Gen 9:6). The rationale for this distinction is that humanity is made in the image of God, which appears to be of great moral significance, a theological reason for treating different species differently. In the light of this passage it does not seem possible to insist that Christians *must* be vegetarians, though presumably it is still a viable option.[30]

It is worth tracing at this point how the rest of the Bible unpacks the issue of eating meat or choosing to be vegetarian. The eating of meat is presupposed in the food laws of Leviticus 11 and Deuteronomy 14, where eating certain animals is taboo, not because they are animals but because they are unclean. Other animals are clean and suitable to be killed and eaten. Some animals were offered in sacrifice, continuing the thread begun in Genesis 4. At times the flesh of these animal sacrifices does not appear to be eaten (for example, Gen 15:7-20, the burnt offering of Lev 1, or the goat on the Day of

---

[29]Eaton, *Circle of Creation*, p. 4, suggests that this is only a post-Fall situation.
[30]Linzey, *Animal Theology*, chap. 9, offers a more persuasive argument for vegetarianism in our culture, based on advances in our dietary knowledge and access to foods, so that we no longer need to eat animal flesh in order to meet our nutritional needs. He regards Genesis 9 as a concession to human sinfulness.

Atonement in Lev 16). However, it is clear that at least some of the sacrificial offerings were eaten by the worshipers and priests (for example, the Passover lamb in Ex 13; the peace offering of Lev 3—see Lev 7:15-16). In New Testament times, the food laws are set aside in Christ, but eating of meat is still permitted (Mk 7:19; Acts 10:9-16; 15:20; Rom 14:1-6, 13-23; 1 Cor 8:1-13; 10:23-33). While there is no explicit mention of Jesus' eating red meat, that would have been an integral part of the Passover meal that was the basis of the Last Supper. The risen Jesus clearly ate fish (Lk 24:41-43).

It is now appropriate to undertake a broader sweep of the place and treatment of animals through the Bible. In the patriarchal era, the clan of Abraham were keepers of animal livestock (Gen 12:16; 13:5-7; 20:14-15; 21:27-30; 24:10-11; 26:19-22; 27:8; 29:1-10; 30:29—31:18; 31:38-41; 32:1-21; 33:13-17; 34:5; 37:2, 12-17; 45:9-11; 46:5-6; 46:31—47:6), in a society where wealth was measured in terms of animal holdings (see, for example, Job 1:3).[31] Even when the Israelites left Egypt, they took with them large numbers of animals (Ex 12:37-38). Thus at this very early stage the descendants of Abraham had domesticated and cared for a large number of animals.

When the Torah was given to Israel, it included a number of laws that dealt with animals. Some of these were food laws (Lev 11; Deut 14) and regulations about animal sacrifices (Lev 1-7), discussed briefly above. However, there were also a number of laws that dealt with the proper care of animals. The sabbath command specifically mentions that animals are to rest as well as people (Ex 23:12; Deut 5:14). The case law of Deuteronomy 25:4 prohibited the muzzling of an ox while it was treading out grain. One principle underlying this law is to take appropriate care of one's domesticated animals. In Deuteronomy 22:1-4 this principle is broadened to involve care for a neighbor's animal, from which one gains no profit. Care for animals is not simply based on the fact that they are profitable possessions. Indeed in Deuteronomy 22:6-7 the recognition of human responsibility to animals is said to extend even to birds. The language of these laws is not, however, that of rights of animals but rather of human responsibility toward the animal world.

The focus at this stage is largely on domesticated animals. It is worth pointing out that the categories right through the Old and New Testaments are domesticated animals and wild animals. There is no evidence supporting (nor, for that matter, any prohibition on) our popular contemporary practice of keeping pets or "companion animals." In fact some common pets like cats are curiously absent from either Testament.[32]

---

[31]While the book of Job is probably written at a much later date, it is given a literary setting in patriarchal times (before the giving of the law) outside of Israel in order to address more universal issues. One indication of the patriarchal setting is the detail in Job 1:5 of the head of the clan acting as the priest.

[32]Eaton notes that the small cat is not mentioned, though there are references to the leopard or lion

The next main stage of Israel's history was entry into the Promised Land. Sometimes the animals of the wicked were destroyed, such as those of Achan, along with all his other possessions, to avoid any possibility of profit (Josh 7:24). However, generally the animals of Israel's enemies were preserved (as in Josh 8:27; 11:14). In any event, it is clear that Yahweh's war had a limited scope. In Deuteronomy 20 its purpose was only to wash the Promised Land clean of the gods of those nations (Deut 20:18), and where an enemy was outside the land (Deut 20:10-15) different rules applied, including preserving the livestock (Deut 20:14). A concern for the environment is evident in that same chapter (Deut 20:19-20). Only occasionally (and only when there was an explicit divine command) were all the inhabitants' possessions, including animals, to be destroyed (as in 1 Sam 15:2-3). While the rationale for this is not explained in Scripture, it is no more morally problematic than the killing of human adults and children. The difficulty is not that animals are treated worse than humans but rather that they are treated in the same way.

Of course, in a fallen world where there was animosity between wild animals and the human world (with its domesticated animals), it is inevitable that wild animals would be killed. One example at this point in Israel's history was the young shepherd David. In 1 Samuel 17:34-36 he describes how he killed both lions and bears in order to preserve his flock.

During the time of the kingdoms of Israel and Judah, God is portrayed as using animals to further his purposes.[33] Thus in 1 Kings 13 (especially verse 24) a wild lion is used to punish a prophet because of his disobedience to God. In 2 Kings 2:23-24 bears maul the young men who mocked the prophet Elisha. God's beneficial purposes are evident in 1 Kings 17:6, where he sends some birds with food to feed Elijah.[34] In Jonah 1:17 God uses a great fish to deliver the prophet. Jonah 4:11 makes the interesting comment in passing that God cares not only for the people in Nineveh but also for the cattle or animals. In the later exilic period, Daniel 6 records how the lions preserved God's spokesman in refusing to eat Daniel but eating those who plotted against him.

(*Circle of Creation*, pp. 56-57). However, there is an exception in the apocryphal letter of Jeremiah in the book of Baruch (6:22), where cats are mentioned in passing. They were common in Egypt. There is more information about dogs, as in Mark 7:28 (dogs cleaning up the scraps under the table) and Job 30:1 (dogs working with flocks of sheep). In the apocryphal book of Tobit (5:15—6:2; 11:4) there is the possible example of a companion animal, or at least a working animal that accompanied his master. A young man, Tobias, sets out on a journey to get a cure for his father, and his dog goes with him and returns.

[33]Of course this did not begin in the monarchy. In Genesis 8:6-12, for example, the raven and dove helped Noah to discover that dry land had appeared, while in Numbers 22:21-38 God was able to use Balaam's donkey.

[34]Eaton argues that Elijah was also sustained by the friendship of the birds (*Circle of Creation*, p. 40), but there is no suggestion of that in the text.

Since the book of Psalms is traditionally linked with David and Proverbs with Solomon, it is appropriate to consider the contribution of the psalm and wisdom material at this point. A number of psalms outline God's attitude to the animals, but it is most clearly set out in Psalm 104. Alongside his concern for the physical world (Ps 104:2-9), God expresses his ongoing care for animals in providing water (Ps 104:11, 13, 16), pasture (Ps 104:14), suitable habitats for birds (Ps 104:16-17) and wild animals (Ps 104:18), and prey for lions (Ps 104:21-22). Even the sea is teeming with life (Ps 104:25). In a summary conclusion in Psalm 104:27-30, God is both the One who gives food to animals and the One who holds the power of life and death over them. The thought of this psalm is that the animals belong to the sovereign God, without any mention of human dominion.[35]

In 1 Kings 4:33 the wise king Solomon is pictured as teaching about animals and birds, reptiles and fish. This is reflected in the wisdom book of Proverbs, such as Proverbs 12:10, where knowing and presumably meeting the needs of one's animals is part of righteousness. In Proverbs 6:6-11 the lazy person is invited to observe the ant and learn from its diligent provision for the future. This concept of learning from and delighting in the animals is behind the use of animal imagery in other parts of the Bible as well.[36]

The mainstream wisdom of Proverbs is qualified or nuanced by the other main wisdom books of Job and Ecclesiastes, but God's delight in the animal world is not qualified. It appears from the words of Eliphaz that part of the wisdom hope is that humans and wild animals will dwell together in peace (Job 5:23), while both Job and his friends use animal analogies (for example, Job 4:7-11; 6:2-7). However, the most significant passage is the majestic description of the animal world in Job 38:39—39:30.[37] This "guided tour" of the animal world is God's way of proclaiming his absolute kingship over all of creation, rather than simply a narrow focus on the (human-centered) doctrine of retributive justice. All the creatures described are not under human control. The possible exception is the horse (Job 39:19-25), but even this creature is a mighty warhorse whose spirit is not tamed by humans. Another interesting aspect of the first Yahweh speech is that it shows that God's concern for his creation is wider than what works best for humans. Thus Job 38:25-27 speaks of rain falling

---

[35]A similar idea is found in Psalm 50:9-12.

[36]For example, the image of an eagle in Exodus 19:4 (God brought his people to himself on eagle's wings), Isaiah 40:29-31 (the weary will rise up like an eagle) and Deuteronomy 32:11 (the eagle's protection of its young). Other examples include a deer panting for water (Ps 42:1), animals recognizing their owner (Is 1:3) and a leopard being unable to change its spots (Jer 13:23).

[37]The second Yahweh speech in chapters 40 and 41 may also refer to natural animals hyperbolically described, or perhaps to mythological creatures.

where no humans live, as part of God's plan for his world.

The book of Ecclesiastes asks hard questions of life in light of the fact of death. While animals are not a prominent focus in the book, an interesting comparison is made between humans and animals in Ecclesiastes 3:18-21. These verses do not assert that humans and animals are alike in every respect, but their common mortality has a leveling effect on human pretensions.[38]

The prophetic writings, emerging during the kingship period, continue through to the end of the Old Testament. While they contain many ideas about animals found in earlier books, a new contribution is their use of animal imagery to depict the future (messianic?) rule of well-being. Prominent here is the picture of wild and domesticated animals lying down together in peace (Is 11:6-9; 65:25). Richard Bauckham has correctly pointed out that this is more than an image of animals in harmony with each other; it shows peace between the human world, represented by domesticated animals, and the wild animals that were then an ongoing threat to human survival and prosperity.[39]

The New Testament continues this positive valuing of animals, as well as noting our human responsibility to care for them. In several passages about the sabbath, Jesus simply assumes that humans should care for animals (Mt 12:11-12; Lk 13:15-16; 14:5) and urges that the sabbath not prevent this. God's own provision for animals is evident in such passages as Matthew 6:29 (God feeds the birds of the air), Luke 12:24 (he feeds even the "unclean" ravens), Luke 12:6 (he does not forget the sparrows) and Matthew 10:29 (not one of them will fall to the ground unless God allows it). Yet he regards humans as of more value than many sparrows (Lk 12:7/Mt 10:31—see also Lk 12:24; Mt 6:26; 12:12). God's valuing of his creatures apparently does not preclude his valuing human beings even more.

Bauckham makes two useful observations at this point. First, these passages do not assert that animals have been created for the sole purpose of serving humans.[40]

---

[38]Ecclesiastes 3:18, 21 is sometimes used to make an even stronger identity between animals and humans. On these verses see the stimulating suggestions of Michael A. Eaton, *Ecclesiastes*, Tyndale Old Testament Commentaries (Leicester, U.K.: Inter-Varsity Press, 1983), pp. 85-89. Other ways of understanding these verses are to propose that they are only true if God is left out of the picture, or that animals and humans are being treated as alike only in certain respects.

[39]Richard Bauckham, "Jesus and the Animals II: What did he Teach?" in *Animals on the Agenda: Questions About Animals for Theology and Ethics*, ed. Andrew Linzey and Dorothy Yamamoto (London: SCM Press, 1998), p. 57.

[40]Richard Bauckham, "Jesus and the Animals I: What Did He Practise?" in *Animals on the Agenda: Questions About Animals for Theology and Ethics*, ed. Andrew Linzey and Dorothy Yamamoto (London: SCM Press, 1998), p. 46. Both of Bauckham's articles in this volume offer thoughtful understandings of Jesus' views in the setting of a first-century Jewish world and are the basis of many of comments in this section.

Second, "Jesus never uses the superiority of humans to animals in order to make a negative point about animals."[41] He is simply arguing from the platform that *since God cares for animals*, he must care for humans to an even greater extent. While the episode of the Gadarene pigs (Mt 8:28-34; Mk 5:1-20; Lk 8:26-39) is still problematic, it must be read in the context of Jesus' constant affirmation of the value of animal life.[42]

It appears that Jesus did not seek to overturn either the place of animal sacrifices or the eating of animals as food. While his death would ultimately obviate the need for animal sacrifices (Heb 10:1-18), his release of cattle, sheep and doves from the temple area (Jn 2:14-16; Mt 21:12) is based neither on opposition to animal sacrifices nor on any insistence that the animals had rights.[43] It is also likely that Jesus ate meat, and he certainly ate fish (Lk 24:32-33).[44]

Yet like the Old Testament prophets, the New Testament looks for the renewing of creation and speaks of the creation as longing for release and liberty (Rom 8:19-22). The picture in Mark 1:13 of Jesus in the wilderness with the wild animals is probably another expression of this longing for a messianic reign of peace. Bauckham argues that the wilderness is seen as the archetypal "nonhuman sphere," where humans cannot live with their domesticated animals.[45] In Jewish tradition this conflict between humans and the wild animals is a consequence of sin's entering the world and will be reversed only in the messianic age of peace. The picture of Mark 1:13, then, suggests that Jesus has come as Messiah and will inaugurate an era in which the ideals of Isaiah 11:6-9 will be fulfilled.[46]

In conclusion, then, the Bible supports a robust and rich theology of the animal world. While God's purposes focus on humanity, indeed on a chosen people, there is always a wider vista of the rest of creation. While language of animal rights is not present, there is a strong emphasis on human responsibility before God to act for the well-being of all of creation, including the animals. As Michael Eaton observes,

---

[41]Ibid., pp. 46-47.

[42]This is dealt with briefly in ibid., pp. 47-48; Bauckham suggests that against the backdrop of Jewish beliefs about demons (including that demons return if they do not find an alternative home), this would be seen as the lesser of two evils.

[43]This is pointed out by Sargent, *Animal Rights and Wrongs*, p. 91. Bauckham, "Jesus and the Animals II," pp. 50-51, also notes that Jesus attended festivals which would involve animal sacrifice (Lk 2:41-42; Jn 2:13; 7:1-10; 10:22-23).

[44]For a brief outline of the evidence, see Bauckham, "Jesus and the Animals II," pp. 51-54. Even Linzey concedes the likelihood of this (*Animal Theology*, p. 135).

[45]Bauckham, "Jesus and the Animals II," p. 55.

[46]Ibid., pp. 56-60. At p. 59 Bauckham suggests that this affirms the value of the wild animals and notes that Jesus did not try to adopt them into the human realm but rather allowed them to remain in their domain, the wilderness.

"The importance of an animal, and indeed of any creature, is that it is part of God's world, loved by him. . . . If you would be servants of the living God you must answer to him for your care of all that lives, the care he has entrusted to you."[47]

Singer in the Light of Ethics and Biblical Theology

In this final section I wish to raise questions more than provide answers. However, the material surveyed above will often suggest a direction to pursue. There are a number of issues that need further exploration.

1. *Where do you draw the line?* Is the morally significant divide between humans and all other creatures or between sentient beings and all other beings? Singer has opted for sentience, largely on the basis of his utilitarian predecessor Jeremy Bentham. Yet it is neither established nor self-evident that the indispensable and sufficient criterion of moral significance is the ability to suffer or experience happiness. If the Bible is right, the image of God in humanity may be a better criterion. Humans alone are moral agents. The thought that animals might "sin" and be judged for their "sin" is at the very least counterintuitive. Humans are normally viewed as morally responsible beings in a way that animals are not. From a Christian perspective, a key focus of moral responsibility is being accountable for our actions before God as judge. While Singer's focus is on the maximization of interests or preferences, the differing moral responsibility of humans and animals provides a *prima facie* justification for viewing the interests of animals and humans differently. While it is true that some humans (infants, children, mentally ill) have diminished or no present responsibility, the human race as a whole is distinguishable from other sentient beings by moral accountability.

2. *Are species valuable?* Does Singer give enough weight to individual species? Charles Pinches has sought to defend a certain kind of "speciesism," suggesting that the word has been plundered by Singer.[48] Pinches mentions a program in Minnesota to revive and restabilize the native gray wolf population, which had been driven out by cattle ranchers. He assumes this is a good thing and argues that a position like Singer's is "simply blind to species distinctions."[49] It gives no reason to wish the wolf population to increase more than the cattle, or any similar species at the expense of another. The Bible shows a concern for species, with animals being created after their own kind (Gen 1:24). Pinches wants to treat wolves as wolf creatures and cattle

---

[47]Eaton, *Circle of Creation*, pp. 2, 111.
[48]Charles Pinches, "Each According to Its Kind: A Defense of Theological Speciesism," in *Good News for Animals*, ed. Charles Pinches and J. B. McDaniel (Maryknoll, N.Y.: Orbis, 1995), pp. 187-205.
[49]Ibid., p. 196.

as cattle creatures; he sees the image of God as the caretaker of this diversity of species. Singer's view gives little ground for preferring one species to another or preserving endangered species or a diversity of species, provided that utility is maintained.

3. *Does utilitarianism lead to justice?* Singer's ethic is technically described as "preference utilitarianism," a position that aims to maximize certain consequences —in his case the preferences of sentient beings. Other moral philosophers have questioned whether consequences (such as preferences and interests) can be all that counts morally. This is too complex an issue to be dealt with in the scope of this essay, and it has been addressed in Andrew Sloane's chapter. However, it is worth pointing out that most people do not believe that a maximization of utility always leads to a just distribution of that utility. Justice is commonly agreed on as a key ethical goal, so this is often regarded as a major obstacle to any purely utilitarian theory.[50]

4. *Do Singer's views have any troubling implications?* While Singer's theory has appeal to those who wish to care for animals, it also has some unattractive implications. First, replaceability (replacing one being with a similar or better one) is a thorny issue, for his views permit in certain circumstances the painless killing of any non-self-conscious being. Not only does this fail to protect young animals, it can also be used, as Singer himself concedes, to justify infanticide, even on a "normal" infant. Furthermore, Singer's reluctance to endorse either animal rights or God as Creator has left him in a position where creation has no intrinsic value. Our care for the environment can be justified only on the basis of the interests and preferences of present and future sentient beings. This is a shaky foundation on which to ground ongoing care for our fragile environment.

5. *What are the positive aspects of Singer's stance?* The objections I have highlighted ought not blind us to the value of Singer's contributions. He has rightly raised some important questions, concerns and challenges. He calls attention to practices in animal raising and the use of animals in research that are clearly unacceptable and contrary to biblical human dominion. Such issues deserve further exploration and action.

Singer's arguments may not always be right, but he has shown in his lifestyle an impressive and costly commitment to his beliefs. His evident care for the fair treatment of animals and activity in urging reform far exceed those of most Christians. He has challenged false understandings of human dominion and supremacy.

6. *Animals as an ethical issue.* As I have read Singer on animals, what I have appreciated most of all is his desire to raise the treatment and use of animals as a

---

[50]See, for example, W. K. Frankena, *Ethics*, 2nd ed. (Englewood Cliffs, N.J.: Prentice-Hall, 1973), pp. 32-43.

legitimate ethical issue. His work points us toward a pressing need for Christian ethicists, biblical scholars and theologians to move toward a fuller theology of animal well-being and human responsibility.[51]

---

[51]An interesting example of movement in this direction is Andrew Linzey and Dorothy Yamamoto, eds., *Animals on the Agenda: Questions About Animals for Theology and Ethics* (London: SCM Press, 1998), which canvasses a wide range of these issues. One that is conspicuously absent, however, is the ethics of pet keeping.

5

Rethinking Singer on Life & Death

GORDON PREECE

In an aging Western world, voluntary euthanasia (VE) will probably be the "life issue" of the early twenty-first century—and Peter Singer its most articulate advocate. The push for VE has been pioneered by highly secularized frontier societies like the Netherlands, Oregon in the United States, and the Northern Territory in Australia. It is now legal in the Netherlands (as of April 11 2001, after two decades in which its illegality was overlooked and VE was regulated), while its legality in Oregon and the Northern Territory has been overturned by federal courts or legislation, respectively. Nonetheless, the issue will not go away, for like abortion it represents a place where the ethical tectonic plates underpinning Western societies are shifting. Singer describes this as the clash between an outdated Sanctity of Life Ethic (SOLE) and a new Quality of Life Ethic (QOLE).

An odd alliance of left and right supports VE. Some are social and some are economic libertarians; all share individualism, a commitment to what Singer calls "the culture of choice."[1] Yet this is merely negative choice, the right not to be coerced; it forgets to ask *how* or *what* we ought to choose. Such poverty of choice neglects questions of the content of choice, the meaning and moral substance that traditional, religious societies were much richer in.[2] Singer's allies are also rationalists who apply principles like economic rationalism to life-and-death decisions, seemingly unaware

---

[1]Sally Blakeney, "The Brave New World of Peter Singer," *The Australian Weekend Review*, September 28-29, 1996, Features, p. 28.
[2]Daniel Callahan, *The Troubled Dream of Life: In Search of a Peaceful Death* (New York: Touchstone, 1993), pp. 35-37.

of the dangers of letting market rationality take over medicine.

For instance, former Australian governor-general Sir Bill Hayden advocated VE and spoke of the rising burden of healthcare costs for the elderly in a speech to surgeons. "Succeeding generations deserve to be disencumbered of some unproductive burdens . . . [like] the Trobriand islanders who celebrated impending death with a feast after which the aged went into the bush to die from the effects of poisoned food."[3] Christians, by contrast, are called to "bear one another's burdens" (Gal 6:2). As the bumper sticker states, "I hope to live long enough to be a burden to my children!" We are all, in all societies, dependent on one another, from womb to tomb. "If it is degrading to be dependent on others then everyone is degraded at some point."[4]

This chapter will critically examine the following aspects of Singer's case for VE: first, definitions; second, the clash between SOLE and QOLE; third, some hard cases used to justify VE; fourth, his abandoning the crucial acts versus omissions distinction; fifth, the role of patient autonomy and choice; sixth, the slippery slope—does it go up or down? will voluntary euthanasia lead to involuntary euthanasia or not?

Definitions

Euthanasia is the intentional bringing about or hastening of death (by act or omission) to relieve someone's suffering. *Intentional* is the key word here. Etymologically, *euthanasia* is composed of two Greek words—*eu*, "good," and *thanatos*, "death"—giving the root meaning "good death."

Active or *passive* euthanasia is a common distinction; the former involves direct intervention, such as by injection or medication, and the latter involves indirectly allowing someone to die by natural causes or as a side effect of pain relief. However, the loaded terminology is better ignored. As Andrew Sloane notes, this is "a misnomer for it lumps together things which are quite different in theory and practice. It implies that if you accept one you must accept the other."[5] Singer and collaborator

---

[3]Quoted in Michelle Grattan, "Hayden Backs Euthanasia, Tests for AIDS," *The Australian*, June 22, 1995, pp. 1-2. Cf. David van Gend, "Euthanasia's 'Unproductive Burdens,'" *Quadrant*, January-February 1997, pp. 15-17.

[4]Jenny Teichman, *Social Ethics: A Student's Guide* (Oxford: Blackwell, 1996), p. 75. Cf. Alasdair MacIntyre, *Dependent Rational Animals: Why Human Beings Need the Virtues* (London: Duckworth, 2000), pp. ix, xi, and chap. 1, on the way most philosophers have focused on independent, adult, mature, rational males and thus ignored large parts of life—birth and childhood, sickness, aging, death etc. Vulnerability, affliction and dependent animality are fundamental to the human condition, though we are made in God's image.

[5]Andrew Sloane, "Doctoring Death: Euthanasia Versus the Withdrawal of Life-Prolonging Treat-

Helga Kuhse write of "passive euthanasia" as part of a strategy of linguistic confusion, for they smuggle in a contested practice, active voluntary euthanasia, as similar to the generally acceptable practice of withdrawing futile treatments when death is inevitable. Actually "passive euthanasia" is better described as "letting die" or "allowing to die."[6]

The unsatisfactory category of active and passive euthanasia is subdivided further as follows.

Voluntary active euthanasia (by patient choice) occurs when people are presumably unable or unwilling to carry out suicide. Euthanasia advocates support living wills specifying circumstances, such as terminal cancer, in which someone wants to be painlessly killed. They do not want such wills specifying that someone does not want euthanasia. The active means may include lethal injection of morphine or another drug.

Involuntary active euthanasia (against one's choice) involves euthanasia of those who have expressed their choice against it.

Nonvoluntary active euthanasia (without one's choice) is a death not asked for because the patient is unconscious or otherwise unable to speak or write. The person may be a child or a senile elderly personal incapable of rational decision whose parents, relatives or doctors are given the right to make the decision.[7]

Each of these three has, in Singerian terminology, a passive equivalent where death is by omission, regarded as the equivalent of an action. Some omissions are culpable equivalents of actions intended to kill. Some involve merely letting death happen without intending it. Crucially, official Dutch definitions ignore these key distinctions based on intention. They use a narrower definition of euthanasia as active VE.[8]

Death with dignity is a common synonym for euthanasia. Presumably everyone desires a dignified death, but dignity depends on what is appropriate to what sort of

---

ment," paper delivered to the Christian Philosophical Society, August 21, 1995, Morling Theological College, New South Wales.

[6]David J. Atkinson, "Causing Death and Allowing to Die," *Tyndale Bulletin* 34 (1983): 201-28.

[7]However, "nonvoluntary killing" would be more accurate, because "nonvoluntary euthanasia" suggests that "the administering agent does not act voluntarily. . . . This highlights the similar infelicity of the (now standard) use of 'non-voluntary euthanasia' and 'involuntary euthanasia' to describe (voluntary) mercy-killing without the consent of the subject" (Suzanne Uniacke and H. J. McCloskey, "Peter Singer and Non-voluntary 'Euthanasia': Tripping Down the Slippery Slope," *Journal of Applied Philosophy* 9, no. 2 [1992]: 217, n. 8). They argue that this may warrant using quotation marks for non- and involuntary "euthanasia" in order to connect with the conventional usage but also challenge it. I will observe this usage from now on.

[8]P. J. van der Maas et al., "Euthanasia and Other Medical Decisions Concerning the End of Life," *The Lancet* 338 (1991): 669.

being—a queen or a slug? When people say, "I wouldn't treat an animal like that—put them [or me] out of their [my] misery," they imply that it is undignified to die in great, uncontrolled pain. With palliative care they should not have to. But humans are more than animals; they are kings and queens of creation and have an "alien dignity" bestowed on them from outside by God's grace. As such they should not be killed.

Mercy killing is a common euphemism for euthanasia. But it is a further example of confusing definitions. First, infanticide has been so described because some of those killed are deformed. But the vast majority of infanticides in history and in our day have been females killed without mercy. Second, sometimes money, not mercy, is the motive, as revealed in statements by some U.K. National Health managers and Australian politicians. Third, Social Darwinists and those in favor of eugenics (selective breeding), including Singer, sometimes refer to the destruction of allegedly inferior babies as euthanasia. None of these can be equated with mercy killing.[9]

Singer himself trades, whether deliberately or not, on the positive emotional and motivational connotations of "mercy killing" and "euthanasia" over the negative connotations of just plain "killing." As other philosophers note: "It is easier to represent killing as euthanasia" than to justify the killing of infants for reasons other than mercy in their suffering, such as for the sake of parents, siblings or society's happiness.

> Killing that would otherwise arouse moral revulsion might be viewed as more acceptable if misdescribed as euthanasia. . . . To cause or allow someone a gentle and easy death for a reason other than the good of the one who dies is not euthanasia. . . . It is crucial to cases of killing/letting die/not saving that are *euthanasia* that death itself and not simply the way in which death is brought about be merciful to the one who dies.[10]

This is a matter not merely of method, which Singer stresses—of quick lethal injection versus long slow, lingering agony—but the actual meaning and desirability of death to *the person herself.* The widely accepted extension of the notion of euthanasia to address quality-of-life considerations

> changes the concept of euthanasia from one relating to *making death easier* to one that refers to terminating a life on the basis of a judgement about its quality. It . . . can be an important contributing factor in a slide towards less morally discriminating justifications of killing.[11]

---

[9]Teichman, *Social Ethics*, pp. 65-67.
[10]Uniacke and McCloskey, "Peter Singer," p. 205.
[11]Ibid., p. 206.

New Commandments for Old

Singer highlights three events in three nations in 1993-1994 as marking earth-shaking moments, an ethical earthquake when the sanctity-of-life ethic gave way to the quality-of-life ethic: the trial by Britain's highest court that allowed doctors to terminate the life of a comatose young man, Anthony Bland; the Dutch Parliament's recognizing the unofficial medical guidelines for euthanasia; and a Michigan court's acquittal of Dr. Jack Kevorkian on charges of assisting a Lou Gehrig's disease sufferer, Thomas Hyde, to suicide.[12]

To change the image, Singer sees us as in the middle of a Copernican QOLE revolution that is overturning the old SOLE. Humanity is no longer at the center of the universe, and the sanctity-of-life ethic is a relic left over from when the scientific revolution did not reach into the ethical arena. It is a form of human moral monarchy in a democratic republic of all animals.

For Singer the real issue in the euthanasia debate is that new medical technology confronts us with questions about the sanctity-of-life ethic against euthanasia which we could hide from before. First we redefined death as whole brain death so we could transplant usable organs; now we are redefining the sanctity of life to evade confronting that ethic's fatal flaws. We distinguish ordinary and extraordinary forms of treatment that allow us to withdraw respirators from comatose patients; we anesthetize patients to pain by giving massive morphine doses that kill them, though we say that is not euthanasia because our intent is to relieve pain; we select severely disabled newborns for nontreatment, leaving them to die but claiming not to kill them. By denying full personhood to fetuses we can give preference to the life and health of their mothers, and by vetoing comparisons of intellectually defective human babies and nonhuman animals we maintain the arbitrary boundary of the *human* SOLE despite all the evidence that they differ only in degree. The SOLE can no longer be patched up, because it is "paradoxical, incoherent, and dependent on pretence. . . . New medical techniques, decisions in landmark legal cases and shifts of public opinion are constantly threatening to bring the whole edifice crashing down."[13]

Before we get swept along by Singer's revolutionary rhetoric, it is worth noting, with Singer, that the Copernican theory triumphed "not because it was more accurate than the old one, but because it was a fresh approach, full of promise." Singer claims no more for his own theory, hardly arguing for its merits but simply setting it

---

[12]Peter Singer, *Rethinking Life and Death* (Melbourne: Text, 1995), p. 1. VE has since been fully legalized in Holland, while Kevorkian is now serving a long jail sentence for assisted suicide.
[13]Ibid., pp. 187-89.

up as the only alternative to a stale SOLE. But surely we can expect more evidence of rational and ethical superiority when asked to take such a risky, revolutionary step. Singer's utopian revolution, like the French, Russian and Chinese revolutions, is potentially dangerous as well as inaccurate or untruthful. Those revolutions led to the deaths of millions and a totalitarian loss of freedom, and Singer's revolution would be no different. Further, Singer's revolutionary view of science, and by implication ethics, caricatures Thomas Kuhn's *The Structure of Scientific Revolutions,* from which he adapts the subheading "The Structure of Ethical Revolutions."[14] Contemporary philosophy of science takes a generally evolutionary view and allows for the development of theories, such as through new technologies and data, as in the case of life issues, while maintaining central or core beliefs, such as SOLE.[15]

In his fascination with new medical technologies for keeping people alive, perhaps against their will and QOL, Singer ignores palliative care as the fast-advancing new alternative to euthanasia as a last resort in terms of pain relief and QOL. The notion of absolute last resort is crucial to the two-thousand-year-old just war tradition. Parallels are often drawn in relation to abortion and euthanasia.

Euthanasia is, in fact, the last resort of the "therapeutically destitute" or doctors ignorant of new possibilities for pain control. In the Northern Territory there were no state provisions for palliative care.[16] The Netherlands has fewer than ten facilities, compared with over two hundred in the United Kingdom.[17] The "subjective opinions" of Dutch doctors justifying their performing non-VE because patients were "suffering grievously" and "palliative care possibilities were exhausted" were of those uneducated about palliative care. "Pain management was independently assessed as inadequate in 54 per cent of patients at The Netherlands Cancer Institute."[18]

The palliative care and hospice movements came into being when fear of cancer was chronic and common. Palliative care successfully addresses the QOL of patients. It neither hastens nor postpones death. Advances in pain control have "won the battle against cancer." So successful has palliative care been that VE supporters no

---

[14]Thomas Kuhn, *The Structure of Scientific Revolutions,* 2nd ed. (Chicago: University of Chicago Press, 1972), esp. Kuhn's postscript. See Singer, *Rethinking Life and Death,* pp. 187-88.
[15]See Gordon R. Preece, *The Viability of the Vocation Tradition in Trinitarian, Credal and Reformed Perspective* (Lewiston, N.Y.: Edwin Mellen, 1998), chap. 1, n. 100, for further discussion and references.
[16]See "Did Bob Dent Receive All Available Medical Treatment?" *News Weekly,* October 19, 1996, p. 7. Concerning the first person to die by legal VE, the verdict by West Australian palliative care specialist Dr. Andrew Dean is no, Dent did not receive a breakthrough palliative care technique that would have relieved his pain.
[17]Teichman, *Social Ethics,* p. 89.
[18]Roger Woodruff, "Is Euthanasia Contagious?" letter to the editor, *The Age,* December 24, 1996, quoting K. L. Dorrepaal, *Cancer* 63 (1989): 593.

longer think of cancer sufferers as their prime example of those needing VE, but AIDS patients. Some still opposing palliative care do so on cost grounds, unaware that it is very inexpensive, averaging less than $10 per person per annum.[19]

Dr. James Gilbert of the Exeter Hospice summarizes the virtues of palliative as an alternative to euthanasia: "The hospice experience of the last three decades is that when high quality care of this type is provided to those with advanced progressive diseases the demand for euthanasia on grounds of compassion disappears."[20] A good death will be better ensured not by a revolutionary legalizing of VE but by small revisions to health budgets to include the act of dying and the palliative care to ease it.

Still, Singer modestly claims that his revolution demands five new QOLE rules or commandments to replace the old SOLE commandments. I will deal with only the three most pertinent to euthanasia and provide critical responses to each.

First Commandment

"First Old Commandment: Treat all human life as of equal worth." Singer argues that no one really believes this rhetoric, as we do not pull out all stops to save humans with poor QOL. For instance, we withdraw nourishment from a person in a persistent vegetative state or a severely malformed baby or do not treat an elderly man with advanced Alzheimer's disease who gets pneumonia.

If we follow the letter of this law, it leads to modern American medical absurdities like Joey Fiori's nearly two decades in a persistent vegetative state. Another absurdity was Nancy Cruzan's eight-year comatose existence until friends conveniently remembered her saying that she would want to die if ever in such a situation. Only then could the feeding tube be withdrawn.[21]

To Singer, extreme cases such as these show that life is not *always* good, sanctified or an end in itself, but is a means to personal existence. In other words, it is a certain quality of life, a rational, chosen existence that includes more pleasure than pain. If life cannot be lived from the inside, consciously and biographically rather than merely biologically, then it is not worth living.

"First New Commandment: Recognize that the worth of human life varies." In Singer's view "we should treat human beings in accordance with their ethically rele-

---

[19]Teichman, *Social Ethics*, p. 72.
[20]Quoted by Teichman, *Social Ethics*, p. 73, on whom this section depends. Gilbert also states that through the charity Hospicecare in southwest England palliative care is provided for an area of 300,000 people at approximately six pounds per head per year. Note that a comparison of Dutch and U.S. health costs found that "less than 0.07% of the total amount spent annually on health care in the US . . . would be saved from allowing doctor-assisted suicide" (Ezekiel Emanuel and Margaret Battin, *The New England Journal of Medicine*, July 16, 1998).
[21]Singer, *Rethinking Life and Death*, pp. 62-63, 190.

vant characteristics"—their rational, relational and experiential capacities. This allows us to recognize, like the British judges in the Tony Bland and Baby C cases, that life without consciousness is worthless. Without consciousness we no longer have the inherent capacity for interest in our personal future or interaction with others or our environment. Singer states baldly that "the best argument for the new commandment is the sheer absurdity of the old one." We would have to have indefinite treatment for everyone, including anencephalic babies like baby K with continued respirator support, even the brain dead. "For if human life is of equal worth, whether it has the capacity for consciousness or not, why focus on the death of the brain, rather than on the death of the body as a whole?"[22]

Response. Many of the extreme cases Singer characteristically cites are tragic, and some involve medically unsound treatments. This is particularly true of Singer's American examples, where, he admits, unlike the rest of the world, illnesses tend to be treated aggressively lest doctors find themselves being sued by grieving relatives and ambulance-chasing lawyers. This leaves doctors in the United States with thousands of technologically maintained comatose patients, more than the rest of the world combined.[23] Law rather than medical wisdom often rules in the United States and occasionally in U.K. cases. But this does not mean that we face a choice between rigidly absolutist SOL-based legal restrictions and sanctions or Singer's vague new QOL commandment. This ignores the biblical leavening of law with wisdom, the medical and familial discernment of "a time to die" (Eccles 3:2). "The case against euthanasia . . . is not a case for compulsory treatment. Compulsory treatment is a distortion produced by an accidental feature of a particular legal system."[24]

SOL stresses the inherent value of human life, not its value "by virtue of others' responses" nor for grand utilitarian purposes irrelevant to itself, as in Singer. Humans are ends, not means. The worth of a human being is unconditional. The SOL erects "a moral obstacle to merely using her or, for example, to killing her . . . in the way one does a sick animal. . . . Each person *is* a value rather than is valuable *because of such and such properties or characteristics.*"[25]

This unconditional value is paramount in the Western medical and legal traditions:

---

[22]Ibid., pp. 190-91.

[23]In the United Kingdom there are 1,000-1,500 persons in a persistent vegetative state. U.S. facilities are stricter about withdrawal of treatment, and 10,000-25,000 adults and 4,000-10,000 children are in a persistent vegetative state. Ibid., p. 59.

[24]Teichman, *Social Ethics*, p. 84.

[25]John Quilter, "The Babies Doe: Sanctity or Quality of Life?" *Ethics Education* 6, no. 3 (2000): 2-5. Cf. John F. Kavanagh, *Who Counts as Persons? Human Identity and the Ethics of Killing* (Washington, D.C.: Georgetown University Press, 2001), on intrinsic individual dignity and inviolability.

The notion of a worthless life is as alien to the Hippocratic tradition as it is to English [read Western] criminal law, both of which subscribe to the principle of the sanctity of human life which holds that because all lives are intrinsically valuable, it is always wrong intentionally to kill an innocent human being. This principle is, by contrast, rejected by the so-called "new" (consequentialist) morality which openly espouses the notion of the "life not worth living."[26]

While there are sometimes difficulties with squaring this with quality-of-life considerations, Singer's straw-man methodology is unfair and unrepresentative of SOL theorists and practitioners. "For nowhere has the sanctity of life position seriously maintained that there are literally *no instances* where letting another die, or even killing another human being, is ethically right," John Quilter notes. Advocates of the SOL who allow for certain exceptional cases appeal to

the "futility" of treatment, a distinction between ordinary and extraordinary treatments, "what the reasonable person would decide" or to the applicability of the principles of the Double Effect. Unfortunately moves such as these, parading as realistic limits on the obligation imposed by the sanctity of life to save lives, often serve only to conceal what really is an appeal to quality of life considerations.[27]

These distinctions are "shot through with moral judgments, and one of the things relevant to these judgments is a patient's quality of life prospect." Extraordinariness or futility depends in part on the benefits to the patient's quality of life by such treatment in compensation for the burden or indignity of the treatment. But this notion of quality of life as a supplement to sanctity or unconditional value of a human life is different from its use by Singer and others who do not hold to its unconditional value.

Further, it is important in recognizing grades of quality not to think, as Singer does, of a lower degree of quality "as a negative amount of quality as if a low-quality form of life is a harm. But this is a deep and dangerous mistake. For to say that something lacks the benefits of some conditions is a far remove from saying that it thereby suffers harm." For example, blindness is not a good thing, but a blind person does not suffer a "moral harm" by living, so that we should either let them die or kill them. Nor is life for a baby necessarily a harm because he is retarded, nor is life for a comatose person.[28]

---

[26]John Keown, "Doctors and Patients: Hard Case, Bad Law, New Ethics," *Cambridge Law Journal* 52, no. 2 (July 1993): 211.

[27]Quilter, "Babies Doe," pp. 3-6. The Roman Catholic doctrine of double effect allows for an action with two effects, one foreseen, such as the death of a person, the other willed, such as the reducing of their pain through morphine.

[28]Ibid., pp. 7-8.

Singer is correct that consciousness and its ending through brain death is the current key marker of death (despite elements of convenience for transplantation purposes). Yet his equation of human worth with consciousness is reductionistic. Significant as consciousness is, it is not just "the thought that counts." The rational is a means to the end of the relational, and the relational can exist even when one member cannot respond or reciprocate, whether to other humans or to God. Such responsiveness is also often very difficult to judge.

Humanity's "alien dignity" resides mysteriously in God's relationship to God's image. This keeps humans from "being finally dissected by reason" as in Singer's view. So

> when we meet another person, however poor, lowly, diseased or dumb, we stand before something which holds the divine—we stand before someone who is mystery and must be reverenced as such, someone who, like Buber's God, is a "You that in accordance with its nature cannot become an it." Of course we can, and do, treat other people like "its," as mere objects, but always to the loss of our own humanity.[29]

As we saw in chapter one, Singer's "moral actualism" and personist antispeciesism means that only persons (human or nonhuman) consciously actualizing or activating their capacities and preferences now have a right to life. This disqualifies the less developed and maldeveloped. But babies have a potential (as humans) that a currently more intelligent ape does not. The small number of elderly who lose their language ability altogether, or those born with severe Down syndrome, are in part analogous to those who are asleep. Keith Ward shows that

> just as a person who is asleep does not use his or her rational powers, so a mentally handicapped person is prevented from using such powers, often throughout a whole lifetime. The subject of their consciousness is not non-human, or that proper to an animal. It is human, belonging to the human species, but is deprived of its proper form of activity.[30]

Finally, and significantly for Singer's whole proposal, his claim that "the best argument for the new commandment is the sheer absurdity of the old one" is simply a rhetorical ploy, the old argument *ad absurdum*. He does not have a good positive argument for his alternative. A truly rational and scientific procedure is to always

[29]Janet Martin Soskice, "Creation and Relation," *Theology*, January/February 1991, p. 37, citing Andrew Louth, "The Mysterious Leap of Faith," in *In Vitro Veritas: More Tracts for Our Times*, ed. Tom Sutcliffe and Peter Moore, St. Mary's (Pimlico) Annual for 1984/1985, p. 89.

[30]Keith Ward, *The Battle for the Soul* (London: Hodder & Stoughton, 1985), p. 152. Note too that Singer's moral actualism is a danger to the anesthetized, the sleeping, the temporarily comatose and so on.

evaluate arguments, theories and paradigms against each other to see if they solve particular problems—for example, the dilemmas of new medical technologies that indefinitely prolong life—better than the alternatives.[31] The old view has some problems adapting to new life-prolonging technologies, but these seem minor compared to the dangers of Singer's largely untried view.

Second Commandment

"Second Old Commandment: Never intentionally take innocent human life." Singer often tries to expose the complexities and contradictions of the SOLE, particularly its inconsistencies regarding killing. He finds this command too absolute to deal with all circumstances and cases. Misquoting the Roman Catholic position as an example of absolutism that costs many mothers' lives, he claims that it condemns killing any fetus (such as one with its head stuck in labor), even at the cost of its mother's life.

Singer then cites the Tony Bland case as showing that the British judges recognized that the second old commandment should be scrapped "when life is of no benefit to the person living it." However, relying on the tenuous thin line between acts and omissions, they refused to go beyond allowing withdrawal of treatment, leaving unaddressed "the problem of cases in which it is better to use active means to take innocent human life." This occurred in the case of Dr. Nigel Cox, who was found guilty of the attempted murder of Lilian Boyes after she begged him to shorten her agony.[32]

Singer's argument is capped off with Arthur Hugh Clough's famous couplet from "The Latest Decalogue": "Thou shalt not kill; but need'st not strive officiously to keep alive." Singer claims this is usually used to support the old ethic but is in fact an ironic attack on our hypocritical adherence to the letter but not the spirit of the commandments. "Clough would therefore have supported an extended view of responsibility. Not killing is not enough. We are responsible for the consequences of our decision not to strive to keep alive."[33]

"Second New Commandment: Take responsibility for the consequences of your decisions." Here Singer argues that we should abandon the traditional acts/omissions distinction and the related importance of intention and look only at consequences.

1. The distinction between killing and letting die is not clear-cut but ambiguous. "By insisting that we are as responsible for our omissions as for our acts—for what we deliberately don't do, as well as for what we do, we can neatly explain why the doctors were wrong to follow the Roman Catholic teaching when a craniotomy was the

---

[31]Alasdair MacIntyre, *Whose Justice? Which Rationality?* (London: Duckworth, 1988), chaps. 18, 20.
[32]Singer, *Rethinking Life and Death*, pp. 192-93.
[33]Ibid., pp. 193-94.

only way to prevent the deaths of both mother and fetus."[34]

2. The above reasons against killing do not apply when a person wants to die and can die more swiftly and easily by an act, such as lethal injection, than by an omission, such as allowing death by pneumonia or starvation through withdrawal of feeding tubes.

Response. First, the case of threat to the mother's life, like many cases Singer cites, is extremely rare and is now avoidable and outdated due to obstetric advances, as he admits.[35] Also, we do not have to defend all aspects of fundamentalist Roman Catholic or Protestant life ethics to recognize Singer's tendency to use the most absolutist and often outdated positions as if representative of all current Christian views. The Roman Catholic doctrine of double effect allows for an action with two effects, one foreseen, here the death of the fetus, the other willed, the saving of the mother's life.

Second, whether Clough's dictum was used according to his intended sense or not, it makes sense in medical circumstances of futile treatments. As taught to medical students it shows that the old ethic was not rigidly absolutist, as the commandment against killing itself was not. Instead it was a *prima facie* absolute, requiring justification of rare exceptions to the general rule.[36] It primarily forbade murder.

Third, Singer admits that to totally abandon the acts/omissions distinction is extremely demanding unless some limitation is agreed upon. There would be no limit on what we should do. For instance, is not giving to World Vision as bad as killing a poor person? Singer qualifies his commandment: "The new approach need not regard failing to save as equivalent to killing. *Without some form of prohibition on killing people, society itself could not survive*" (emphasis mine). You have more to fear from people killing you than from their allowing you to die. So "in everyday life there are good grounds for having a stricter prohibition on killing than on allowing to die."

Also, Singer recognizes limits to our capacity for care and sacrifice. So for "a viable ethic . . . a moderate degree of partiality for ourselves, our family and our friends" is needed. "These are the grains of truth in the view that we are responsible only for what we do, and not for what we fail to do."[37] But these giant "grains" of truth outweigh Singer's argument against the acts/omissions distinction, as shown in chapter one.

Furthermore, the biblical and traditional ethic has always taken seriously sinful

---

[34]Ibid., p. 195.
[35]Ibid., p. 193.
[36]See W. D. Ross, *The Right and the Good* (Oxford: Clarendon, 1930).
[37]Ibid., pp. 195-96.

omissions (Mt 25:31-46), and the Anglican/Episcopal general confession asks forgive-
ness for "what we have left undone." Yet it does not regard all omissions as equally
culpable as deliberate actions. But more on this crucial distinction later.

Fourth, Singer manipulatively blurs the linguistic and legal distinction between
"killing" and "not saving."[38] This is despite his reliance on a commonsense distinction between them, which cannot be squared with the scorn he heaps on people's
drawing such distinctions or "fine lines" elsewhere.

Third Commandment

*"Third Old Commandment: Never take your own life, and always try to prevent others
taking theirs."* Singer correctly states that the traditional ethic condemns suicide as
sin. The decision when to die is God's decision, not ours, according to Thomas
Aquinas. Suicide was even made a crime as part of Christendom's state enforcement
of morality. Singer agrees with neither the theological notion of sin against God,
since he is an atheist, nor with state sanctions against sin, since he is a liberal utilitarian.

In classical Enlightenment fashion, Singer asserts human autonomy against God
and the state, unless, in his secularized notion of sin, harm is done to others. In John
Stuart Mill's classic *On Liberty* the state can coerce a person against their will only for
this reason. "His own good, either physical or moral, is not a sufficient warrant." Terminally ill people who consistently ask for assisted suicide are not harming others.

"Third New Commandment: Respect a person's desire to live or die." The key word
here is *person*. Singer draws on John Locke's definition of a person as having reason
and a sense of continuous identity over time. Only a person wants to go on living,
hoping and planning for the future. "This means that to end the lives of people,
against their will, is different from ending the lives of beings who are not people."
Nonpersons do not have a will or a right to life.[39] Further, "since neither a newborn
human infant nor a fish is a person, the wrongness of killing such beings is not as
great as the wrongness of killing a person."[40]

Response. The crucial issue of autonomy will be addressed in more depth later,
but for now let us note the irony that in the name of human autonomy Singer has
defined away the personhood of many unconscious or non-self-conscious human
beings—fetuses, babies, the comatose and Alzheimer's sufferers. In this way volun-

---

[38]Anna Wierzbicka, "The Language of Life and Death," *Quadrant*, July-August 1995, pp. 21-25. This
    professor of linguistics at the Australian National University scorns Singer's misuse of language,
    absence of moral norms, and metaphorical extension of notions of persons and morality to animals.
[39]Singer, *Rethinking Life and Death*, pp. 196-98.
[40]Ibid., p. 220.

tary euthanasia leads to "nonvoluntary" and "involuntary euthanasia." This form of death by definition also contradicts Singer's general desire to avoid deciding ethical issues by definitions.[41]

Further, Singer seems unaware of the postmodern critique that definitions of personhood are expressions of power by the definers. If there are, as Rowan Williams says,

> criteria for "counting" as a human being . . . to be decided by others unilaterally: the question has become one of power, the profound power of definition. The power to decide the human claims of others is, of course, precisely what feminism rightly rebels against—the long and shameful history of educating people to ignore, distort or minimise certain kinds of biological community and the recognitions that are or should be bound up with them.[42]

It seems that God might well be the best safeguard of human personhood and a relative form of human autonomy. God's service, as the Anglican collect or prayer puts it paradoxically, "is perfect freedom." The argument from absolute autonomy leads to the idea of an autonomous wish imputed to incompetent patients—"what he'd have done if only he'd told us." U.S. courts resort to this to defend withdrawal of treatment from the incompetent. Singer uses it to justify withdrawal of treatment from newborns. But it is no more than a projection of our own preferences or defense mechanisms when we have no explicit wishes from the patient to go on. Once an imputed view of autonomy justifies "nonvoluntary euthanasia," its extension to the very old, demented or chronically ill is likely. Expressed autonomy will seem less important under pressure to drop the legal requirement for explicit request. If personal autonomy is the overriding concern, why not let VE or assisted suicide happen in nonterminal situations and not just when no palliative care is available?

Further, it could still be held that sin, including (attempted) suicide, is morally wrong but that in some cases the state should not punish it. We in the West live in democracies (government by the people), not theocracies (direct government by God). Therefore not all sins, for example adultery, are crimes. But some sins, such as murder, are and should be crimes, as they harm others and can be prevented or punished appropriately. A sin like suicide or self-murder deserves (merciful) state sanction because of the severe harm to the person herself and others, as anyone knows who has delivered the news of a suicide or led the funeral of a suicide, as I have. It is

---

[41]Herlinde Pauer-Studer, "Peter Singer on Euthanasia," *The Monist* 76, no. 2 (April 1993): 153 n. 2.
[42]Rowan Williams, *Lost Icons: Reflections on Cultural Bereavement* (Edinburgh: T & T Clark, 2000), pp. 43-44.

not a "victimless crime." This is particularly important in relation to the danger of exacerbating the current epidemic of youth suicide in some Western societies.

In fact, the common law punishing suicide and aiding and abetting it is grounded in both civic and theological principles. A classic late-seventeenth-century legal text argues against suicide that "no man hath the absolute interest of himself, but 1. God almighty hath an interest and propriety in him, and therefore self-murder is a crime against God. 2. The king [or state now] hath an interest in him."[43] Presumably the latter is through being a subject or citizen of a country. Even atheists like Singer may be bound by it.

Singer argues that the state has no right to interfere in or block a patient's being assisted to suicide by his doctor. However, he fails to note that "assisted suicide" is a misnomer—suicide is a "do-it-yourself" job.[44] The moment you ask someone's assistance, it becomes a public, not a private, issue. This is especially so when that person is a doctor or nurse, an accredited instrument of the state, whereby it is already interfering. The real question, which Singer begs, is *how* should the state interfere—to facilitate or prevent the death of the patient? Singer rightly raises the question whether the patient should be prevented from carrying out suicide if she has young children who would be harmed by her inability to care for them. What if the doctor were prevented from effectively caring for his patients because he was changed from being primarily a carer and curer to a killer? Surely that too would constitute harm to future fiduciary doctor-patient relationships, if not to doctors themselves, many of whom in the Netherlands are reluctant to continue practicing euthanasia.[45]

As chapter one showed, Singer's atheistic, evolutionary assumption that rational and technological progress will leave a religiously based SOL ethic on the dust heap of history is highly debatable. Singer has little understanding for "the complex moral and religious tradition"[46] of SOLE and its adaptability to changing medical technologies and practices. Doctors have to make relatively new judgments, first about

[43]John Warwick Montgomery, "Whose Life Anyway? A Re-examination of Suicide and Assisted Suicide," in *Christian Perspectives on Law Reform*, ed. Paul R. Beaumont (Carlisle, U.K.: Paternoster, 1998), p. 87, quoting Sir Matthew Hale, *History of the Pleas of the Crown*.

[44]Even Richard Taylor, who is something of a Singer supporter, argues thus in "The Singer Revolution," *Philosophy Now* 28 (August-September 2000): 10-13.

[45]Australian bioethicist Sue Sherston spent a study tour with doctors in Holland who practiced VE and spoke (at the Death and the State Conference, Centre for Public Policy, University of Melbourne, August 23-24, 1995) of the great cost to doctors of performing VE and its difference from natural death. She cited a Dutch doctor who said that if he had to practice euthanasia more than three times per year he would quit medicine. After all, it is not what medicine is meant to be about.

[46]Raimond Gaita, "On the Sanctity of Human Life," *Quadrant*, April 1995, p. 53.

whom to place on life-support machines and second about whether or when to withdraw them. But that is no reason to demand a new ethics as Singer does.

> There is no more reason to want a "new" ethics here than there was when the cause of malaria was discovered, or when penicillin, or vaccines, were discovered. We just need to take new and more careful thought about the "old" ethics. . . . It is not necessary or sensible to try to redefine death. . . . For we do not need a "new ethics" to tell us that curing a patient is not the same thing as prolonging his death. The philosophy teachers who argue that a "new ethics" is needed here do so because they have an inadequate understanding of what it is to kill.[47]

Nonetheless Singer challenges the more rigid absolutists of the old ethic to such "new and more careful thought." The great Christian ethicist Paul Ramsey has rightly warned fundamentalist Christian and sanctity-of-life absolutists that "if the breadth and depth and flexibility of good moral reason is lost from view, then all that once passed for rationality is bound to seem a cruel master."[48] Extreme absolutists could drive sensitive people to become Singerian consequentialists to escape from legalism. There are just enough legalists to give some substance to the largely strawman SOLE Singer has set up in order to drive people to his QOLE as the only alternative, when in fact there are several. Still, one of the main reasons we have to argue in terms of (at least some *prima facie*) absolutes is the human tendency toward sin, something Singer is extraordinarily naive about.

Hard Cases That May Justify Euthanasia

Singer's method is to draw on hard legal and medical cases such as those of Tony Bland and Karen Ann Quinlan to show inconsistencies in the current SOLE. He particularly cites as a legal precedent for his "Copernican revolution" the House of Lords court (not the upper house) decision concerning seventeen-year-old Bland. Bland was crushed in the Hillsborough soccer stadium tragedy in Sheffield, United Kingdom. He was in a persistent vegetative state (PVS) with only brain-stem function, chronically awake but with no prospects of return to conscious awareness. According to Singer it is normal in most Western countries that when doctors and family are agreed, a PVS patient's feeding tube can be withdrawn. But this time the coroner intervened because of the public focus on the Hillsborough disaster, and appeal was made to the House of Lords court.[49]

---

[47]Teichman, *Social Ethics*, pp. 76-77.
[48]Paul Ramsey, "The Case of the Curious Exception," in *Norm and Context in Christian Ethics*, ed. Gene Outka and Paul Ramsey (New York: Charles Scribner's Sons, 1968), p. 92.
[49]Singer, *Rethinking Life and Death*, pp. 57-60.

Singer highlights three ways in which the House of Lords court decision and the Quinlan case broke new ethical and legal ground.

1. The Lords decided not to prolong Bland's life pointlessly on grounds of lack of QOL or consciousness, because there was "no therapeutic, medical or other benefit," as Sir Stephen Brown said in the initial judgment. Bare biological life versus biographical life was seen as no benefit to him.

2. They also declined to uphold the SOLE, because the aim of the action, withdrawal of the feeding tube, was specifically designed to end an innocent life.[50]

3. In the now quite old (1976) Karen Quinlan case, Singer shows some difficulties with distinguishing between ordinary and extraordinary means of treatment. Withdrawal of Quinlan's respirator was approved by her Roman Catholic parents and a bishop because the respirator was seen as "extraordinary" treatment disproportionate to any benefit to her, as she had no prospect of return to normal life. Singer rightly argues that the "extraordinary/ordinary" distinction was based on prior QOL considerations. He highlights cases where a respirator would not be considered extraordinary, such as where there are prospects for recovery. Singer also asks, "Why is a respirator extraordinary and a feeding tube ordinary?"[51]

Response. As argued earlier, QOL considerations concerning proportions of benefit and harm to a patient may supplement but not substitute for SOL considerations. They may justify "letting die" decisions of withdrawal of some futile or extraordinary treatment but not active killing or withdrawal of basic treatment. The moral issue in the Bland case was not whether everything needed to be done to keep a patient alive. It was that "a patient neither ill nor dying receiving basic healthcare necessary to continue living had this discontinued with the intention of causing his death because it was not in his best interest to live." If someone has no conscious awareness, "it does not follow that he has no gain from continued living. Not all value is experienced value: we can gain and maintain benefits without experiencing them. Without a doubt Bland gained from his nursing care, and could he gain from this without his being alive . . . ?"[52] The Lords mistakenly took over the Lord's role by claiming that Bland's life should be ended because he could no longer benefit from it and could not be harmed by its ending.

The judges, like Singer, distinguished between human, biological or corporeal life and personhood, biographical or conscious life in their descriptions of Bland as a

[50]Ibid., pp. 64-67.
[51]Ibid., p. 71.
[52]Hayden Ramsay, "The Case of Tony Bland," *Res Publica* 4, no. 1 (1995): 8, in reply to Brian Scarlett, "On the Death of Tony Bland," *Res Publica* 3, no. 2 (1994).

"shell" without a "spirit," as "not living a life at all," a nonpersonality.[53] Subjectivity and a dualistic dismissal of embodiment abounds in these judgments. They open the door to such controversial conclusions as that those not yet dead, or those who are unconscious, are not alive. They make "medical termination of such un-dead human beings conceivable." It is impossible to judge certainly from the outside whether another's life is worth living. "When judged from inside virtually every type of human life turns out to be worth living for many or most of those who are living it." Judgments from outside are "all too often a violation of autonomy."[54]

The views of Singer and the judges involve a long-discredited (biblically and philosophically) Platonic and Cartesian dualistic view of the self. This view conceives the self or person not as a body/mind-soul unity but as a core consciousness without which a living but damaged body is disqualified from personhood and protection.

John Finnis correctly argues that "Bland remained a person because he could still be subjected to indignities such as being treated as rubbish or as a sex object." In this a person is different from, for example, a painting, which can be damaged but not suffer indignity.[55] Dignity and indignity are derivative of personhood. To illustrate from the treatment of the terminally comatose: to harvest sperm so that their partners

---

[53]Singer, *Rethinking Life and Death*, pp. 66-67. For the distinction between valueless biological (e.g., comatose) and valuable biographical life, cf. James Rachels, *Created from Animals: The Moral Implications of Darwinism* (Oxford: Oxford University Press, 1990), pp. 198-99, and his *The End of Life* (Oxford: Oxford University Press, 1986), pp. 5-6, 24-27, 64-66, 77. Neither Rachels nor Singer explains, as Gilbert E. Meilaender writes (*Body, Soul and Bioethics* [Notre Dame, Ind.: University of Notre Dame Press, 1995], p. 58), "why one's period of decline is not part of one's personal history, one's biography. . . . From zygote to irreversible coma, each life is a single personal history." John Kleinig (*Valuing Life* [Princeton, N.J.: Princeton University Press, 1991], p. 201) notes that "Karen Ann Quinlan's biography did not end in 1975, when she became permanently comatose. It continued for another ten years. That was part of the tragedy of her life." Meilaender paraphrases Kleinig: "We may . . . distinguish different points in this story—from potentiality to zenith to residuality. But the zenith is not the person." As Kleinig writes: "Human beings are continuants, organisms with a history that extends beyond their immediate present, usually forward and backward. What has come to be seen as 'personhood,' a selected segment of that organismic trajectory, is connected to its earlier and later phases by a complex of factors—physical, social, psychological—that constitutes part of a single history." Further, Meilaender, quoting Holmes Rolston II ("The Irreversibly Comatose: Respect for the Subhuman in Human Life," *Journal of Medicine and Philosophy* 7 [1982]: 352), writes, "Indeed, it is not strange at all to suggest that even the unaware living body has 'interests.' For the living body takes in nourishment and uses it, the living body struggles against infection and injury . . . and if we remember 'the somatic dimensions of personality, as expressed for instance in face and hands,' we may recognize in the living body the place—the only place—through which the person is present with us."
[54]Teichman, *Social Ethics*, p. 74.
[55]John Finnis, "Bland: Crossing the Rubicon," *The Law Quarterly Review* 109 (1993): 329-37, quoted in Ramsay, "Case of Tony Bland," pp. 7-8, from which I have drawn much of this argument.

or even parents can have their children is to depersonalize and dishonor them as ends in themselves.[56]

Both the new-fangled theory of value as experienced benefit and the theory of personhood as consciousness "require close scrutiny given the drastic changes, conceptual and practical, which [they] would entail. When the mind is as severely impaired as Bland's what has ended: life or normal life, conscious life? To equate the two without prejudice would require a consideration of questions of value and personhood not evident in the House of Lords judgment."[57] Nor Singer's either.

Even more fundamentally, behind the question "who is a person?" lies something like the lawyer's self-justifying question to Jesus, "Who is my neighbor?"—an attempt to evade the force of the Great Commandment. This precipitated Jesus' parable of the good Samaritan (Lk 10:29-37). We cannot know anyone speculatively. We must first commit ourselves to care for them. And contrary to dualistic personists who want "some secret knowledge about a 'real' humanity," beyond appearances, the only ground we have for risking this commitment is [human] 'appearance.'"[58]

As a precedent for his Copernican revolution, Singer makes some judges' imprecise statements against an "abstract" or "absolute" SOL principle in *one* case into a

---

[56]See *Sperm Wars*, a documentary shown on BBC TV on September 20, 2000. The dead can also be treated with indignity, but this is derivative of their bodily connection with a once living person. Ramsay, "Case of Tony Bland," p. 8.

[57]Ramsay, "Case of Tony Bland," p. 8.

[58]Oliver O'Donovan, "And Who Is a Person?" in *Begotten or Made?* (Oxford: Oxford University Press, 1984), chap. 4, p. 8 in my manuscript version. Cf. Stanley Hauerwas, "Must a Patient Be a Person to Be a Patient? Or, My Uncle Charlie Is Not Much of a Person, But He Is Still My Uncle Charlie," in *On Moral Medicine: Theological Perspectives in Medical Ethics*, ed. Stephen E. Lammers and Allen Verhey (Grand Rapids, Mich.: Eerdmans, 1987), pp. 278-81. Hauerwas distinguishes protective uses of the notion of person, as in the Kantian deontological view of Paul Ramsey (*The Patient as Person* [New Haven, Conn.: Yale University Press, 1970]), from "a permissive notion that takes the heat off certain quandaries raised by modern medicine." While having problems with the former, he has more with the latter. (1) It makes a dualistic distinction between the personal and bodily dimensions of life (more fully explored by Meilaender, *Body, Soul and Bioethics*, chap. 2, "How Bioethics Lost the Body: Personhood," and chap. 3, "Producing Children." (2) It does "violence" to the "first-order moral language through which we live our lives." We rarely think or speak of ourselves or loved ones as "persons." Instead of "persons" we use language of trust between doctors and patients, which would be undermined if we knew a utilitarian doctor would use us as means to the end of caring for another.

While I am willing to use such "person" language in Hauerwas's first sense against the second, I agree that it is often strangely impersonal and unengaged. Brenda Almond (*Exploring Ethics: A Traveller's Tale* [Oxford: Blackwell, 1998], p. 152) finds it counterintuitive when used to deny some humans personhood. More important, she argues "that 'personhood' is a wholly artificial construct, replacing in some ways the historic concept of the soul, but freeing it from its theological connotations." However, for a sophisticated theological defense of "person" language see Stanley Rudman, *Concepts of "Person" and Christian Ethics* (Cambridge: Cambridge University Press, 1997).

manifesto for a sea change in the *whole* English legal tradition. This focuses on the intention to kill or not in both acts and omissions as distinguishing murder and manslaughter. Singer does not mention that the more circumspect House of Lords Select Committee on Medical Ethics (Walton Committee), set up in the wake of the Bland case, strongly affirmed "the prohibition of intentional killing" as still "the cornerstone of law and social relationships" and thus rejected VE.[59] Nor does Singer note that the count of the "House of Lords in effect acknowledged its unease at its own decision by insisting that further cases of a similar kind should not be decided on the precedent they were setting, but must be brought to the courts also."[60]

Singer seems unaware of the consequences of changing this fundamental aspect of the law in the light of one extreme case. He cavalierly dismisses concerns that the judgment illustrates the legal maxim "hard cases make bad law," is based on a dangerously "consequentialist ethic" and effectively "declared non-voluntary euthanasia lawful."[61]

However, the Lords did not go far enough for Singer, who notes that "the judges did not think they were legalizing euthanasia." As Lord Goff said, they had no intention of crossing the ethical and legal "Rubicon" leading to active killing or euthanasia. Yet they unintentionally moved in that direction because they refused to challenge the artificial line between "positive actions" and culpable "omissions intended to terminate life," though they "admitted its legal misshapenness and moral irrelevance."[62]

Singer shows that decisions about withdrawal of extraordinary versus ordinary treatments are clearly contextual and involve weighing up consequences and benefits/costs of continued treatment or withdrawal of treatment, primarily for the patient. However, that does not mean that QOL considerations should overwhelm SOL considerations and carry over to active euthanasia. Singer assumes that they should because he sees no validity in the standard acts/omissions distinctions and therefore sees treatment withdrawal as equivalent to active killing. I will deal with this large question in the next section.

For now, one way of tidying up some of the ordinary/extraordinary treatment anomalies is to instead distinguish morally obligatory and optional treatments. It helps keep a sense of proportion regarding the prolongation of life in relation to

---

[59]House of Lords Paper 21-I of 1993-1994, para. 237.
[60]Roy Clements, "Officiously, to Keep Alive? Euthanasia: Definitions and Consequences," *Cambridge Papers* 2, no. 3 (1993): 3.
[61]Singer, *Rethinking Life and Death*, pp. 68-69, 74-76.
[62]See John Finnis, "A Philosophical Case Against Euthanasia," in *Euthanasia Examined: Ethical, Clinical and Legal Perspectives*, ed. John Keown (Cambridge: Cambridge University Press, 1995), p. 25, and his "Bland."

other values, in order to prevent an almost indefinite prolongation of death, "corpses with cords" that have lost all promise of a return to self-sustaining, relational life. However, this must be based on definite medical criteria, such as brain death or an inability to sustain integration of the main life organs, rather than spurious subjective definitions of "meaningful life."[63]

Regarding withdrawal of feeding tubes versus withdrawal of respirators, again contextual distinctions can be made. There is a higher level of artificiality or extraordinariness involved in permanent breathing technology, because we do not normally breathe for someone else but we do often feed others regularly. Although an asthmatic can be resuscitated, it is occasional and extraordinary, not permanent or ordinary. In fact "breathing is one of the activities constitutive of human life, and not just the ventilation of a cage conveniently related to a person."[64] This difference between extraordinary breathing and ordinary feeding for others justifies the decision to discontinue Quinlan's ventilator as opposed to Bland's feeding tube.

> Food, water, warmth and sanitation are surely the basics of all humanitarian care; moreover, the procedures by which Bland was supplied with these are employed long term and uncontroversially for the benefit of many sorts of helpless persons. His means of feeding, upon which the Law Lords . . . concentrate, did involve a naso-gastric tube, but this addresses no medical condition, but rather the normal need for food. It is . . . a simple technique. It is an artificial process, but not, as the Lords thought, equivalent to a ventilator: it does not perform the natural function for the patient, but artificially supplies food after which the natural function, digestion, occurs normally. The naso-gastric tube in no way keeps the patient alive.[65]

Jenny Teichman argues that "drip-feeding an unconscious person isn't the same thing as [normally wrongful] force-feeding; it is more akin to reviving someone who can't be asked what he wants."[66]

---

[63]Such as the one Judge Johnson used in a Georgia court case where Larry McAfee, a quadraplegic former outdoorsman on a ventilator who was unable to go outdoors anymore, had his life arbitrarily and judged nonmeaningful or a living death ("Death Wish," *Time*, September 18, 1989, p. 55). Cf. P. Painton and E. Taylor, "Love and Let Die," *Time*, March 19, 1990.

[64]Ramsay, "Case of Tony Bland," p. 8.

[65]Ibid. Cf. Elisabeth Ohlenberg's account in *RN (Registered Nurse)* about the case of a PVS patient, "John Levine," at Brooklyn Veterans Hospital in New York. The family requested that food and hydration be withdrawn. "It took twenty days for Mr. Levine to die—an unusually long time." Despite being in PVS, "we would talk to him and sometimes he would smile. I'm almost sure he understood what we were saying. When we came near the bed his eyes would look at you as if he knew you were there." Richard John Neuhaus, who quotes this in "The Public Square," *First Things*, February 1998, p. 72, says, "Presumably the nurses did not tell him they were killing him, though ever so caringly."

[66]Teichman, *Social Ethics*, p. 70.

The real strategy behind Singer's arguments can be seen in his collaborator Helga Kuhse's comments at a Right to Die conference: "if we can get people to accept the removal of all treatment and care—especially the removal of food and fluids—they will see what a painful way this is to die and then . . . in the patient's best interests, they will accept the lethal injection."[67] Again the means, malicious treatment of patients, are justified by the end, bringing in euthanasia.

Singer indulges in mind-reading when he says that the death of the patient is the real "intention" in the Quinlan respirator withdrawal, against the parents' and bishop's stated intention to not disproportionately/extraordinarily prolong her dying. Further, in agreeing with Lord Browne-Wilkinson's loose and dangerous statement that the "whole purpose" of withdrawal of feeding in the Bland case was Bland's death, Singer is contradicted by the judge's further statement that "what is being done is to omit to feed or to ventilate; the removal of the nasogastric tube or the switching off of a ventilator are merely incidents of that omission.[68] Singer, and some of the judges, cannot see the important common moral and legal distinction between foreseeing the effect of an action and intending it, though Browne-Wilkinson belatedly remembered.

Acts and Omissions

In the name of consequences Singer wants to abandon the Judeo-Christian roots of the old commandments as "simple rules that allow for no exceptions." He claims that SOLE supporters hold to it absolutely—"it is not a principle to be balanced against conflicting considerations."[69]

Singer's use of the category of passive euthanasia depends on the utilitarian banning of the distinction between acts and omissions. So either not starting medical treatment or terminating it is an omission that Singer describes as passive euthanasia. Because the only moral currency in Singer's wallet is consequences, omissions are effectively actions, because they count equally in terms of consequences.

In Bland's case, Singer argues that removing a feeding or ventilating tube is "a positive act [i.e., actively causing his death], and not merely an omission" of feeding or ventilating, where the positive act of withdrawing the feeding tube is incidental, as Lord Browne-Wilkinson argued. Singer objects that if a patient with good prospects of recovery needed a respirator temporarily and "an interloper who had his own reasons" for wanting him dead turned it off, he would have committed the perfect crime—there is no positive act counting as murder. Singer asks what is a positive act,

---

[67]Quoted in ibid., p. 178.
[68]Singer, *Rethinking Life and Death*, pp. 68, 77-79.
[69]Ibid., p. 221.

apart from giving a lethal injection with intent to kill, if withdrawing breathing and feeding assistance is not?

Based on the judges' muddled philosophizing, Singer sees great difficulty in predicting what will count as positive acts and what will not. Singer cites Lord Goff's reluctance "to cross the Rubicon which runs between on the one hand the care of the living patient and on the other hand euthanasia—actively causing his death to avoid or to end his suffering." But for Singer, "This 'Rubicon' . . . is clearly no broad river! It is at best a meandering creek, one that seems about to dry up in a series of waterholes."[70]

Response. In contrast to Singer's one-size-fits-all consequentialism, a biblical triple A[71] or C mixed ethical theory (corresponding to and confirmed by the best philosophical traditions of deontological, virtue and teleological ethics, respectively) is not an absolute or arbitrary ethics of law and command. Instead it includes consequences within a more complete theory made up of

acts	commands
agents	character (including intention)
aftermath	consequences

The consequentialist position abstracts and isolates the aftermath or consequence from the narrative flow of motivation, character and the intrinsic nature or value of an act in itself. Every act has a story that enables us to understand and ethically evaluate it. Singer simply ignores the clear role of narrative, character and intention in moral judgments in the law (e.g., distinguishing manslaughter and murder) and everyday life.

Contrary to Singer's stereotype, the SOLE includes commands, character and consequences within a narrative and relational framework that explains their purpose. God's relational purposes for people made in his image are bigger than consequences or people's personal preferences for pleasure over pain, though they include aspects of these.

A mixed ethical framework recognizes the significance of both acts and omissions, in terms of commands, character and consequences, without confusing them. Contrary to Singer's claim, most SOLE supporters recognize a difference between acts and omissions, *sometimes* but *not always.*

Careful definition of acts and omissions is crucial. Singerians see "a positive action" as like a bodily movement such as lifting your arm and an omission as doing

---

[70]Ibid., pp. 76-78.
[71]The framework of Graham Cole, author of chapter three.

nothing, like sitting still. But this represents, as Teichman shows,

> an impoverished view of actions and activities. Some actions involve no overt physical movements. Many actions include purpose as well. . . . It is better to define actions and activities as: *items which can be meaningfully mentioned in answering the questions* "What are you . . . [they] doing (etc.)." Some possible answers are: They are lifting their arms. They are voting. . . . He is waving goodbye. I am getting rid of a bee on my hand. I am warning someone.[72]

"Omissions are parasitic on actions . . . because reference to an omission implies that some action . . . is *expected*" but fails to occur, according to a rule, an activity one is engaged in, a responsibility or purpose one has or standards of ordinary human decency. "It follows that the simple not-doing of something that might have had good results is not an omission at all, strictly speaking."[73]

"More generally, failing to do what is expected or rational or owed *can* be morally bad." "*Some* omissions are as bad as positive actions. It does not follow that their badness is due solely to their consequences."[74] Consequences are part but not the whole of moral judgment. The reasons that some failures to act are as good or evil as positive acts, apart from consequences, have to do with "intention; knowledge; skill; difficulty; responsibility; and certain facts about time." Regarding responsibility, for instance,

> suppose that it is decided that a certain man's life can only be saved by putting him onto a life-support machine. Suppose that the doctor or nurse in charge fails to connect the patient to the machine. Here the fact that the medical worker has accepted responsibility for connecting the machine makes a huge difference to the character of the omission. The whole point of using the machine . . . was to save the patient's life; hence if someone with responsibility deliberately fails to make the connection the omission is not just like a murder, it is murder.[75]

Some omissions, like the one above or refusing heart pills to a dying person, are

---

[72] Teichman, *Social Ethics*, p. 79.

[73] Ibid., pp. 79-80.

[74] Consequentialists like Singer argue that not giving to World Vision is a bad as killing people when the consequent number of deaths is the same. But failing to donate is clearly not as bad as sending poisoned food to refugees (ibid., p. 80, adapting Philippa Foot's example). Most omissions are morally minimal, actions morally maximal—if we equalize them we make letting things happen as praiseworthy as doing good things. We thereby encourage moral passivity. If we reverse the logic: "Since my failure to kill my neighbours goes on every day and every minute of every day the praise I deserve, if this 'omission' really deserved praise, would be enormous. But that idea is ludicrous. If the failure to do something which would have had bad results does not always deserve praise we have no reason to think that failure to do something that would have good results always deserves blame" (ibid., p. 81, drawing on Elizabeth Anscombe).

[75] Ibid., pp. 81-82.

morally culpable. Making people like Bland die by the increasingly practiced starvation or dehydration methods is wrong because feeding was owed to him and
expected of responsible people.

Further, the consequentialist view against distinguishing letting die from active
killing

> is a piece of logic that no logician could accept. There is no inconsistency in saying that
> (i) when a doctor has no obligation to prolong treatment it is (ii) also the case that he
> must not kill his patient. The technical (logical) reasons are as follows. First, saving and
> killing are not opposites, they are not contradictories, but merely contraries. Hence not-
> saving is not equivalent to killing. Secondly, killing and treating are not even contraries;
> logically they are wholly independent [like green and rectangular]. Hence not-treating
> is not equivalent to killing.[76]

In that case, when is it right to not start or stop life-saving treatment? Among several considerations the first key one is "ought implies can." Letting several swimmers
drown when there is time to rescue only one is not blameworthy. We can be responsible only for what we have the resources or ability to do. Christians recognize our
limits as finite creatures, limits even on the obligation to do good. Singerian utilitarians do not. The second reason is that it becomes clear in certain situations that a
patient will die unless constantly resuscitated, a taxing procedure for patient and doc-
tor/nurse alike. At some stage the treatment changes character from a life-saving
treatment to a prolongation of the dying process. The obligation to continue presumably ends then.

In denying this distinction between acts and omissions or active killing and letting die, Singer again twists normal language. There is a clear difference between
doing and not doing or not preventing and deliberately causing (as Singer himself
recognized earlier).[77] Given that death is physically inevitable one day, not caused by
our actions, we cannot be said to intend death when we recognize we can no longer
stop it.

The utilitarian position minimizes the role of motivation. It does not allow the
different moments of moral action their own integrity. Singer is blind to the sometimes difficult to determine but nonetheless definite difference between intending
and foreseeing or permitting. Others are not. The Bible distinguishes between God's
original purpose of one husband, one wife, for life in Genesis and his permission for
divorce mentioned by Jesus in Matthew 19:3-9. The Roman Catholic catechism and
its doctrine of double effect says that discontinuing treatment is allowable if "death is

---

[76]Ibid., pp. 82-83.
[77]Wierzbicka, "Language of Life and Death," p. 22.

not willed" but only "foreseen and tolerated."[78] There is a real difference in some cases between the effect *desired* and another associated effect *foreseen* but reluctantly permitted that is parasitic upon it or a side effect of it. For instance, in administering pain-killing drugs like morphine there comes a point where one will foresee that death may result, but the aim is still to minimize pain. The biblical, Catholic and classical ethical distinction between desired and expected effects does justice to the tragic and nonideal nature of ethics, which Singer ignores.

To equate letting die and active killing, malevolent motivation is required. For instance, Singer's case of the interloper unplugging the life-support machine mentions "his own reasons."[79] This omission is equivalent to murder because it includes intent to kill. Culpable intention makes some omissions as bad as some actions. In Bland's case the admitted purpose of withdrawing his feeding tube was death by starvation.

Intention is the difference between actions we invest with personal involvement and those that run through us passively without poisoning our character.[80] Killing corrupts character, both the personal character of individual doctors and nurses and the institutional character of medicine and the law where people have particular responsibilities for care. If we personally invest in killing, it will bring disastrous dividends in the rest of our lives.

A narrowly consequentialist ethic sees no intrinsic moral norms for the practice of medicine, nor does a postmodern social constructionism that says medicine can be

---

[78]*Catechism of the Catholic Church* (Homebush, N.S.W.: St. Paul's, 1994), p. 549, para. 2279.

[79]Compare James Rachels's case that Singer uses: a person who sees another hit her head when she slips in the bath and is consequently drowning, and does nothing about it because he stands to inherit the drowning person's wealth. Singer's defense of the equivalence of acts and omissions is not very full and seems to depend on Rachels's fuller version. But Pauer-Studer shows that Rachels's thesis "does not hold generally for all cases of killing and letting die. Rachels understands 'letting die' in the sense that *we could have saved someone* (easily as, e.g., in the Jones case), but he did not want to do so. . . . This sense of 'letting die' is not presupposed when passive euthanasia is considered . . . (in the sense of abstaining from further life-prolonging measures). . . . Even if we take the equivalence thesis for granted, . . . in all cases, can this really confirm what advocates of active euthanasia want it to show, namely that active euthanasia is allowed? I do not think so" ("Peter Singer on Euthanasia," pp. 144-48).

[80]Cf. Jorge Garcia, "Intentions in Medical Ethics," summarized in the introduction to *Human Lives: Critical Essays on Consequentialist Bioethics*, ed. David S. Oderberg and Jacqueline A. Laing (London: Macmillan, 1997), p. 10. He argues that "there is a genuine psychological difference between intending something to result from one's behaviour and merely expecting it to." He provides criteria for distinguishing intention and foresight. He also "argues that there is more to the psychological reality of intention than the mere 'redirection of one's will,' and sketches a view according to which intentions, as real and profound mental phenomena, fit centrally into a life of planning and execution of projects." See also Finnis, "Philosophical Case," pp. 25-30, on how and why "intention counts."

whatever we call it or make it to be. But a broader biblical and Aristotelian teleological ethics based on the *teloi* (purposes or goals) of nature, human nature and social practices and institutions affirms natural norms and goals. "The goal of medicine is health," for human health exists as a natural, objective kind of entity, not just subjectively in the mind. From this it follows that some activities, like euthanasia or administering capital punishment, are not appropriate activities of a doctor as a doctor.[81]

An ethic of "letting die" must be based first on a doctor's consideration of the patient's health interests rather than on a utilitarian cost/benefit analysis for society or even the family. In the moral division of labor a doctor's primary (though not exclusive) covenantal or fiduciary duty is to the patient, not to the health of the whole of society, just as a lawyer's primary duty is to her client. We are bound into particular relationships by a kind of nearest-neighbor principle that recognizes where we are placed as part of God's providential care for the world or ordinary human finitude. God, not we, can care for the whole world at one time.

Asking for Death: Absolute or Relative Autonomy?

Singer supports his third new commandment "to respect a person's desire to live or die" with four standard liberal reasons for restricting the law's role in relation to individual liberty.

1. *States should not interfere with individual liberty unless to avoid harm to others.* Having argued for non-VE for comatose patients like Bland with no personal prospects, Singer now asks, if conscious, autonomous patients (not their doctors, families, ministers or philosophers) make an informed, sustained decision that their QOL is intolerable and ask for assistance in their suicide, and if a doctor is willing, why should the law stop it?[82]

2. *If a person needs assistance for voluntary euthanasia, the state should allow it.* Singer details the legal and practical difficulties (e.g., fear of arrest and unsuccessful suicides) of various U.S., U.K. and Australian cases where assisted suicide is still prohibited. He reinforces the plea for allowing people their choices and rights through

---

[81]Summary of John Cottingham, "Medicine, Virtues and Consequences," summarized in the introduction to *Human Lives: Critical Essays on Consequentialist Bioethics*, ed. David S. Oderberg and Jacqueline A. Laing (London: Macmillan, 1997), p. 9. Cf. Oliver O'Donovan, "The Natural Ethic," in *Essays in Evangelical Social Ethics*, ed. D. F. Wright (Exeter, U.K.: Paternoster, c. 1978), pp. 19-25, on "kinds." Lance Simmons draws on Alasdair MacIntyre's *After Virtue: A Study in Moral Theory*, 2nd ed. (London: Duckworth, 1985) to similarly focus on health "as a good internal to the practice of medicine, which the doctor can only promote if he possesses certain virtues. The conclusion, then, is that good doctors do not intentionally attack or destroy the health of their patients, even if this is to promote some other end" (Oderberg and Laing, introduction to *Human Lives*, p. 10).

[82]Singer, *Rethinking Life and Death*, p. 132.

touching stories of people like Janet Adkins with Alzheimer's disease and Thomas Hyde with Lou Gehrig's disease. Both were assisted to suicide by the heroic pioneer Dr. Jack Kevorkian.

In Holland, the case of Dr. Geertruida Postma, convicted of voluntary mercy killing her long-suffering mother (but let off lightly) in 1971 and the 1984 Alkmaar case of ninety-five-year-old Mrs. B. voluntarily euthanized by her family doctor led to a mass movement and to gradual change in medical and legal attitudes. Such cases were allowed euthanasia by the Royal Dutch Medical Association and regularized by the Dutch Parliament in 1993. There were four conditions: unbearable and hopeless suffering; a clear patient request; no alternative measures of pain relief; approval by a second medical opinion.[83]

3. *A sane individual is best positioned to judge whether to continue his or her life.* Singer recites the Dutch case of Carla, who was voluntarily euthanized even with the approval of her Roman Catholic counselor. Carla's death is seen as clearly better than the examples above because she was conscious and had the best medical, family and spiritual care till the end. There was nothing furtive, no fear of failure, no police. Singer then paints a very rosy picture of the development and state of euthanasia practice in Netherlands against the dark background of less enlightened regimes.

4. *Opinion polls are in favor of voluntary euthanasia.*[84] Despite religion's role in formulating the old rules of our society, Singer asks what right any religion has to stop someone carrying out suicide in a democratic, pluralist society where the majority are in favor of VE and choose to live by the new rules.

Response. Individual liberty is a relative, not an absolute good which can sometimes be interfered with to avoid serious self-harms and indirect harm to others. We should first note again the peculiarity of Singer's procedure of using a liberal view of polity and legality to argue to what is moral rather than working from morality to polity or legality, as Singer himself argues in justifying the civil disobedience of animal activists.[85] Singer and Helga Kuhse argue from hidden liberal premises that the soundness of the SOL doctrine should be tested against liberal political morality. So liberal laws regarding abortion should lead consistently to allowing VE of the old and nonvoluntary "euthanasia" of the very young, or infanticide. But this proves nothing, because the analogy's moral force could be a reason to oppose both abortion and euthanasia. On the grounds of consistency and Singer's correctly noting the

[83]Ibid., pp. 138-48.
[84]Ibid., pp. 132, 196-97.
[85]Peter Singer, *Practical Ethics* (Cambridge: Cambridge University Press, 1979), chap. 9.

arbitrary line between born and unborn, if we oppose infanticide, as the overwhelming majority do, then we should oppose abortion.

In support of the centrality of their view of rational autonomy and personhood, Singer makes no argument. He simply presupposes the authority of an assumed social consensus about autonomy and the philosopher John Locke's (disputed) definition of a person, "that having future hopes and desires about one's existence is exhaustive of the moral significance of human life. Saying that some people do believe that *p* or that it is entirely reasonable to believe that *p* does not amount to 'offering a ground' for believing that *p*."[86]

Singer's basic argument from autonomy assumes that we own our own lives, as if life were a form of property that we could dispose of when we tire of it or no longer want to invest in or repair. One response of many ancient and non-Western societies is that individual lives, at least partly, belong to the community. Others, perhaps a majority of the world's population, believe that they belong to God. But assuming for argument's sake that we do own our own individual lives, does it follow that I should be allowed to destroy it? One may have a right to destroy trivial possessions, but not everything, especially valuable or unique things. For instance, as Teichman shows:

> If I was the legal owner of a collection of works of art would many art lovers agree that I had a right to destroy it? If I was the legal owner of the last pair of peregrine falcons in the whole world should I be allowed to kill them? The notion of "owning" one's life is in any case rather peculiar. We speak of "my" life or "your" life but that doesn't necessarily imply genuine ownership. After all, I can speak of *my* uncle and *my* aunts, and so on, but that doesn't mean that I own my uncles and aunts. . . . It would be preposterous to argue that I may kill my uncle just because he is my uncle. . . . In other words not all uses of the possessive pronouns my, yours, and so on, imply a property right.[87]

Individual autonomy or liberty is thus not a moral trump card. It is a necessary but not sufficient condition for justifying voluntary euthanasia. Other values, such as

---

[86]Hans S. Reinders, "Debunking the Sanctity of Life," chap. 2 of "Should We Prevent Handicapped Lives? Reflections on the Future of Disabled People in Liberal Society," unpublished manuscript, pp. 6-9 (on Locke see Singer, *Rethinking Life and Death*, pp. 162, 180, 197, 233). Cf. Reinders's similar example of Kuhse and Singer's allegedly rigorous argument against the sanctity of life regarding Down syndrome children, which amounts to a combination of "widely accepted values" supporting their abortion, disputed "anecdotal evidence" from those living with the disabled, and most decisive, Singer and Kuhse's personal attitudes which lead them to disbelieve positive anecdotal accounts about living with Down syndrome and disabled children (Reinders, "Debunking the Sanctity of Life," p. 10, citing Helga Kuhse and Peter Singer, *Should the Baby Live? The Problem of Handicapped Infants* [Oxford: Oxford University Press, 1985], pp. 144, 152, 158). I write as one who once worked as a bus driver for disabled, especially Down syndrome children, and found great delight in them as many of their parents did, despite their difficulties.

[87]Teichman, *Social Ethics*, pp. 70-71.

loving relationships, faith, or the protection of the vulnerable and easily influenced such as the elderly or potential youth suicides, may have priority. Autonomy is a relative, not an absolute value.[88] It is ironic that "many modern bioethicists can be consequentialist, and yet elevate respect for autonomy to the status of an almost absolute value."[89]

Freedom should be defined not as unfettered freedom to pursue individual preferences (without harming others) but by whether it expresses the nature of a thing. With regard to humans, we can ask, does it further the relational purpose of human nature and the common good? This is a conviction shared not just by Christians but by Aristotelians and communitarians and republicans.[90] Creation-based notions of covenant, neighbor and relationship provide a better basis for community and society than the liberal-contractual, rational-individualistic notion of persons.

On the basis of the liberal argument Singer cites and the pioneering U.K. Wolfenden Committee Report, most Western societies have decriminalized a range of allegedly victimless crimes such as private homosexual acts between consenting adults on the basis that "it is not the law's business." Yet the Wolfenden Committee went on to say that the law should "provide sufficient safeguards against exploitation and corruption of others, particularly those who are specially vulnerable because they are young, weak in body or mind or inexperienced." Since then the public health consequences of such activities, even smoking, and the slogan "the personal is political" show that there is no pure or absolute privacy. "Even John Stuart Mill himself, the apostle of liberty and personal autonomy, was distinctly ill-at-ease with autonomously selling oneself into slavery."[91]

Pluralist democratic states do make moral interventions in people's allegedly private lives. The state intervenes by banning or preventing such things as drug taking, rape, bigamy, female genital mutilation, dueling, youth suicide, smoking in public

---

[88]Cf. Gordon R. Preece, "Ethics and the End of Life," in *The Ethics of Life and Death*, ed. Barry Webb (West Homebush, N.S.W.: Lancer, 1990), pp. 103-5, 116-18, 122-24.

[89]Janet Smith, "The Pre-eminence of Autonomy in Bioethics," summarized in the introduction to *Human Lives: Critical Essays on Consequentialist Bioethics*, ed. David S. Oderberg and Jacqueline A. Laing (London: Macmillan, 1997), pp. 10-11. She traces the contemporary exaltation of autonomy to skepticism about ethics.

[90]See Robert N. Bellah et al., *Habits of the Heart* (Berkeley: University of California Press, 1985); *The Good Society* (New York: Vintage, 1991); *Individualism and Commitment in American Life: Readings on the Themes of Habits of the Heart* (New York: Harper & Row, 1988); D. L. Gelpi, ed., *Beyond Individualism: Toward a Retrieval of Moral Discourse in America* (Notre Dame, Ind.: University of Notre Dame Press, 1989).

[91]W. J. U'Ren, "Euthanasia and Autonomy," in *Death and the State*, papers presented to a conference on Euthanasia at the Centre for Public Policy, University of Melbourne, 1995, p. 20, quoting *Report of the Committee on Homosexual Offences and Prostitution* (London: HMSO, Cmd. 247, London, 1957), paras. 61 and 13. This is known as The Wolfenden Report, after its chairperson.

spaces, driving or riding without seatbelts or bike helmets. The question then arises: is VE more like private homosexual acts, exempt from prosecution, or more like "suicide pacts, duelling . . . and youth suicide and should equally with them be proscribed by the law?"[92]

The right to assisted suicide is even more questionable than the right to suicide. Before asking about the right to assisted suicide, we should ask whether people have a right to self-destruction or suicide, as Singer assumes. The very notion of such a right in our rights-intoxicated world is self-contradictory, because it implies a correlative social duty. Yet suicide seems to deny all such duties to others. Rights do not exist in individualistic isolation but in social and political settings.

Even if people do have a right to suicide, there can be no presumed right to *assisted* suicide, which I noted earlier is a misnomer—suicide means self-killing. Homicide is not excusable just because the victim has consented. Singer's answer that suicide is messy or could fail is possibly tragic but insufficient and even wrong. Even the bedridden can refuse food, which, especially in cases of serious illness, soon ends one's life relatively painlessly.[93] No nanny state, unless it is Singer's utopian one charged with the elimination of all human suffering, can take on such a task. This contradicts the thrust of Mill's liberal concern to minimize state interference.

Who guards the assistants' and medical profession's liberty and conscience once we allow doctors and nurses to become, or make them into, aiders and abetters of suicide or VE? Singer claims to respect their autonomy and cites evidence of surveys, including his own, to argue that many doctors and nurses support VE and that many have already been involved in informally administering it to patients.[94] But even if his disputed figures are correct, majorities are not always respectful of minorities. Doctors and nurses must make up their own minds and consciences as professional groups and individuals, despite the Dutch Remmelink Report and Singer's regarding them as mere instruments of the patient. Choices shape our very selves. A doctor who kills is a different kind of doctor, if a doctor at all.

Even if we adopt a conscience clause for medical professionals in relation to euthanasia, the precedents are not promising. Many doctors, anesthetists and nurses have been institutionally coerced into participating in abortions or denied passes in exams, promotions or lists of patients. Twenty-three percent of nurses were asked by doctors to euthanize patients and 80 percent did so in Australia, according to

[92]Ibid.
[93]Teichman, *Social Ethics*, p. 69.
[94]Ibid., pp. 155-57.

Singer.[95] How many of these were freely informed decisions of conscience? Or were they like the concentration camp guards, merely going on orders from above? The power politics of doctor-nurse relationships are notorious and leave little likelihood that coercion will not be brought to bear on tender consciences to conform to doctors' orders.

Doctors and nurses are not just private individuals but members of relatively autonomous but partly state recognized and regulated professions and institutions. The demand by consequentialists like Singer that doctors justify their traditional standards by the methods of secular philosophical reason not only puts doctors at a disadvantage in that discourse but often shows little respect for the tacit knowledge built up over years, even centuries, of medical practice and doctor-patient relationship, which is not always easily articulated in philosophical terms. The boom in bioethics that Singer has spearheaded, and the attempted marginalization of traditional medical standards, could be seen as merely a form of professional rivalry. This is not to argue for completely self-regulating professions, nor to deny the need for public accountability and scrutiny. But the latter is not the same as accountability to other, more academic professional groups, like utilitarian bioethicists.

A disturbing feature of the Northern Territory's attempted legalization of VE was its removal of the autonomy and authority of professional medical associations to discipline members who break their professional rules "for anything done in good faith in compliance with this Act."[96] This is a chilling reminder of fascist and communist governments' attempts to destroy the independence of intermediate associations and voluntary groups, against the long-term interests of their citizens. In a technological society people and politicians often assume that doctors can be trusted because of their special technical skills. But many business people have specialist skills, and in business we say "caveat emptor—let the buyer beware." The fact that most doctors can be trusted mostly is due not merely to their skills nor to some "natural virtuousness." It is more to do with the medical profession's self-imposed taboos, summed up in the two-millennia-old Hippocratic Oath, whose most important command is "Do not kill."[97] If this taboo is ignored, our new motto could well be "let the patient beware."

---

[95]Singer, *Rethinking Life and Death*, pp. 154-55.

[96]Rights of the Terminally Ill Act of the Northern Territory, para. 20. The chief minister and major proponent of the bill angrily dismissed the Australian Medical Association's opposition to the act as "a dinosaur approach." "Address by Marshall Perron," in *Death and the State*, papers presented to a conference on Euthanasia at the Centre for Public Policy, University of Melbourne, 1995, p. 38.

[97]Teichman, *Social Ethics*, pp. 89-91. A trans-Atlantic group recently published a charter for doctors' ethics that develops the Hippocratic oath in the light of technological advances in medicine. Its core values concerned with healing the patient appear to have been maintained. See "Medical Professionalism in the New Millennium: A Physician's Charter," *The Lancet* 359 (2002): 520-22. On the

Such a shift could well tear the delicate tissue of trust between doctor and patient. Teichman notes that legalized euthanasia would reduce that level of trust. She suggests that if society insists on legalizing euthanasia, perhaps we should invent another profession to do it, akin to the ancient executioner. If medical specialties in voluntary, nonvoluntary and involuntary euthanasia develop, "their existence, and the identity of the practitioners might have to be disguised. After all, it would be scary, and very bad for those with weak hearts, to see the hospital specialist in involuntary euthanasianism walking through the ward!"[98]

Singer's claim that the autonomous, sane patient is the best judge of his or her own continued life prospects underestimates the power of professional medical judgment (positive and negative) and others on informed consent, as well as the patient's responsibilities to others, and is applied only to some individuals. Singer's claim in effect challenges the autonomy of professional medical judgment and care. For all its problems of paternalism, the ideal of professionalism acknowledges that professionals usually know more than patients or clients. Compare the old legal adage about the person who defended himself who had a fool for a lawyer. Anchorless autonomy in a market-driven society will mean that the "customer is always right" current will direct medical decisions. Professionals will be pressured to abdicate their responsibility to help patients make informed decisions about their health needs, not merely wants.[99] Choices need to be informed choices to be truly free; ignorance constrains. Doctors, counselors (sacred and secular) and families will hopefully be key sources of helpful information and guardians of the patient's autonomy.

On the other hand, there is also a danger of professional and other power subtly undermining the patient's will to live. That allegedly only 4 percent of Dutch doctors question euthanasia does not augur well for a process of objectively informed autonomy, given the institutional power doctors have in relation to sick patients. While I will leave a full treatment of the Dutch situation to the next section on slippery slopes, there is evidence of strong and subtle forms of coercion and even murder by doctors and nurses, not to mention families.[100] In this situation, who guards the guardians of the patient's autonomy when all of these have been shown to be sometimes corruptible or untrustworthy?

Hippocratic oath as the basis for neutral, scientific medicine based on the study of nature and no specific religion, see Owsei Tomkin, *Hippocrates in a World of Pagans and Christians* (Baltimore: Johns Hopkins University Press, 1991). Christianity, however, added a much stronger concern for the vulnerable at both ends of life.

[98]Ibid., p. 86.

[99]Hans S. Reinders, "Why It Matters to Care About 'Care,'" *Zadok Papers* S 117 (Autumn 2002).

[100]See Isaac van der Sluis, "The Practice of Euthanasia in the Netherlands," *Issues in Law and Medicine* 4, no. 4 (1989): 455-65.

While the patient herself has primary responsibility for her own life, she still has responsibilities to others. A patient can manipulate loved ones who may have strong interests in their loved one's continued life. Even in Singer's ideal case of Carla, her husband was clearly shocked and "visibly upset" by the request for euthanasia, as was her eldest son, but eventually she persuaded them.[101] One wonders where the line between persuasion and coercion should be drawn in such cases.

More generally, despite Singer's apparent advocacy of individual choice, it is only the choice of *some* individuals. Singer is more a utilitarian than a liberal, as his philosophy is deeply demeaning of the intrinsic worth of the individual which liberalism seeks to safeguard. He defines a potentially large number of human beings as nonpersons without preferences for ongoing life, thus defining away their individuality, autonomy and irreplaceability. As Suzanne Uniacke and H. J. McCloskey show, under cover of euthanasia Singer's idea of replaceability aims to justify killing and replacing "many non-defective babies and those who will lead what he admits are worthwhile lives like haemophiliacs," not to increase their own happiness but their replacements', parents', siblings' or society's happiness. This can also justify nonvoluntary "euthanasia" at the end of life. Singer's extraordinarily illiberal replacement proposal on total utilitarian grounds is really totalitarian. "His position is essentially one not of *mercy* or kindness—to the infants themselves or their parents and siblings—but rather one of *culling* in order to increase the total happiness."[102]

However, contrary to Singer's indifference to individuals,

individual sentient beings are not replaceable or interchangeable in the way that pencils, cars, beads, socks and plants are said to be replaceable. . . . Most human infants [or all] are not simple experiencers, receptacles and causes of happiness and unhappiness. They have unique personalities, characters, lives of intrinsic worth which are lives of their own . . . that . . . cannot be replaced by different infants. Even if we accept Singer's view that, because it has no preference for continued life, we do an infant no "personal wrong" by killing it, as a potential person an infant is irreplaceable in the important sense in which an individual *person* cannot be replaced by a different person. We can (with varying degrees of success) replace potential and actual persons in their roles and jobs—as children, as parents, as teachers, as clerks, etc. As persons they cannot be replaced by different people.[103]

Brenda Almond notes the speculative nature of Singer's replaceability argument

---

[101]Singer, *Rethinking Life and Death*, pp. 141-42.

[102]Suzanne Uniacke and H. J. McCloskey, "Peter Singer and Non-voluntary Euthanasia: Tripping Down the Slippery Slope," *Journal of Applied Philosophy* 9, no. 2 (1992): 216-17, drawing on Singer's *Practical Ethics*.

[103]Ibid.

against the specialness of individual persons. It is quite possible that parents choosing infanticide would not replace their child. "And how soon would they have to do so for this to count as replacement? Or what if someone *else*—a relative, for instance— had an extra child instead? Would this be a 'replacement'? It is by no means certain, either, that someone who has a handicapped child would not go on anyway to have another [healthy] child." Further, when the replaceability argument is used to support abortion, the usual case cited is the disabled. But in practice "abortion is frequently used to postpone child-bearing. The real 'replacement' then, is of children of mothers in their prime child-bearing years—their twenties—with children of mothers in their thirties who are statistically more likely to have [disabled] children, thus *adding* to the problem of handicapped births."[104]

Even on Singer's own grounds of replaceability his argument thus proves too much, putting all persons potentially under threat. Michael Lockwood is alarmed at just how far the notion of replaceability might lead because the preference utilitarian defenses (in terms of a general preference to go on living) Singer mounts against replaceability of existing adults are too weak.[105]

> You can always hope to create someone better, so the Replaceability Argument could be drafted in to do double service as an argument for getting rid of the old, the infirm or the disabled. The only utilitarian argument offered is that this would worry ordinary people who were not old, infirm or disabled, but might become so; and worrying a person in the prime of life is widely accepted as wrong by a large number of philosophers who happen to fit this description![106]

From a German context justly wary of Singer's views, Herlinde Pauer-Studer agrees that "Singer has to concede the 'replaceability of persons' if he holds to the

---

[104]Almond, *Exploring Ethics*, pp. 156-57. Unlike Singer, I do not see disabled births as all bad, nor may Almond. I am merely using this argument to show the problems of his argument on his own consequentialist grounds. We should also note the unintended consequences of state interference with birth, such as in China, where the one-child policy has led to a massive disproportion between males and females due to the abortion of many more females than males.

[105]As Michael Lockwood says: "According to Singer, it is not directly wrong to kill 'non-self-conscious beings,' such as lower animals, human foetuses and newborn infants, provided that any consequent loss of happiness is made good by the creation of new sentient life. In contrast, normal adult humans, being 'self-conscious,' generally have a strong preference for going on living, the flouting of which cannot, Singer argues, be morally counterbalanced by creating new, equally happy individuals. . . . It proves difficult, however, to find a formulation of 'preference utilitarianism' which, while lacking other obviously unacceptable consequences, supports Singer's 'non-replaceability principle.' Also, Singer's position fails adequately to accommodate our conviction that the lives of human beings are, in general, more valuable than those of other animals. Finally, his thesis that lower animals (let alone human infants) are replaceable, has decidedly counterintuitive implications" ("Singer on Killing and the Preference for Life," *Inquiry* 22 [1979]: 157).

[106]Almond, *Exploring Ethics*, p. 157.

'replaceability of infants.'" It is not necessary to argue that Singer plans to expand his categories for ethically justified killing, merely that he has no rational reason, on his premises, not to. As a colleague of mine joked, "It's easier to argue for the person-hood of a four-week-old than a fourteen-year-old!" "Somehow a change in Singer's starting premises seems inevitable . . . whether this amounts to giving up his distinction between persons or to giving up his utilitarianism."[107]

Singer's moral priorities are upside down. Our primary task should be to improve the lives and conditions of Down syndrome and hemophiliac children rather than guesstimating whether their "euthanasia" and replacement by a healthy child might marginally increase the sum total of human happiness.

Singer's argument from opinion polls favoring VE confuses political and moral categories, ignores the problems of such polls on ethical issues and the unrepresentability of the dying person, and seeks to banish Christian reasons from the public realm. There are major questions about the suitability of the survey questions, their outdated nature, the definitions of euthanasia used, and the extent to which people were well-informed about the Dutch practice and euthanasia generally.[108]

Singer's overreliance on polls is, like many of our poll-iticians' similar overreliance, a denial of moral leadership and a confusion of categories. As legal scholar John Warwick Montgomery argues, legal judgments are prescriptive or "ought" statements. For judges (or ethicists like Singer) to base their opinions on a sociological or statistical basis is to commit the naturalistic or sociologist's fallacy: deriving an "ought" from an "is"—the morally normative or prescriptive from the statistically normal or democratically descriptive. To allow VE merely because opinion polls show a majority of doctors or people favor it is no different from allowing the death penalty because a majority of people favor it. Yet most Western nations, besides the United States, where it is increasingly questioned, reject the death penalty on moral grounds, as Singer would.

Opinion-poll morality, as Montgomery notes,

> is the functional equivalent of decriminalizing tax evasion because most people hate income tax. And to reason that because many people now think suicide or assisted suicide is permissible and that a certain number of physicians do in fact help the terminally ill on their way, such practices are legally justifiable, is utterly fallacious. *Vox populi* has never been, and has not suddenly become, *vox Dei.*[109]

Singer relies on a democratic argument from "the majority of society." This does not

[107]Pauer-Studer, "Peter Singer on Euthanasia," p. 143.
[108]Brian Pollard, *The Challenge of Euthanasia* (Crows Nest, N.S.W.: Mount, 1994], chap. 10.
[109]Montgomery, "Whose Life Anyway?" pp. 85-86.

prove anything unless you believe you can transfer a principle of the liberal political sphere, majority rule, to the medical sphere, which, rather than political representation, involves the unrepresentable, literal reality of your own life or death, if you are the patient."[110]

Singer's argument against the role of religion in promoting laws restraining personal autonomy has been partly responded to earlier. Not all sins are crimes, but some are, like murder. Singer is simply wrong to say that because a religious doctrine of SOL cannot be the basis of legislation in a pluralistic society, it cannot be the basis of our moral thinking on euthanasia. Morality and political plurality are not identical.

Singer, however, wants to effectively limit the liberty to use religious reasons in public. Believers would be confined to an allegedly pure secular or public reason long subject to critique, most recently by postmodernists (see chapter one). On liberal democratic grounds, given the large numbers of religious believers (especially in the United States), there is no reason that religious reasons cannot be used, as long as no particular religion or denomination is established.

Singer's claim that SOL is nonsensical without a Christian framework is only partly true. Christians and those of other religions or none should be allowed to speak their "thick" native languages of particular moral communities and spell out their frameworks in public moral debates to understand where the real differences lie. But there is still a need to translate this into the "thinner" rational language of natural law or human rights to highlight areas of commonality, supporting SOL, though always seeking to thicken the brew.

For example, Singer's argument from autonomy is refuted on nonreligious grounds by Jenny Teichman, a philosophical follower of Immanuel Kant, who first developed the principle of autonomy. For Kant autonomy does not mean having your apparently "rational self-regarding desires treated as absolutely paramount. Moreover, . . . Kant believes suicide to be a violation of the moral law and therefore essentially irrational. . . . Medical practice follows Kant in this matter. . . . The instinct for survival is very strong and its apparent absence is a *prima facie* reason to conclude that the individual is not thinking rationally."[111] This latter argument is an argument from natural law, not a religious argument.

As Teichman argues in relation to Singer's view of non-VE or infanticide:

---

[110]Reinders, "Debunking the Sanctity of Life," pp. 10-11. See Peter Singer on majority rule in his "Can We Avoid Assigning Greater Value to Some Human Lives Than to Others?" in *Moral Issues in Mental Retardation*, ed. R. S. Laura and A. F. Ashman (London: Croome Helm, 1985), p. 96.
[111]Teichman, *Social Ethics*, pp. 68-69.

If Singer's reasoning leads us where we intuitively know that we don't wish to go (the dispatch of the unwanted) it is sensible for us to reject it. Singer rejects the sanctity of life because it is based on the religious belief of our "being made in the image of God" and this he says is now part of "a set of beliefs that most people have laid aside." Many humanists and atheists would argue that their conviction that human life has a unique and intrinsic value has less to do with religious sanctity than it has with their humanism. . . . It was people's humanity that was shocked when the gates of Auschwitz were opened, as it is our human-ness that is revolted by "ethnic cleansing"—that more recent example of dispatching the unwanted.[112]

Slippery Slope Arguments

In response to the common question whether the legalization of VE will put us on a slippery slope leading to non-VE, Singer asks whether the slippery slope runs up or down. As the only test case for slippery slope effects where VE is openly practiced is the Netherlands, Singer cites the Dutch experience to substantiate his case for VE. Others dispute the so-called success of the Dutch experiment with euthanasia. So the debate hinges on the Dutch evidence.

First, Singer argues that we have unregulated nonvoluntary euthanasia already, but we can have regulated VE if we legalize it. "Three Australian studies have shown that active voluntary euthanasia is relatively common" there, though illegal. In my home state of Victoria 29 percent of doctors surveyed said they had taken active steps to hasten a patient's death on request, 80 percent more than once. Singer cites similar figures from the neighboring state of New South Wales and the U.S. state of California. Similar ratios were found among Australian nurses also. Non-VE is guesswork, but likely to be more than in the more open Netherlands, Singer claims.[113]

---

[112]Ibid., p. 179. Cf. Almond, *Exploring Ethics*, p. 155, who critiques the expansive liberal use of the First Amendment (proscribing establishment of any state's religion for all states) as a justification of free, nonreligious choice regarding abortion. "Apart from the general implausibility of this as a defence of abortion, it reinforces an erroneous view of the issue as a religious one, rather than as a moral issue of much more general significance. The fact that Catholics and other Christian groups have a well-defined absolutist position on the matter is, of course, important, but it does not make this broad ethical issue, with its implications for people of all religions or of none, a narrowly and exclusively religious or theological question." These comments apply also to infanticide and euthanasia. Oderberg and Laing likewise contradict the claim of many consequentialists like Singer "that there is something essentially religious about anti-consequentialist thinking" (introduction to *Human Lives*, p. 4). Cf. Samuel Scheffler, ed., *Consequentialism and Its Critics* (Oxford: Oxford University Press, 1988). In fact the claim of modern utilitarianism to some kind of rational, nonreligious neutrality is belied by an 1801 letter from its founder, Jeremy Bentham, saying, "A new religion would be an odd sort of thing without a name," and so he suggested "Utilitarianism." Quoted in Mary Warnock's introduction to John Stuart Mill's *Utilitarianism* (Glasgow: Collins/Fontana, 1962), p. 9 n. 1.

[113]Singer, *Rethinking Life and Death*, pp. 154-55.

Second, Singer argues that we cannot compare Dutch euthanasia statistics with the lack of statistics from their situation preregulation nor with other countries pre-VE. The Dutch government's Remmelink Report provides no basis for comparison with prelegalization of VE figures in Holland. So one cannot prove increases in non-VE since regulated VE was allowed. Singer admits that a "limited amount of non-voluntary euthanasia is being practiced in the Netherlands in extreme circumstances" but that no examples of "involuntary euthanasia came to light" in Remmelink.

Third, Singer admits a much larger number of cases, as many as eight thousand, where doctors gave painkilling drugs but "hastening death was . . . part of the purpose of giving the drugs." He diminishes the significance of this by claiming that determining "one's primary or secondary purpose" is obviously difficult.

Singer claims that determining the incidence of non-VE is guesswork. But he admits that 70 percent (15,750 deaths) of cases of withdrawal of treatment were without consent. In 12 percent of these cases the patient "was capable of being consulted but was not." Singer argues that the greater openness in the Netherlands allows for fewer life-shortening decisions without consent than elsewhere. He cites a two-year review of Remmelink as definitive: "We conclude that no empirical data can be marshalled to support the slippery slope argument against the Dutch."[14]

Finally, Singer cites history and contemporary sophistication against the slippery slope argument. He claims that

> there is . . . little historical evidence to suggest that the permissive attitude towards the killing of one category of human beings leads to a breakdown of restrictions against killing other humans. Ancient Greeks regularly killed or exposed infants, but appear to have been at least as scrupulous about taking the lives of their fellow-citizens as medieval Christians or modern Americans. In traditional Eskimo societies it was the custom for a man to kill his elderly parents, but the murder of a normal healthy adult was almost unheard of. If these societies could separate human beings into different categories without transferring their attitudes from one group to another, we with our more sophisticated legal systems and greater medical knowledge should be able to do the same.[15]

Response: The logical slippery slope. Singer's critique of the "slippery slope argument" only deals with the less clear empirical half of the issue, not the more clear logical half.

First, when we play around with slippery or promiscuous definitions of person-

---

[14]Ibid., pp. 153-56.
[15]Singer, *Practical Ethics*, p. 157.

hood, we inevitably slip into discounting of the personhood and autonomy of many of the economically nonessential or nonefficient. As Bernard Williams notes:

> What degree of what characteristic will count in a given context for being a person may very well turn out to be a function of the interests involved—other people's interests, in many cases. Certainly there is no slippery slope more perilous than that extended by a concept which is falsely supposed not to be slippery.[116]

Second, Daniel Callahan describes "the boundless logic of private killing." When the crucial premises of the argument for VE and assisted suicide are accepted,

> there will remain no logical way in the future to: (1) deny euthanasia to anyone who requests it for whatever reason, terminal illness or not; or to (2) deny it to the suffering incompetent, even if they do not request it. We can erect legal safeguards and specify required procedures to keep these things from happening. But over time the safeguards will provide poor protection if the logic of the moral premises upon which they are based are fatally flawed. They will appear arbitrary and flimsy, and will invite covert evasion or outright rejection.[117]

The two key VE premises, our right to self-determination and our claim to merciful relief of suffering, are usually joined to strengthen them against abuse, not for any inherent reason. Both premises have no limits built in. Why should one have to be suffering to receive VE? After all, to paraphrase the old song, "it's my body and I'll die if I want to." Why should the incompetent be unfairly excluded from mercy if they suffer? The joining of the argument is "perfectly arbitrary, a jerry-rigged combination. . . . Each has its own [unlimited] logic. There is no principled reason to reject such logic, and no reason to think it could long remain suppressed by the expedient of an arbitrary legal stipulation that both features, suffering and competence, be present."[118] VE on the basis of patient autonomy logically leads to VE for

---

[116]Bernard Williams, "Which Slopes Are Slippery?" in *Moral Dilemmas in Modern Medicine*, ed. Michael Lockwood (Oxford: Oxford University Press, 1985), p. 137.

[117]Callahan, *Troubled Dream of Life*, p. 107.

[118]Ibid., p. 108. John Keown ("Euthanasia in the Netherlands," in *Euthanasia Examined: Ethical, Clinical and Legal Perspectives*, ed. John Keown [Cambridge: Cambridge University Press, 1995], p. 262) likewise shows there is a good logical case that doctors' judgments of the worth of a patient's life are more determinative of decisions regarding euthanasia than the patient's autonomy. No responsible doctor will euthanize a patient if they think they have a life worth living, no matter how much they are asked. "And, if a doctor can make this judgment in relation to an autonomous patient, he can, logically, make it in relation to an incompetent patient. Moreover, if death is a 'benefit' for competent patients suffering certain conditions, why should it be denied incompetent patients suffering from the same conditions?"

Henk Jochemsen argues that it is "the condition of the patient, not the request, which is the real ground for euthanasia in many cases." The request is logically irrelevant. "The practice of Eutha-

any reason. VE on the basis of the patient's condition logically leads to non-VE on the same basis.

The logical likelihood of increased non-VE has thus led a number of commentators and authorities to oppose legalization of VE. This was partly why the House of Lords Select (Walton) Committee of 1994 rejected VE for Britain. It is also why the U.S. Supreme Court on June 26, 1997, unanimously reversed the decision in the Kevorkian case *Compassion in Dying* v. *State of Washington,* which Singer cites approvingly as a precedent for allowing assisted suicide. Quoting a New York task force, Justice Anthony Kennedy told assisted-suicide supporters that "the autonomy for the individual that you seek is illusory. . . . In fact you will be introducing fear [of non VE] into medical facilities."[119]

The empirical slippery slope. It is time now to respond to Singer's disputing of the empirical form of the argument that even if a line can be drawn in principle between nonvoluntary and VE, a slippage will occur because of ineffective safeguards.

In response to Singer's first argument, that VE would open up practices that are already occurring—covert VE and "non-VE"—there are five main arguments.

First, we should acknowledge some of the problems of the present situation which Singer raises. Illegality doesn't stop some from practicing assisted suicide, VE and even "non-VE." There are tragic cases where loved ones or doctors are prosecuted for what fits the term "mercy killing." But the courts generally exercise mercy in punishment while upholding the law.

Second, however, Singer simply assumes that the more VE takes place the less involuntary or nonvoluntary "euthanasia" will occur. This is a flawed interpretation of the experience of Dutch, English and American law.

A Dutch source argues that

> transgression of a law is not a reason to abolish the law; a large part of Dutch euthanasia practice and probably the worst part has not become controllable; there is no proof of a comparable number of cases of euthanasia in countries where the law is maintained in this respect; the acceptance of euthanasia leads to an extension of its practice almost certainly far beyond what was going on in the Netherlands before.[120]

---

nasia in the Netherlands seems to entail an inherent slippery slope" ("Euthanasia in Holland: An Ethical Critique of the New Law," *Journal of Medical Ethics* 20 [1994]: 213).

[119]Quoted by Montgomery, "Whose Life Anyway?" p. 84 n. 3.

[120]Jochemsen, "Euthanasia in the Netherlands: A Critique of Its Practice and Policy," unpublished manuscript, abstract. VE has not led to greater openness, for deaths are routinely falsified as due to natural causes on death certificates by 65-75 percent of Dutch doctors—as many admit, to save administration and the family's feelings (Jochemsen, "Euthanasia in Holland," p. 214). The most detailed study of the Netherlands situation found that "euthanasia is being practiced on a scale

From an English perspective, John Keown noted that the Dutch Penal Code prohibited providing VE (until 2001). However, exceptions were allowed in 1984 (the *Alkmaar* case) and 1986 for the "necessity" of relieving severe distress (article 40) leading to a doctor's "conflict of duties" between obeying the law not to kill (article 293) and being faithful to the duty to relieve pain. However, these exceptions are strange: first, the necessity defense traditionally justifies breaching the law only "to *save* life [as in the case of speeding to get an injured person to hospital], not to take it. Secondly, the judgment fails to explain *why* the doctor's duty to alleviate suffering overrides his duty not to kill. Finally, the Court appears to abdicate to medical opinion the power to determine the circumstances in which killing attracts the necessity defence." This in effect made doctors judges in their own cases before 2001 as to whether they had broken the law. And giving such enormous discretionary powers to unelected experts in a context of ambiguity inevitably led to abuse. "Despite a 1987 State commission on euthanasia allowing VE by 'careful' doctors, the maintaining of article 293 and the lack of clear directions regarding 'when and where' provides Dutch doctors with a motive to dishonestly fill out cause of death on death certificates."[121]

This "grotesque" reasoning is not applied to property or blue-collar crime. "In the present context it has to do with the alleged behaviour of doctors and nurses—educated, middle-class, professional people. It is an argument which secretly and silently distinguishes between citizens of different social status and is therefore in conflict with natural justice."[122]

Third, John Warwick Montgomery argues that American court cases like the infamous abortion-legalizing decision of *Roe v. Wade* and the assisted-suicide-legalizing decision of *Compassion in Dying* "are not classic common-law jurisprudence at all, but a relatively recent [yet dominant] deviant." This is known as American legal realism, which replaces objective values and formal reason with seeing the law as a mere means to certain sociologically surveyed ends. Law becomes a form of ad hoc social engineering driven by polls.[123]

---

vastly exceeding the 'known' (truthfully reported and recorded) cases. As Leenen has observed, there is an 'almost total lack of control on the administration of euthanasia' and 'the present legal situation makes any adequate control of the practice of euthanasia virtually impossible'" (John Keown, "The Law and Practice of Euthanasia in the Netherlands," *Law Quarterly Review* 108 [1992]: 51-78). Cf. John Keown, "Euthanasia in the Netherlands: Sliding Down the Slippery Slope?" *Notre Dame Journal of Law, Ethics and Public Policy* 9 (1995): 407, and his essay of the same title in J. Keown ed., *Euthanasia Examined*, p. 286.

[121]Teichman, *Social Ethics*, p. 88.

[122]Ibid., p. 66.

[123]Montgomery, "Whose Life Anyway?" p. 85.

Fourth, this is hardly realistic about human nature. As Montgomery notes,

The Christian position on suicide and assisted suicide is grounded in an acidly realistic
view of fallen human nature. Because of the self-centredness characteristic of all
human beings since the fall, . . . to normalize or legalize the aiding and abetting of suicide is an act of utter naivety and folly. Owing to original sin, we are all subject to falli-
bility, laziness, and perversity. Where voluntary euthanasia is allowed a gilt-edged
invitation is provided for the manifestation of these characteristics. The patient and/or
physician may err in diagnosis of the true medical condition and the chances of survival. The patient and/or his loved ones may simply tire of life and of the care needed to
sustain it. Those who will survive the patient may even be motivated by greed. . . . All of
these considerations are particularly magnified in our modern secular society, with the
intense psychological and social pressures it puts on its members: the supposed absolute
right to health, success, and happiness. No one should have to endure a moment of
unnecessary suffering![124]

Utilitarian utopianism has no place for suffering, based on a narrow notion of
human happiness. Humans are mainly sentient creatures (topped off with rational
preferences), and therefore suffering is always evil and must be reduced,[125] regardless
of other relational aspects of humanity (such as the willingness to suffer for love).
Certainly we should seek to minimize suffering, and Christian-based hospices are at
the forefront of such efforts. But Singer's naive vision of an end without suffering justifies all manner of immoral means. There are evils, such as killing, that are greater
than suffering. Only at the true end will God "wipe every tear from their eyes" and
wipe out death (Rev 21:4).

Yet while both Christian and utilitarian eschatologies (or views of the end) are
statements of faith, awareness of original sin is not. Reinhold Niebuhr, the great
theological realist, often quoted the *Times Literary Supplement* stating that "the doctrine of original sin is the only empirically verifiable doctrine of the Christian
faith."[126] Philosopher Jenny Teichman substantiates this concerning the VE lobby:

These well-meaning people, alas, are not living in the real world. . . . Their ideal world
contains no sons and daughters, or . . . in-law[s], who fail to love and respect their old
folk. . . . Kith and kin do not have debts that could be easily paid if only Grand-dad
would hurry up and die. The ideal world contains doctors and nurses who need no

---

[124]Ibid.

[125]Taylor, "Singer Revolution," p. 11.

[126]Reinhold Niebuhr, *Man's Nature and His Communities* (London: Geoffrey Bles, 1966), p. 16. The
statement would perhaps be better if it read "the most" rather than "only." Karl Barth describes the
doctrine of original sin as "the doctrine which emerges from all honest study of history" (*The Epis-
tle to the Romans* [New York: Oxford University Press, 1933], pp. 85-86).

taboos because they are *naturally* more virtuous and noble and intelligent than other people. . . . Doctors and nurses never treat patients in a condescending fashion and never get fed up with dirty, troublesome old people . . . [or] misdescribe the causes of death on death certificates and would never break the law. . . . Even doctors who have . . . broken existing laws against euthanasia can be trusted never to break or bend any proposed new laws.[127]

I can support this from personal experience as a pastor who had a cemetery in my parish and presided at many funerals. Long-lost relatives often came out of the woodwork when an aged relative was dying and there was a sniff of a possible inheritance. It is hard not to see pressures being brought to bear on aged or chronically ill people to give up the ghost and let loved ones have an easier life.[128] As this amusing but dangerously truthful piece of doggerel puts it:

They bumped old grannie off you know:
She only had a cold,
Her sufferings, they told in court,
Were dreadful to behold.
The judge was kind—"besides," he said,
"She's getting rather old."
So they left the court and went away
To share old grannie's gold.[129]

Fifth, Teichman rightly takes on consequentialists on their own grounds:

Euthanasia is supported by many consequentialists like Singer, yet there are powerful consequentialist objections to allowing the practice. . . . Although imaginary counter-examples can test a generalization it is well-known that imaginary "pro"-examples cannot establish truth. Consequentialists ignore this principle and try to draw positive conclusions from the *imagined* effects of proposed actions. They reason on the basis of speculations about the *possible* effects of future events while ignoring ordinary common-sense estimates of probability and hard evidence about actual real-life conse-

---

[127]Teichman, *Social Ethics*, pp. 84-85.
[128]For instance, "an old man was dying from disseminated lung cancer. His symptoms were well controlled and he asked if he could go and die at home. When his four children were told about his wish, they would not agree to take care of him. Even after repeated discussion, they refused. Instead, they pointed to their father's suffering and the need to finish things quickly 'in the name of humanity.' When the doctor refused they threatened to sue him. Because the patient insisted on going home, a social worker went to investigate. She discovered that the patient's house was empty and that every piece of furniture had been taken by the family" (Robert G. Twycross, "Where There Is Hope, There Is Life: A View from the Hospice," in *Euthanasia Examined: Ethical, Clinical and Legal Perspectives*, ed. John Keown [Cambridge: Cambridge University Press, 1995], p. 161, based on Z. Zylicz, personal communication from Holland).
[129]Quoted in John Searle, *Kill or Care?* (Exeter, U.K.: Paternoster, 1977), p. 20.

quences. . . . What are the probabilities here? . . . If doctors are allowed to kill it is probable that other people (for instance, nurses, social workers and the relatives of patients) will eventually be allowed to do the same. . . . It is not difficult to see how pragmatic or anti-elitist ideas could push society onto that slippery slope. . . . There are other slippery slopes here too. Legalizing euthanasia is virtually certain to make ordinary murder much easier to disguise than it is at present.[130]

Singer's second argument is a dangerous argument from silence to show that we cannot compare present Dutch euthanasia statistics with absent statistics from the preregulation Dutch situation nor with any other countries' current situation.

First, however, the argument from silence usually works in favor of the status quo, not a radical change as Singer wants. Even more damaging, Singer breaks the silence, admitting that more than half of Dutch doctors interviewed had performed euthanasia or assisted suicide. Another 34 percent considered it feasible in certain circumstances. Only 4 percent refuse to have anything to do with euthanasia. This latter figure is astonishingly small, considering that the World Medical Association reaffirmed its condemnation of euthanasia in 1987. A more than 50 percent rate of Dutch doctors performing euthanasia is nearly twice the Australian rate of 29 percent that Singer cites from surveys.[131] The evidence from these statistics, backed up by many stories and arguments, shows a probability that Dutch doctors' overwhelmingly positive attitude toward euthanasia and willingness to terminate lives without consent is quite different from Australian or American doctors' attitudes. The slippage rate is very high. What is maverick medicine elsewhere has become mainstream in Holland.

Second, Singer is quite parochial in seeing the Netherlands as the new world standard, not the World Medical Association. Yet he recognizes that his idyllic Dutch situation of euthanasia performed by caring family doctors in a strong welfare state is not easily replicable elsewhere, especially in the individualistic United States.[132] In the context of modern industrialized medicine and managed care, we will surely get euthanasia clinics or factories with euthanasia specialists like the large abortion clinics we now have. There hurried and ill-informed decisions are often induced, though the U.S. Supreme Court had anticipated abortion's being a very private, well-considered decision with the woman's family doctor. As Almond

---

[130]Teichman, *Social Ethics*, pp. 85-87. See, for instance, Rita Marker, *Deadly Compassion: The Death of Ann Humphry and the Case Against Euthanasia* (London: HarperCollins, 1994), for the story of leading VE advocate Derek Humphry of the Hemlock Society. He was accused by his second wife's suicide note of having murdered his first wife and driven her to her own death also.
[131]Singer, *Rethinking Life and Death*, pp. 155-57.
[132]Ibid., pp. 157-58.

Table 1. 1990 Dutch Euthanasia Statistics
129,000 (100 percent) died of all causes.

2,300 (1.8 percent) cases involved active VE.
400 (0.3 percent) cases were medically assisted suicides.
1,000 (0.8 percent) cases were "non-VE"—ending life unrequested, which 27 percent of doctors admitted.

Because of their definitional ignoring of the role of intention in euthanasia, both in acts and in omissions, Singer and van der Maas ignore the following:

22,500 (17.5 percent) cases involving life-support withdrawal or withholding without patient request—that is, stopping or not starting treatment (including tube feeding).
4,275 (11.45 percent) of these were partly to quicken death.
3,600 (2.8 percent) were explicitly to quicken death.

22,500 (17.5 percent) cases involved possible lethal pain medication, about 20 percent of all deaths.
8,100 (6.2 percent of total) of these cases involved doctors' primarily (5.2 percent) or partially (1 percent) intending to hasten death through medication, without patient request.

In all, adding the 2,700 admitted euthanasia cases to the 23,350 cases of quickening death by act or omission without patient permission gives 26,350 cases of shortening life intentionally; that is, an astonishing 20 percent of Dutch deaths were by euthanasia.[133]

---

argues concerning infant "euthanasia,"

> even if there is a case for infanticide, there is still a question about whether what is right or at least condonable when prompted by personal feeling should come to be viewed as a matter of ordinary practice [or] routinised clinical killing.[134]

Singer's denial of a slippage to nonvoluntary "euthanasia" is overreliant on the P. J. van der Maas report to the Dutch government's Remmelink Commission in its 1990 survey of Dutch euthanasia statistics. This seems fair in its statistics but is selective and apologetic in its proeuthanasia interpretation.[135] This is to be expected, given that it is

---

[133]Keown, "Euthanasia in the Netherlands," pp. 270-71. Cf. Jochemsen, "Euthanasia in Holland," p. 213; Pollard, *Challenge of Euthanasia*, pp. 132-33; Robert Manne, "Euthanasia: The Last Right," in *Death and the State*, papers presented to a conference on Euthanasia at the Centre for Public Policy, University of Melbourne, 1995, p. 43.

[134]Almond, *Exploring Ethics*, p. 158. The New York State Task Force of Life and Law's supplement to *When Death Is Sought: Assisted Suicide and Euthanasia in the Medical Context* (April 1997) found that most people, especially the poor, have no access to the "sensible and caring doctor familiar with all the circumstances" of Singer's "idyllic" Dutch situations.

by Dutch doctors strongly in favor of and implicated in the practice of euthanasia.

In contrast to Singer, I outline the statistical survey results independently, as they are extrapolated in relation to the total number of deaths in Holland for 1990, listed in table 1. I also tease out from the statistics those cases of intentional "euthanasia" by act or omission which the Dutch defined away because of their narrow definition equating euthanasia with active VE.

This shows a massive increase over the 1,000 "non-VE" cases or "barely 2 per cent" of all medically determined deaths which Singer, like van der Maas, unconvincingly minimizes as involving some (mainly verbal and early) consultation.[136] Even the 2 percent of his reckoning is significant if it includes you! Further, 41 percent of 157 patients reported by Loes Pijnenborg et al. were euthanized without their discussion or consent.[137]

The alleged regulation of VE has led to a slippery slope of significantly reduced personal autonomy at the hands of Dutch doctors, and it would do so elsewhere as well.

The autonomy principle is expandable not only logically (as seen earlier) beyond terminal illness but empirically in Holland and elsewhere. So euthanasia for children, for HIV-positive patients who are not yet terminally ill, and for physically healthy persons with depression is accepted and increasing. Van der Maas found that "euthanasia and assisted suicide were more often found in deaths in relatively young men and in the urbanised western Netherlands [many being HIV+ patients] and this

---

[135]For example, van der Maas's gratuitous claim that doctors' reluctance to euthanize again denies the slippery slope effect may simply show a remnant of a SOLE or may evidence the sheer horror of euthanasia (van der Maas et al., "Euthanasia and Other Medical Decisions," p. 673).

[136]Singer (*Rethinking Life and Death*, p. 153) claims that 600 of these cases involved some discussion, though no explicit request, because the patients were mainly incompetent. Van der Maas says of the 0.8 percent of all deaths where drugs were administered to explicitly speed death that "in more than half of these cases the decision had been discussed with the patient, or the patient had expressed in a previous phase of the disease a wish for euthanasia if his/her suffering became unbearable." The glass was obviously half full! They ignore the fact that in approximately half of these cases of life termination *it had not been discussed*. Further, among the half who had allegedly discussed it, many had been in an earlier stage of the disease.

Later, van der Maas's report undermines his own and Singer's defense. It says of the many requests for euthanasia and assisted suicide by patients suffering unbearably that "about two-thirds of these requests never end up as a serious and persistent request at a later stage of the disease, and of the serious and persistent requests about two-thirds do not result in euthanasia or assisted suicide since physicians can offer alternatives" (van der Maas et al., "Euthanasia and Other Medical Decisions," pp. 671-73). In fact this means that two-thirds of the 0.4% or so where there was some discussion or view voiced for euthanasia could have changed their minds, in addition to the other 0.4 percent who had no say at all.

[137]Loes Pijnenborg et al., "Life-Terminating Acts Without Explicit Request of the Patient," *The Lancet* 341 (1993): 1196-99.

may be an indication of a shift towards a more demanding attitude of patients in matters concerning the end of life."[138] Dutch doctors who euthanize AIDS patients claim the maximum life shortening is three months. "However, five patients were euthanased at the time of the initial AIDS-defining illness when the life-expectancy should be two to three years"[139]—and that expectancy is probably higher now. "It is estimated that some 25% of deaths in AIDS patients in the Netherlands are now due to euthanasia."[140] As palliative care for cancer has improved, VE societies have shifted from cancer as their paradigm case to AIDS. In my former home state of New South Wales, AIDS groups were proposing VE legislation without a terminal stage of illness requirement.

Dutch courts already accept depression or psychiatric illness as grounds of necessity for euthanasia.[141] At a euthanasia conference in Australia, a reporter asked a Dutch doctor what sort of circumstances would justify euthanasia. She expected to hear a description of some excruciatingly painful disease. Instead she was told of a former diplomat's wife with no physical health problems who had toured the world with her husband and led a very interesting life but lapsed into chronic loneliness, depression and suicidal thoughts after his death. The reporter suggested getting her a cat for company, to which the doctor replied, "That's a good idea, unfortunately it's too late."[142]

A survey of the seven cases of VE before the federal rescinding of the Northern Territory Rights of the Terminally Ill Act (ROTI) found disturbing evidence of depression.

> All seven patients had cancer, most at advanced stages. Three were socially isolated. Symptoms of depression were common. . . . Medical opinions about the terminal nature of illness differed. . . . Provision of opinions about the terminal nature of illness and the mental health of the patient, as required by the ROTI Act, created problematic gatekeeping roles for the doctors involved. . . . Pain was not a prominent clinical issue. . . . Fatigue, frailty, depression, and other symptoms contributed more to the suffering of patients. . . . Studies in Australia, Canada and the USA, have all found an association between depressive disorder and the desire to die.[143]

---

[138]Van der Maas et al., "Euthanasia and Other Medical Decisions," p. 673.
[139]Woodruff, "Is Euthanasia Contagious?" citing Patrick Bindels, *Lancet* 347 (1996): 499.
[140]Pollard, *Challenge of Euthanasia*, p. 133.
[141]Jochemsen, "Euthanasia in Holland," p. 217 n. 26. Cf. A. D. Ogilvie, *British Medical Journal* 309 (1994): 492.
[142]A report broadcasted by Australian Broadcasting Commission radio, n.d.
[143]David W. Kissane, Annette Street and Philip Nitschke (the doctor who administered VE), "Seven Deaths in Darwin: Case Studies Under the Rights of the Terminally Ill Act, Northern Territory, Australia," *Lancet* 352 (1998): 1097, 1101-2.

Further, there are grave doubts about doctors' and even psychiatrists' ability to accurately make a length-of-life prognosis and diagnose possible depression under time and other pressures.[44] So how informed a choice do those suffering depression really make?

Behind the percentages and statistics are real people with real stories. People do change their minds, and their condition can change. In Australia on March 3, 1999, a very weak cancer patient, June Burns, appeared in TV ads for VE, but eight months later she had entered remission and looked healthy. She still wanted to keep the option of VE, though. A nurse told me of a case she knew firsthand on her ward of a young man with AIDS who was given a lethal injection. While dying he was told of a party coming up, and he unsuccessfully tried to change his mind so he could go. A Sydney palliative-care nurse reports that under three percent of patients beginning palliative care request euthanasia, and usually because they do not know what can be done to ease their condition. Once palliative care is under way, under one percent request euthanasia.

Further, the allegedly strict safeguards that van der Maas and Singer claim will prevent a slippery slope are like the little boy's finger in the dyke of increased demand. In van der Maas's report, the grounds patients cited and doctors accepted for requesting voluntary euthanasia and assisted suicide were so vague and subjective that anything could be justified at almost any stage of life: 57 percent cited loss of dignity, 46 percent pain, 46 percent unworthy dying, 33 percent being dependent on others, 23 percent tiredness of life.[45] Without denying the extreme difficulties some people face, we must recognize that all of these are part of life to some extent. Many feel tired of life every Monday morning, but we do not euthanize them.

Keown concludes that the Dutch guidelines are "vague, loose and incapable of preventing abuse. The [van der Maas] Survey bears out this conclusion by indicating that cardinal safeguards—requiring a request which is free and voluntary; well-informed; and durable and persistent—have been widely disregarded. Doctors have killed with impunity . . . shorten[ing] the lives of over 10000 patients in 1990, the

---

[44]"A total of 1375 [Oregon] physicians (50 per cent) were not confident that they could predict that a patient had less than six months to live. Moreover, 761 (28 per cent) indicated that they were not confident they could recognize depression in a patient who requested a prescription for a lethal dose of medication" (Melinda A. Lee et al., "Legalizing Assisted Suicide: Views of Physicians in Oregon," *New England Journal of Medicine*, February 1, 1996, pp. 310-15). "Only 6% of [Oregon] psychiatrists were very confident that in a single evaluation they could adequately assess whether a psychiatric disorder was impairing the judgment of a patient requesting assisted suicide" (Linda Ganzini et al., "Attitudes of Oregon Psychiatrists Towards Physician-Assisted Suicide," *American Journal of Psychiatry*, November 1996, pp. 1469-75.
[45]Van der Maas et al., "Euthanasia and Other Medical Decisions," p. 672.

majority without the patient's explicit request."[46]

Singer's argument for infanticide from ancient and crosscultural precedents "indulges the jejune sort of cultural relativism which argues that if any culture anywhere once performed a practice, then the practice must be morally permissible."[47] This goes against his own criticism elsewhere of cultural relativism regarding animals.[48] Singer's dangerous phrase "separate human beings into different categories" should give us pause. A large part of Greek society was subjected to slavery, a living death, due to the Greek practice of categorizing human beings.[49]

Moreover, when infanticide is sanctioned it is nearly always at the behest of a male head of household in the context of a strongly patriarchal society, such as ancient Rome, where the *paterfamilias* had the power of life and death. It often applies to their children with prostitutes or slaves, or to female children as in contemporary China and India. As Michael Gorman notes, "That the fetus is not a person was fundamental to Roman law. Even when born, the child was valued primarily for its usefulness to the father, the family and especially the state."[50] Early Christians rescued many children left to die by the Romans and rescued Western society from barbarism in the process.

The Inuit people have had extraordinarily high levels of suicide in recent times, due partly, it could be argued, to the precedent set by their treatment of their elderly. This is something to be remembered when Western societies face high rates of youth suicide. Such high rates are particularly common among indigenous peoples like American Indians, Northern Territory Aboriginals and New Zealand Maoris. Both latter groups are among those most strongly opposed to VE and eventually succeeded in opposing it. The prejudicial application of laws (such as mandatory sentencing for repeated petty crime) in that state to Aboriginals, or for that matter to

---

[46]Keown, "Euthanasia in the Netherlands," p. 282.

[47]J. Bottum, "Facing Up to Infanticide," *First Things*, February 1996, p. 43, in reference to Peter Singer's article "Killing Babies Isn't Always Wrong," *Spectator* (London), September 16, 1995, pp. 20-22.

[48]"If there really is no basis for ethics except one's own culture, what is the meaning of the claim that we should not impose our culture on others? Is that view just a reflection of the speaker's culture?" Peter Singer, "Cultural Clash Sets Rite Against Reason" *The Age*, Higher Education sec., June n.d., 1993. Singer is a nonrelativist on ecological and animal issues, for example Japanese killing of whales, but not, it seems, on human life issues.

[49]While Plato, Aristotle and Seneca were great ancient philosophers, this lends no respectability to their views on abnormal or useless humans, despite Kuhse and Singer's claim in Peter Singer and Helga Kuhse, *Should the Baby Live? The Problem of Handicapped Infants* (Oxford: Oxford University Press, 1985), pp. 11-12. Singer admits in "Cultural Clash" that slavery contradicts the universal law of "do unto others."

[50]Michael Gorman, *Abortion and the Early Church: Christian, Jewish and Pagan Attitudes in the Greco-Roman World* (Downers Grove, Ill: InterVarsity Press, 1982), p. 32.

blacks in the United States, does not augur well for how they might be treated by VE laws. There is good historical precedent in Hitler's Germany for minority racial groups to fear VE.

In relation to this, it is worth noting that pro-VE forces are primarily secular Western elites, not the majority of the world's religious people. When a New York lawyer advocated the right to die at the International Institute of Human Rights in Strasbourg, France, she expected a positive response from the international student audience. However, she received the opposite, especially from Third World students; in their countries "the struggle for the right to life had hardly been won—after ages of paganism in which the individual counted for next to nothing. Anything that would facilitate death at the expense of life was therefore anathema." This is far from a parochial Christian concern, despite Singer's claims. Christian perspectives linked with creation-based universal natural law embodied in international declarations of human rights (e.g., the United Nations and European Union declarations including the right to life) provide the basis for a life ethic for a globalized society. Singer's views, by contrast, are a parochial, elitist perspective intent on returning the West back beyond its Christian heritage to a pagan one of infanticide and sanctioned suicide. Singer fails to recognize that "because of the seamless garment of human dignity, facilitating death in any way, facilitates it in every way."[51]

Singer's confidence in our sophisticated legal system's ability to resist slippery slopes by demarcating where human life can be devalued and where not is arrogant and naive. The twentieth century's wholesale disregard for human life in war and peace provides little justification for his assumptions. Proabortion legislation has led to dramatically increased numbers of abortions. Singer himself uses it to justify the next logical steps to euthanasia and infanticide.

> If I accept that it is justifiable for a woman to kill her foetus in the womb because she considers her family complete or would rather have a child at a time that would better suit her career plans I know that I cannot continue to hold conventional views about the sanctity of human life at other times and in other states. . . . Parents should be permitted to kill small infants of one month or younger.[52]

The Netherlands's decriminalization of drugs, pornography and prostitution, which has made it a mecca for all three, also indicates the likelihood of a slippery slope. The law has a modeling or educative effect. People's autonomy is not absolute but is influenced by various sources including, to a large part, the law.

Another secular Jew (like Singer), Robert Manne, always wary of another Holo-

---

[51]Montgomery, "Whose Life Anyway?" pp. 101-2.
[52]Singer, "Killing Babies," pp. 20-22.

caust, notes that relaxation of the prohibition against killing is nearly certain to have a spillover effect to nonvoluntary "euthanasia." Laws allowing VE are not "single, isolated legal acts" as assumed by proponents but are linked with other laws and build up an irresistible momentum. The slippery slope argument recognizes that

society has been built around certain traditional prohibitions and taboos; . . . in the past thirty years or so we have passed through a vast cultural revolution, where many of these taboos have been breached at their most vulnerable points; . . . once breached, we have been drawn inexorably down a path which few citizens, at the point of the initial breach, either anticipated or desired, and which many now, in whole or part, regret. I am already old enough to have witnessed a number of such passages down such slippery slopes. Pornography is the most obvious instance. . . . Or take the more complex case of abortion, which is more directly relevant to euthanasia. . . . These moral journeys had certain features in common. At each way-station liberals claimed that the next step forward would be the last. Even more importantly, during the course of these journeys most citizens gradually lost the sense of what they had once believed or why. As Peter Singer has rightly pointed out, the fundamental direction of the moral journey we have undertaken during the past generation is from a society founded upon the idea of "the sanctity of human life" to one founded, instead, upon the idea of "quality of life." In this journey euthanasia is merely the most recent proposal of the liberals.[153]

There is also a likelihood that the tendency toward a utilitarian calculus of the greatest good for the greatest number in healthcare will be reinforced as Western societies age and more resources of struggling health systems are expended at the end of life. Combined with a market or economic rationalist view of medicine, this raises the question, who will restrict VE from becoming nonvoluntary and even involuntary once the cultural bridge leading to officially sanctioned killing is crossed?

As Teichman notes:

Philosophy teachers [like Singer] tend to be whole-hoggers in this as in other areas, hence those who support euthanasia tend to argue in favour of all three varieties. . . . Politicians, on the other hand, usually insist that they wish only to legalize voluntary euthanasia. But they soon let the cat out of the bag, as it were, by mentioning the shortage of hospital beds, the increasing number of old people "taking up space" on the planet, and the tax burdens of middle-aged middle–income earners. These circumstances . . . have nothing to do with mercy.[154]

---

[153]Manne, "Euthanasia," pp. 42-43.
[154]Teichman, Social Ethics, p. 87.

To illustrate:

> A Dutch woman with disseminated cancer told her doctor she would never choose
> euthanasia because of her beliefs. A second doctor ordered a 20-fold increase in mor-
> phine, following which the patient quickly died. When challenged, he replied "It could
> have taken her another week before she died; I just needed this bed."[55]

Robert G. Twycross sums up twenty-four years of palliative care experience and
displays the pragmatic case for a slippery slope effect from VE legislation in table 2.

Table 2. A case against voluntary euthanasia. Robert G. Twycross, "Where There Is Hope, There Is Life: A View from the Hospice," in *Euthanasia Examined: Ethical, Clinical and Legal Perspectives*, ed. John Keown (Cambridge: Cambridge University Press, 1995), p. 165. Used by permission.

Reason	Comment
Many requests stem from inadequate symptom relief.	Patients no longer ask [for euthanasia] when their symptoms are adequately relieved.
Other requests relate to a sense of uselessness or feeling a burden.	Good palliative care restores hope by giving the patient a sense of direction.
Persistent requests often reflect a depressive illness.	Depression requires specific treatment, not euthanasia.
Patients frequently change their minds.	Many patients have transient periods of despair.
Prognosis is often far from certain.	Some patients live for years longer than originally anticipated.
A "euthanasia mentality" results in voluntary euthanasia extending to imposed euthanasia.	This is indisputably the case in the Netherlands.
If voluntary euthanasia were permitted, elderly and terminally ill patients would feel "at risk."	Anecdotal evidence and the results of a survey of elderly people in the Netherlands . . . support this.
Pressure on doctors from relatives to impose euthanasia could be irresistible.	The Remmelink Report demonstrates that relatives do put pressure on doctors.
Doctors who find it hard to cope with "failure" will tend to impose euthanasia regardless of patients' wishes.	Anecdotal evidence from the Netherlands supports this contention.
Voluntary euthanasia will remove the incentive to improve standards of palliative care.	Palliative care is still in its infancy in the Netherlands; improvements are undoubtedly being hindered by the de facto acceptance of voluntary euthanasia.

[55]Woodruff, "Is Euthanasia Contagious?" citing Robert G. Twycross, "Euthanasia: Going Dutch?" *Journal of the Royal Society of Medicine* 89, no. 2 (1996): 61-63.

In Montgomery's succinct terms, "there is ample evidence of the slippery slope, practically, logically, legally, and ethically."[56]

Conclusion

This chapter has critically examined Singer's use of euthanasia as a test case for his proposed revision of the Western sanctity-of-life ethic. We have found that Singer's case fails on a number of fronts. First, Singer's deliberately ambiguous and misleading definitions of terms like *mercy killing, passive euthanasia* and *persons* disguises the culling of newborns and nonconscious others defined as nonpersons for reasons related not to mercy but to total social utility.

Second, the revolutionary overthrow of the sanctity-of-life ethic by a quality-of-life ethic ignores the way evolutionary changes in traditions and theories can incorporate aspects of other theories and show themselves to be stronger. Singer warns against a rigidly absolutist sanctity-of-life ethic, but his particular warnings have largely already been taken to heart, in a way that does not deny the heart of the sanctity-of-life ethic, the inherent God-given dignity of the individual. Sanctity of life is not absolute for Christians; we seek first God's kingdom and put Christ before life itself. However, sanctity of life is fundamental to other rights and responsibilities.

Third, Singer's hard cases used to justify euthanasia can be dealt with by similar adjustments involving supplementary quality-of-life criteria. Singer neglects the legal maxim that hard cases make bad law and tries to use a sledgehammer (abandonment of the sanctity-of-life basis of Western law) to crush a nut (some hard cases caused by new technologies for keeping people alive). It is also misleading to talk of a continuum of legislative changes from allowing withdrawal of treatment for futile cases to allowing active voluntary euthanasia. They are different.

Fourth, Singer's attempt to abandon the distinction between crucial acts and omissions fails. There is a difference of substance or kind, not degree, both in act and motivation, between active, deliberate killing and letting die.

Fifth, patient autonomy and choice is not an absolute, even for Singer, who is more a utilitarian than a liberal. His priority on total social utility or pleasure means that while a small number of people might gain some autonomy, there would likely be a large loss of autonomy by others, especially those defined as nonpersons having no preferences.

Sixth, this is backed up by the Dutch evidence of a slippery slope leading from voluntary euthanasia to widespread nonvoluntary and involuntary euthanasia.

Despite attempts at building in safeguards, theological, philosophical and pragmatic considerations are against legalization of voluntary euthanasia and so-called

---

[56]Montgomery, "Whose Life Anyway?" p. 100.

assisted suicide. As Robert Twycross aptly sums up his twenty-four years' experience in palliative care: "When everything is taken into account (physical, psychological, social and spiritual) euthanasia is *not* the answer, either for the patient, the family, the professional carers or society."[157]

As Bruce Kaye notes, the main concerns of euthanasia advocates can be addressed in other, less dangerous ways:

> Given the common law protection for a competent person to decline treatment, the distinction between heroic and ordinary, or ordinarily indicated treatment, the difficulties of legislation in this area and a more public and accountable professional ethics for medical practitioners, there would appear to be no basis for enshrining in legislation any so-called right to die, and absolutely no case for the acceptance of active euthanasia.[158]

Behind Singer's specific proposal is a more far-reaching assault on our creation- and Christian-based intuitions and convictions concerning the sanctity of life. Singer's attempt to marginalize Christian views from mainstream debate is an attack on the public freedom of religion and the relative autonomy and reality of people's deep-seated intuitions. These convictions of belonging to a community of mutually dependent beings through which we discover our own personhood are more fundamental than Singer's rationalistic definition of conscious, planned personhood. When this basic sense of mutual dependence in all our vulnerability in birth, sickness and death is violated, we experience moral revulsion.

> Moral revulsion occurs whenever the deep structure of our moral personality is threatened in its foundations. That is why many people in our society—religious and otherwise—cling to the notion of life's sacredness in order to make the point that killing of disabled infants [or the elderly] is to transgress a moral boundary that ought not to be transgressed, even if they do not hold that all human lives in all cases should be saved by all means.[159]

Moral intuition and revulsion is often expressed in taboos. These maintain the sense of transgression, that once a certain point has been crossed it is very difficult to go back against the stream. As Almond says, "at the very least it is worth bearing in mind that a taboo against killing—or, put the other way round, a belief in the right of any human being not to be killed by others—is harder to reinstate, reinforce and preserve than it is to ignore or set aside. Hesitation on the matter is therefore a reasonable reaction to proposals to make changes in the law, even if this leaves difficult decisions for individuals."[160]

---

[157]Twycross, "Where There Is Hope," p. 164.
[158]Bruce Kaye, "The Right to Die," *St. Mark's Review*, March 1988, p. 27.
[159]Reinders, "Debunking the Sanctity of Life," p. 19.
[160]Almond, *Exploring Ethics*, p. 160.

Against this Singer and Kuhse claim that

The principle of the sanctity of life is a legacy of the days when religion was the accepted source of all ethical wisdom. . . . Now that religion is no longer accepted as the source of moral authority in public life, however, the principle has been removed from the framework in which it developed. We are just discovering that without this framework it cannot stand up.[161]

However, numerous philosophers like Jenny Teichman, Mary Midgely, Brenda Almond, Raimond Gaita and Margaret Sommerville accept a still-standing "concept of the secular sacred" involving radical intuitive respect for human life.[162] Along with their insights, our creation-based intuitions and sense of the sacredness of life also need reframing and reinforcement by Christian premises and reasons, found in the doctrines of creation, humanity made in God's image, the Fall, and the incarnation, cross, resurrection and return of Christ. This is a task begun here but which needs the attention of another book.

Singer's lauded consistency—for example, if we practice late-term abortion we should also practice infanticide or infant nonvoluntary "euthanasia"—should lead us not to capitulate but to question his unargued premises in practices like abortion. We can with good reason reject the morality of late-term (or early) abortion. Singer is right to question our society's inconsistency at points on choices of life and death; he is wrong not to question his own premises.

Singer shows up the inconsistencies of Western culture as it holds on to a remnant of a Christian sanctity-of-life ethic. This remnant should remind us of the whole Christian worldview behind our secularized sanctity-of-life ethic and call us back to consistency with it. Singer's stark challenge will do us a service if it pushes our society to rediscover the Christian roots for many of the commitments to the maintenance of the dignity of individual, personal, human life that we take for granted but are now under threat. So as we engage in rethinking Peter Singer, we are forced to rethink the roots of what is most valuable in Western society.

---

[161]Quoted in ibid., p. 160.
[162]Margaret Sommerville, *The Ethical Canary: Science, Society and the Human Spirit* (New York: Viking, 2000), p. 35: "Applying a concept of the secular sacred would mean that, whether we are religious or not, our moral and ethical views would include a recognition that the passing on of human life to the next generation deserves the deepest respect." She says the same thing of the "passing on of human life" in death, in her opposition to euthanasia, chaps. 5-6.

Index of Names & Subjects